JOHN BURNET OF BARNS

JOHN BUCHAN (1875-1940) was born in Perth on 26th August 1875, the eldest son of a minister in the Free Church of Scotland. He spent part of his childhood in Fife, before the family moved to Glasgow in the 1880s. In 1894 he went to Oxford University and began to write, publishing several books and many articles while still a student. After Oxford he had a successful career as a barrister and Member of Parliament, while continuing to write highly acclaimed novels such as *The Thirty-Nine Steps*, *Greenmantle* and *The Three Hostages*. He also wrote widely on other subjects, including biographies of Cromwell and Montrose, and an autobiography *Memory Hold-the-Door*. John Buchan was created Baron Tweedsmuir in 1935 and became Governor-General of Canada the same year. He died in Canada in 1940, soon after completing his last great novel, *Sick Heart River*.

JAMES ROBERTSON studied history at Edinburgh University, later returning to complete a doctorate on the works of Sir Walter Scott. His critically acclaimed first collection of short stories, *Close*, was published in 1991 and his second collection, *The Ragged Man's Complaint*, in 1993. He is the first holder of the Brownsbank Writing Fellowship based at the former home of Hugh MacDiarmid near Biggar.

JOHN BURNET *of* BARNS

JOHN BUCHAN

Introduced by James Robertson

EDINBURGH
B&W PUBLISHING
1994

First published 1898
This edition published 1994
by B&W Publishing, Edinburgh
Introduction © James Robertson 1994
ISBN 1 873631 31 6
All Rights Reserved.
No part of this publication may be reproduced
or transmitted in any form or by any means
without the prior permission of B&W Publishing.

The publisher acknowledges subsidy
from the Scottish Arts Council towards
the publication of this volume.

British Library Cataloguing in Publication Data:
A catalogue record for this book is available
from the British Library.

Cover design by *Hamman, Delvaux & Palmer*

Cover illustration: Detail from
The Drumhead Courtmartial, by John Pettie (1839-93)
Photograph by kind permission
of The Graves Art Gallery, Sheffield.

Printed by Werner Söderström

CONTENTS

BOOK III—THE HILLMEN

BOOK IV—THE WESTLANDS

INTRODUCTION

James Robertson

John Buchan already had one novel (and three other books) to his name when *John Burnet of Barns* was published in 1898, but this was his first full-length and fully realised work of fiction. *Sir Quixote of the Moors*, written while he was still at Glasgow University and published in 1895, is a competent but slight effort by comparison. *John Burnet* was also mostly written while Buchan was still nineteen, and completed when he went on to Oxford University, but it shows the touch of a writer who has learned quickly and easily from his first attempt—a fact wittily acknowledged when the French hero of *Sir Quixote*, the Sieur de Rohaine, makes a brief appearance in a meeting with John Burnet in the Low Countries:

> If I were to tell all the benefit I derived from this man I should fill a volume and never reach the end of my tale. Suffice it to say that from him I learned many of the tricks of sword play, so that soon I became as nigh perfect in the art as it was ever in my power to be.

"He did much kindness to me," John concludes, and it is true. Both novels are set in the Borders in the same period of Scottish history, but one is mere prentice work for the other.

Buchan himself used a similar phrase to describe these early works, in the posthumously published musings of *Memory Hold-the-Door* (1940):

> My chief passion in those years was for the Border country-side, and my object in all my prentice writings was to

reproduce its delicate charm, to catch the aroma of its gracious landscape and turbulent history and the idiom of its people. . . . I asked for nothing better than to spend my life by the Tweed.

Likewise, his note at the start of later editions of *John Burnet* states modestly that it was the charm of the delectable Tweeddale countryside which had "won for a simple story a certain degree of favour". There is no question but that the description of landscape and its effect upon the moods and actions of humans is central to the novel, and it is interesting to see this fascination with landscape, one of the defining characteristics of Buchan's style, so clearly in his earliest fiction. Later, in books as varied as *The Thirty-Nine Steps*, *Midwinter* and *Sick Heart River*, he would use the skills exhibited here to make landscape a living and active agent, as important to theme and plot as any character. Even in *Sir Quixote*, right from its opening lines, the land had played its part:

> Before me stretched a black heath, over which the mist blew in gusts, and through whose midst the road crept like an adder. Great storm-marked hills flanked me on either side, and since I set out I had seen their harsh outline against a thick sky, until I longed for flat ground to rest my sight upon. . . . Sometimes the fog would lift for a moment from the face of the land and show me a hilltop or the leaden glimmer of a loch, but nothing more—no green field or homestead; only a barren and accursed desert.

Here the moor is dark and threatening, alien to the foreign adventurer M. de Rohaine. By contrast, *John Burnet* opens with a scene in which the young Scots hero is at one with the landscape, knowing and loving it as he goes after the trout in the Tweed:

> A stretch of green turf, shaded on all sides by high beeches, sloped down to the stream side. The sun made a shining

pathway down the middle, but the edges were in blackest shadow. At the foot a lone gnarled alder hung over the water, sending its long arms far over the river nigh to the farther side. Here Tweed was still and sunless, showing a level of placid black water, flecked in places with stray shafts of light.

But in both cases, Buchan is not just describing the natural surroundings with precision and authority, he is also using them to inform the mood of his protagonists. It is this ability to create an interactive relationship between characters and land that, when combined with his great knowledge of a particular countryside, its topography and climate, raises Buchan's style out of mere locality. There *is*, of course, a local dimension to *John Burnet of Barns*: to be able to identify the many places mentioned in the text and follow John's journeys through southern Scotland is an added bonus—indeed, sitting in MacDiarmid's cottage here at Brownsbank, there are times when it seems one could watch the novel's events unfold from the front door. But, crucially, one does not have to know Tweeddale to feel drawn into the landscape Buchan creates: he neither exaggerates nor understates the land; the reader gets it at face value.

The MacDiarmid connection is of more than passing interest. Not only was Buchan an early supporter of the MacDiarmid-driven revival of Scottish literature (contributing poems to *Northern Numbers* and writing an introduction to MacDiarmid's 1925 book of lyric poems *Sangschaw*), but in an essay in *Contemporary Scottish Studies* (also 1925) MacDiarmid gave one of the fairest assessments of Buchan's own literary worth. He described him as "Dean of the Faculty of Contemporary Scottish Letters", but "only incidentally a man of letters" who had "somehow found time to make fairly successful hobbies of almost every branch of literature." Praising the "excellence of his writing in every direction his pen has taken him", he refused however to flatter:

I can agree with all the grateful things that can be said about Buchan's novels: I owe them many happy hours: but it is essential despite one's private likes and dislikes to preserve a sense of proportion: some people apply such adjectives to Buchan that one wonders how their stock would last out if they had to deal with the literary world as a whole.... In our literary history Buchan as a novelist will be of the respectable but unexciting company of James Grant, William Black, and George MacDonald—well above the Crocketts and Ian MacLarens. His fiction well deserves its vogue: would that many whose popularity is greater wrote half so well. But that is saying little!

It was a forthright opinion with which the unpretentious Buchan almost certainly concurred.

He was himself very dismissive of *John Burnet*. In a letter to Gilbert Murray he wrote:

To tell the truth I am rather ashamed of it, it is so very immature and boyish. I had no really serious interest in fiction when I wrote it, and the result is a sort of hotch-potch.

For a novel written by a nineteen-year-old, it is in fact remarkably mature, exhibiting the rounded knowledge of Buchan's classical Scots education to great effect, as Burnet looks back from middle age on the adventures of his youth. And a hotch-potch it may be, but only because it is a kind of clearing-ground for so many of the themes to which Buchan would return again and again in his later fiction. Among these we find:- The hero is a man of moderation caught between opposing forces, or facing a single force of great evil. In this Buchan writes in the tradition of Scott, but with his heroes having more of the panache, activity and decisiveness of Stevenson's fiction (Buchan is truly the disciple of Stevenson, and only in passing that of Scott).—The wild land is both threat and sanctuary. The "black horrific hill" by its very ferocity lends protection from the dragoons; the "bleakest place in God's creation" can appear in the moonlight like "a fantastic fairyland"; and in the "steep craigs and screes" are "caves and holes where one might lie hid for months".

Perhaps in the hide-and-seek sequences of *The Thirty-Nine Steps* this duality of the high land, and especially of the Scottish moors, is most clearly drawn.—A mysterious stranger appears, and in some way assists or simply refreshes the spirit of the hero. In *Sir Quixote* a man of honour among a band of thieves enables the hero to escape assault at a lonely inn. In *Midwinter*, "the Spainneach", a man "as secret in his ways as the woodcock blown shoreward by the October gales", appears at a fortuitous moment to save Alastair Maclean from death. Francis Birkenshaw, the hero of *A Lost Lady of Old Years*, is met in a desolate place en route to the field of Culloden by a pedlar who advises him, "when ye meet a man in thae camsteery times ye'll let on that ye're no quite wise." John Burnet's encounter is with a one-eyed man in the green cleuch of a narrow glen: they cross swords in a good-natured contest to test each other's skills, and then the stranger rides out of the tale altogether. "It was a ray of amusement in the perils and hardships of my wanderings", John concludes, and in other novels too, shadowy figures enter and vanish leaving a brightness or a warning in their wake.—An "other" society is entered by the hero. In this case history supplies the society of the Hillmen or Covenanters, who live not just outwith settled society but *under* the world, in the Cave of the Cor Water; and John also falls in with gypsies, the Baillies of No Man's Land. In *Midwinter* and *The Blanket of the Dark* the underworld is similarly crude but honest, represented by "Old England" in the former and the "Parliament of Beggars" in the latter. But in *The Power-House* and *The Thirty-Nine Steps* the conspiracy is subversive and evil, and threatens the very foundations of society which these honest brotherhoods support.

We also find, in Nicol Plenderleith, the first appearance of the faithful servant, a figure often to appear in Buchan's work. And Cousin Gilbert is the first in a line of admirable villains—brave but guilty, honourable but self-serving, scheming but magnificent in their designs—among whom might be counted (with variations on the theme) Lord Lovat in *A Lost Lady of Old Years*, Lumley in *The Power-House*, Castor in *The Courts of the Morning*, and Nicholas Kyd in *Midwinter*. Also, in the chapter titled "I Spend My Days in Idleness", just before John departs the Low Countries, there is that mood of *ennui* which so often precedes a burst of Buchanite activity. Finally, in the various movements of the characters through the Scottish landscape we are constantly reminded of Buchan's fascination with what he called, in *Memory Hold-the-Door*, "the notion of hurried journeys":

> We live our lives under the twin categories of time and space, and when the two come into conflict we get the great moment. Whether failure or success is the result, life is sharpened, intensified, idealised. A long journey, even with the most lofty purpose, may be a dull thing to read of if it is made at leisure; but a hundred yards may be a breathless business if only a few seconds are granted to complete it.

It was this, Buchan's understanding of how to create suspense through action, that so impressed Alfred Hitchcock when he filmed *The Thirty-Nine Steps* and thought seriously about adapting other Buchans for the cinema. Buchan rated his historical fiction well above his "shockers", but this technical skill is common to the best of both, and *John Burnet* is no exception.

As might be expected for such an early work, *John Burnet of Barns* did not sell well until its author's name became established. Serialised in *Chambers' Journal* prior to publication, in book form it sold about six hundred copies in its first year, and over the next twenty years about the same number of that edition were sold. But a cheap shilling edition issued in 1915 in the wake of *The Thirty-Nine Steps* sold in thousands. Thereafter *John Burnet* was regularly reissued, but, like the other historical fiction, it never sold as well as the shockers. Maurice Lindsay, in his *History of Scottish Literature*, has commented rather sweepingly that, with Buchan, the last connection between the historical novel and "anything that might reasonably be considered as literature, was severed." Buchan himself would have agreed at least that his truly literary energies were invested in the historical novels.

J.R.
Brownsbank
April 1994

TO THE MEMORY OF MY SISTER

VIOLET KATHERINE STUART

Ἀστὴρ πρὶν μὲν ἔλαμπες ἐνι ζωοῖσιν Ἐῶος,
νῦν δὲ θανὼν λάμπεις Ἕσπερος ἐν φθιμένοις.

BOOK I

TWEEDDALE

CHAPTER I

THE ADVENTURE WHICH BEFELL ME
IN THE WOOD OF DAWYCK

I HAVE taken in hand to write this, the history of my life, not without much misgiving of heart; for my memory at the best is a bad one, and of many things I have no clear remembrance. And the making of tales is an art unknown to me, so he who may read must not look for any great skill in the setting down. Yet I am emboldened to the work, for my life has been lived in stirring times and amid many strange scenes which may not wholly lack interest for those who live in quieter days. And above all, I am desirous that they of my family should read of my life and learn the qualities both good and bad which run in the race and so the better be able to resist the evil and do the good.

My course, by the will of God, has had something of a method about it, which makes the telling the more easy. For, as I look back upon it from the vantage ground of time, all seems spread out plain and clear in an ordered path. And I would but seek to trace again some portion of the way with the light of a dim memory.

I will begin my tale with a certain June morning in the year 1678, when I, scarcely turned thirteen years, set out from the house of Barns to the fishing in Tweed. I had escaped the watchful care of my tutor, Master Robert Porter, the curate of Lyne, who vexed my soul thrice a week with Cæsar and Cicero. I had no ill-will to the Latin, for I relished the battles in Cæsar well enough, and had some liking for poetry; but when I made a slip in grammar he would bring his great hand over my ears in a way which would make them tingle for hours. And all this, mind you, with the sun coming in at the window and whaups whistling over the fields and the fish plashing in the river. On this morn I had escaped by hiding in the cheese closet; then I had fetched my rod from the stable loft, and borrowed tackle from David Lithgow, the stableman; and now I was creeping through the hazel bushes, casting, every now and then, a glance back at the house, where the huge figure of my teacher was looking for me disconsolately in every corner.

The year had been dry and sultry; and this day was warmer than any I remembered. The grass in the meadow was browned and crackling; all the foxgloves hung their bells with weariness; and the waters were shrunken in their beds. The mill lade, which drives Manor Mill, had not a drop in it, and the small trout were gasping in the shallow pool, which in our usual weather was five feet deep. The cattle were *stertling*, as we called it in the countryside; that is, the sun was burning their backs, and, rushing with tails erect, they sought coolness from end to end of the field. Tweed was very low and clear. Small hope, I thought, for my fishing; I might as well have stayed with Master Porter and been thrashed, for I will have to stay out all day and go supperless at night.

I took my way up the river past the green slopes of Haswellsykes to the wood of Dawyck, for I knew well that there, if anywhere, the fish would take in the shady, black pools. The place was four weary miles off, and the day was growing hotter with each passing hour; so I stripped my coat and hid it in a hole among whins and stones. When I come home again, I said, I will recover it. Another half-mile, and I had off my shoes and stockings and concealed them in a like place; so soon I plodded along with no other clothes on my body than shirt and ragged breeches.

In time I came to the great forest which stretches up Tweed nigh to Drummelzier, the greatest wood in our parts, unless it be Glentress, on the east side of Peebles. The trees were hazels and birches in the main, with a few rowans, and on the slopes of the hill a congregation of desolate pines. Nearer the house of Dawyck were beeches and oaks and the deeper shade, and it was thither I went. The top of my rod struck against the boughs, and I had some labour in steering a safe course between the Scylla of the trees and the Charybdis of the long brackens; for the rod was in two parts spliced together, and as I had little skill in splicing, Davie had done the thing for me before I started. Twice I roused a cock of the woods, which went screaming through the shadow. Herons from the great heronry at the other end were standing in nigh every pool, for the hot weather was a godsend to them, and the trout fared ill when the long thief-like bills flashed through the clear water. Now and then a shy deer leaped from the ground and sped up the hill. The desire of the chase was hot upon me when, after an hour's tough scramble, I came to the spot where I hoped for fish.

A stretch of green turf, shaded on all sides by high beeches, sloped down to the stream side. The sun made a shining pathway down the middle, but the edges were in blackest shadow. At the foot a lone gnarled alder hung over the water, sending its long arms far over the river nigh to the farther side. Here Tweed was still and sunless, showing a level of placid black water, flecked in places with stray shafts of light. I prepared my tackle on the grass, making a casting line of fine horsehair which I had plucked from the tail of our own grey gelding. I had no such fine hooks as folk nowadays bring from Edinburgh, sharpened and barbed ready to their hand; but rough, home-made ones, which Tam Todd, the land grieve, had fashioned out of old needles. My line was of thin, stout whipcord, to which I had made the casting firm with a knot of my own invention. I had out my bag of worms, and, choosing a fine red one, made it fast on the hook. Then I crept gently to the alder and climbed on the branch which hung far out over the stream. Here I sat like an owl in the shade, and dropped my line in the pool below me, where it caught a glint of the sun and looked like a shining cord let down, like Jacob's ladder, from heaven to the darkness of earth.

I had not sat many minutes before my rod was wrenched violently downwards, then athwart the stream, nearly swinging me from my perch. I have got a monstrous trout, I thought, and with a fluttering heart stood up on the branch to be more ready for the struggle. He ran up the water and down; then far below the tree roots, whence I had much difficulty in forcing him; then he thought to break my line by rapid jerks, but he did not know the strength of my horsehair. By-and-by he grew wearied, and I landed him comfortably on a spit of land—a great red-spotted fellow with a black back. I made sure that he was two pounds weight if he was an ounce.

I hid him in a cool bed of leaves and rushes on the bank, and crawled back to my seat on the tree. I baited my hook as before, and dropped it in; and then leaned back lazily on the branches behind to meditate on the pleasantness of fishing and the hatefulness of Master Porter's teaching. In my shadowed place all was cool and fresh as a May morning; but beyond, in the gleam of the sun, I could see birds hopping sleepily on the trees, and the shrivelled dun look of the grass. A faint humming of bees reached me, and the flash of a white butterfly shot, now and then, like a star from the sunlight to the darkness, and back again to the sunlight. It was a lovely summer's day, though too warm for our sober country, and as I sat I thought of the lands I had read of and heard of, where it was always fiercely hot, and great fruits were to be had for the pulling. I thought of the oranges and olives and what not, and of silver and golden fishes with sparkling scales; and as I thought of them I began to loathe hazelnuts and rowans and whortleberries and the homely trout, which are all that is to be had in this land of ours. Then I thought of Barns and my kinsfolk, and the tales of my forbears, and I loved again the old silent valley of Tweed—for a gallant tale is worth many fruits and fishes. Then as the day brightened my dreams grew accordingly. I came of a great old house; I, too, would ride to the wars, to the Low Countries, to Sweden, and I would do great deeds like the men in Virgil. And then I wished I had lived in Roman times. Ah, those were the days, when all the good things of life fell to brave men, and there was no other trade to be compared to war. Then I reflected that they had no fishing, for I had come on nothing as yet in my studies about fish and catching of them. And so, like the boy I was, I dreamed on, and my thoughts chased each other in a dance in my brain, and I fell fast asleep.

I wakened with a desperate shudder, and found myself floundering in seven feet of water. My eyes were still heavy with sleep, and I swallowed great gulps of the river as I sank. In a second I came to the surface, and with a few strokes I was at the side, for

I had early learned to swim. Stupid and angry, I scrambled up the bank to the green glade. Here a first surprise befell me. It was late afternoon; the sun had travelled three-fourths of the sky; it would be near five o'clock. What a great fool I had been to fall asleep and lose a day's fishing! I found my rod moored to the side with the line and half of the horsehair; some fish had taken the hook. Then I looked around me to the water and the trees and the green sward, and surprise the second befell me; for there, not twelve paces from me, stood a little girl, watching me with every appearance of terror.

She was about two years younger than myself, I fancied. Her dress was some white stuff which looked eerie in the shade of the beeches, and her long hair fell over her shoulders in plentiful curls. She had wide, frightened blue eyes and a delicately featured face, and as for the rest I know not how to describe her, so I will not try. I, with no more manners than a dog, stood staring at her, wholly forgetful of the appearance I must present, without shoes and stockings, coat or waistcoat, and dripping with Tweed water. She spoke first, in a soft southern tone, which I, accustomed only to the broad Scots of Jean Morran, who had been my nurse, fell in love with at once. Her whole face was filled with the extremest terror.

"O sir, be you the water-kelpie?" she asked.

I could have laughed at her fright, though I must have been like enough to some evil spirit; but I answered her with my best gravity.

"No, I am no kelpie, but I had gone to sleep and fell into the stream. My coat and shoes are in a hole two miles down, and my name is John Burnet—of Barns." All this I said in one breath, being anxious to right myself in her eyes; also with some pride in the last words.

It was pretty to see how recognition chased the fear from her face. "I know you," she said. "I have heard of you. But what do you in the dragon's hole, sir? This is my place. The dragon will get you without a doubt."

At this I took off my bonnet and made my best bow. "And who are you, pray, and what story is this of dragons? I have been here scores of times, and never have I seen or heard of them." This with the mock importance of a boy.

"Oh, I am Marjory," she said, "Marjory Veitch, and I live at the great house in the wood, and all this place is my father's and mine. And this is my dragon's den"; and straightway she wandered into a long tale of Fair Margot and the Seven Maidens, how Margot wed the Dragon and he turned forthwith into a prince, and I know not what else. "But no harm can come to me, for look, I have the charm," and she showed me a black stone in a silver locket. "My nurse Alison gave it me. She had it from a great fairy who came with it to my cradle when I was born."

"Who told you all this?" I asked in wonder, for this girl seemed to carry all the wisdom of the ages in her head.

"Alison and my father, and my brother Michael and old Adam Noble, and a great many more—" Then she broke off. "My mother is gone. The fairies came for her."

Then I remembered the story of the young English mistress of Dawyck, who had died before she had been two years in our country. And this child, with her fairy learning, was her daughter.

Now I know not what took me, for I had ever been shy of folk, and, above all, of womankind. But here I found my tongue, and talked to my new companion in a way which I could not sufficiently admire. There in the bright sunsetting I launched into the most miraculous account of my adventures of that day, in which dragons and witches were the commonest portents. Then I sat down and told her stories I had read out of Virgil and Cæsar, and all that I had heard of the wars in England and abroad, and the tales of the countryside which the packmen had told me. Also I must tell the romances of the nettie-wives who come to our countryside from the north—the old sad tale of Morag of the Misty Days and Usnach's sons and the wiles of Angus. And she listened, and thanked me ever so prettily when I had done. Then she would enlighten my ignorance; so I heard of the Red Etin of Ireland, and the Wolf of Brakelin, and the Seven Bold Brothers. Then I showed her nests, and gave her small blue eggs to take home, and pulled foxgloves for her, and made coronets of fern.

We played at hide-and-go-seek among the beeches, and ran races, and fought visionary dragons. Then the sun went down over the trees, and she declared it was time to be going home. So I got my solitary fish from its bed of rushes and made her a present of it. She was pleased beyond measure, though she cried out at my hardness in taking its life.

So it came to pass that Mistress Marjory Veitch of Dawyck went home hugging a great two-pound trout, and I went off to Barns, heedless of Master Porter and his heavy hand; and, arriving late, escaped a thrashing, and made a good meal of the remnants of supper.

CHAPTER II

THE HOUSE OF BARNS

The house of Barns stands on a green knoll above the Tweed, halfway between the village of Stobo and the town of Peebles. Tweed here is no great rolling river, but a shallow, prattling stream, and just below the house it winds around a small islet, where I loved to go and fish; for it was an adventure to reach the place, since a treacherous pool lay not a yard below it. The dwelling was white and square, with a beacon tower on the top, which once flashed the light from Neidpath to Drochil when the English came over the Border. It had not been used for half a hundred years, but a brazier still stood there, and a pile of rotten logs, grim mementoes of elder feuds. This also was a haunt of mine, for jackdaws and owls built in the corners, and it was choice fun of a spring morning to search for eggs at the risk of my worthless life. The parks around stretched to Manor village on the one side, and nigh to the foot of the Lyne Water on the other. Manor Water as far as Posso belonged to us, and many a rare creel have I had out of its pleasant reaches. Behind, rose the long heathery hill of the Scrape, which is so great a hill that while one side looks down on us another overhangs the wood of Dawyck. Beyond that again came Dollar Law and the wild fells which give birth to the Tweed, the Yarrow, and the Annan.

Within the house, by the hall fire, my father, William Burnet, spent his days. I mind well his great figure in the armchair, a mere wreck of a man, but mighty in his very ruin. He wore a hat, though he seldom went out, to mind him of the old days when he was so busy at hunting and harrying that he had never his head uncovered. His beard was streaked with grey, and his long nose, with a break in the middle (which is a mark of our family), and bushy eyebrows gave him a fearsome look to a chance stranger. In his young days he had been extraordinarily handsome and active, and, if all tales be true, no better than he should have been. He was feared in those days for his great skill in night foraying, so that he won the name of the "Howlet," which never left him. Those were the high days of our family, for my father was wont to ride to the Weaponshow with seven horsemen behind him; now we could scarce manage four. But in one of his night rides his good fortune failed him; for being after no good on the hills above Megget one dark wintry night, he fell over the Bitch Craig, horse and all; and though he escaped with his life, he was lamed in both legs and condemned to the house for the rest of his days. Of a summer night he would come out to the lawn with two mighty sticks to support him, and looking to the Manor Water hills, would shake his fist at them as old enemies. In his later days he took kindly to theology and learning, both of which, in the person of Master Porter, dined at his table every day. I know not how my father, who was a man of much penetration, could have been deceived by this man, who had as much religion as an ox. As for learning, he had some rag-tag scraps of Latin which were visited on me for my sins; but in eating he had no rival, and would consume beef and pasty and ale like a famished army. He preached every Sabbath in the little kirk of Lyne, below the Roman camp, and a woeful service it was. I went regularly by my father's orders, but I was the only one from the household of Barns. I fear that not even my attendance at his church brought me Master Porter's love; for I had acquired nearly as much Latin as he possessed himself, and vexed his spirit at lesson hours with unanswerable questions. At other times, too, I would rouse him to the wildest anger by singing a profane song of my own making:

"O, ken ye his Reverence Minister Tam,
Wi' a heid like a stot and a face like a ram?"

To me my father was ever kind. He was never tired of making plans for my future. "John," he would say, "you shall go to Glasgow College, for you have the makings of a scholar in you. Ay, and we'll make you a soldier, John, and a good honest gentleman to fight for your king, as your forbears did before you." (This was scarce true, for there never yet was a Burnet who fought for anything but his own hand.) "No damned Whig for me. Gad, how I wish I were hale in the legs to be off to the hills with the Johnstones and the Keiths. There wouldna be one of the breed left from Tweedwell to the Brig o' Peebles." Then he would be anxious about my martial training, and get down the foils to teach me a lesson. From this he would pass to tales of his own deeds till the past would live before him, and his eyes would glow with their old fire. Then he would forget his condition, and seek to show me how some parry was effected. There was but one result: his poor weak legs would give way beneath him. Then I had to carry him to his bed, swearing deeply at his infirmities and lamenting the changes of life.

In those days the Burnets were a poor family—a poor and a proud. My grandfather had added much to the lands by rapine and extortion—ill-gotten gains which could not last. He had been a man of a violent nature, famed over all the South for his feats of horsemanship and swordsmanship. He died suddenly, of overdrinking, at the age of fifty-five, and now lies in the kirk of Lyne beneath an effigy representing the angel Gabriel coming for his soul. His last words are recorded: "O Lord, I dinna want to dee, I dinna want to dee. If ye'll let me live, I'll run up the sklidders o' Cademuir to a' eternity." The folk of the place seldom spoke of him, though my father upheld him as a man of true spirit who had an eye to the improvement of his house. Of the family before him I had the history at my finger-ends. This was a subject of which my father never tired, for he held that the genealogy of the

Burnets was a thing of vastly greater importance than that of the kings of Rome or Judah. From the old days when we held Burnetland, in the parish of Broughton, and called ourselves of that ilk, I had the unbroken history of the family in my memory. Ay, and also of the great house of Traquair, for my mother had been a Stewart, and, as my father said often, this was the only family in the countryside which could hope to rival us in antiquity or valour.

My father's brother, Gilbert, had married the heiress of a westland family, and with her had got the lands of Eaglesham, about the headwaters of Cart. His son Gilbert, my cousin, was a tall lad some four years my senior, who on several occasions rode to visit us at Barns. He was of a handsome, soldierly appearance, and looked for an early commission in a Scots company. At first I admired him mightily, for he was skilful at all sports, rode like a moss-trooper, and could use his sword in an incomparable fashion. My father could never abide him, for he could not cease to tell of his own prowess, and my father was used to say that he loved no virtue better than modesty. Also, he angered every servant about the place by his hectoring, and one day so offended old Tam Todd that Tam flung a bucket at him, and threatened to duck him in the Tweed: which he doubtless would have done, old as he was, for he was a very Hercules of a man. This presented a nice problem to all concerned, and I know not which was the more put out, Tam or my father. Finally it ended in the latter reading Gilbert a long and severe lecture, and then bidding Tam ask his pardon, seeing that the dignity of the family had at any cost to be sustained.

One other relative, though in a distant way, I must not omit to mention, for the day came when every man of our name was proud to claim the kinship. This was Gilbert Burnet, of Edinburgh, afterwards divinity professor in Glasgow, Bishop of Salisbury, and the author of the famous *Bishop Burnet's History of his Own Times*. I met him often in after days, and once in London he had me to his house and entertained me during my stay. Of him I shall have to tell hereafter, but now he was no more than a name to me, a name which my father was fond of repeating

12

when he wished to recall me to gravity.

Tam Todd, my father's grieve, who managed the lands about the house, deserves more than a passing word. He was about sixty years of age, stooped in the back, but with long arms and the strength of a giant. At one time he had fought for Gustavus, and might have risen high in the ranks, had not a desperate desire to see his native land come upon him and driven him to slip off one night and take ship for Leith. He had come to Peebles, where my father met him, and admiring his goodly stature, took him into his service, in which Tam soon became as expert at the breeding of sheep as ever he had been at the handling of a pike or musket. He was the best storyteller and the cunningest fisher in the place, full of quaint foreign words, French and Swedish and High Dutch, for the army of Gustavus had been made up of the riddlings of Europe. From him I learned to fence with the rapier, and a past-master he was, for my father told how, in his best days, he could never so much as look at Tam. *Bon pied bon œil* was ever his watchword, and I have proved it a good one; for, short though it be, if a man but follow it he may fear nothing. Also, he taught me a thing which has been most useful to me, and which I will speak of again—the art of using the broadsword or claymore, as the wild Highlanders call it. My school was on a strip of green grass beside Tweed, and there I have had many a tough encounter in the long summer nights. He made me stand with my back to the deep pool, that I might fear to step back; and thus I learned to keep my ground, a thing which he held to be of the essence of swordsmanship.

My nurse, Jean Morran, was the only woman body about the place. She and Tam did the cooking between them, for that worthy had learned the art gastronomical from a Frenchman whose life he saved, and who, in gratitude, taught him many excellent secrets for dishes, and stole ten crowns. She had minded me and mended my clothes and seen to my behaviour ever since my mother died of a fever when I was scarce two years old. Of my mother I remember nothing, but if one may judge from my father's long grief and her portrait in the dining-hall, she had been a good and a gentle as well as a most beautiful woman. Jean, with her uncouth tongue and stern face, is still a clear figure in my memory. She was a kind nurse in the main, and if her temper was doubtful from many sore trials, her cakes and sugar were excellent salves to my wronged heart. She was, above all things, a famous housewife, keeping the place spotless and clean, so that when one entered the house of Barns there was always something fresh and cool in the very air.

But here I am at the end of my little gallery, for the place was bare of folk, and the life a lonely one. Here I grew up amid the woods and hills and the clean air, with a great zest for all the little excellences of my lot, and a tolerance of its drawbacks. By the time I had come to sixteen years I had swum in every pool in Tweed for miles up and down, climbed every hill, fished in every burn, and ridden and fallen from every horse in my father's stable. I had been as far west as Tintock Hill and as far south as the Loch o' the Lowes. Nay, I had once been taken to Edinburgh in company with Tam, who brought me a noble fishing-rod, and showed me all the wondrous things to be seen. A band of soldiers passed down the High Street from the Castle with a great clanking and jingling, and I saw my guide straighten up his back and keep time with his feet to their tread. All the way home, as I sat before him on the broad back of Maisie, he told me tales of his campaigns, some of them none too fit for a boy's ear; but he was carried away and knew not what he was saying. This first put a taste for the profession of arms into my mind, which was assiduously fostered by my fencing lessons and the many martial tales I read. I found among my father's books the chronicles of Froissart and a history of the Norman kings, both in the English, which I devoured by night and day. Then I had Tacitus and Livy, and in my fourteenth year I began the study of Greek with a master at Peebles. So that soon I had read most of the *Iliad* and all the *Odyssey*, and would go about repeating the long, swinging lines. I think that story of the man who, at the siege of some French town, shouted a Homeric battle-piece most likely to be true, for with me the Greek had a like effect, and made me tramp many miles over the hills or ride the horses more hard than my father permitted.

14

But this bookwork was, after all, but half of my life, and that the less memorable. All the sights and sounds of that green upland vale are linked for me with memories of boyish fantasies. I used to climb up the ridge of Scrape when the sun set and dream that the serried ranks of hills were a new country where all was strange, though I knew well that an hour of the morning would dispel the fancy. Then I would descend from the heights, and for weeks be so fiercely set on the sports of the time of year that I had scarcely time for a grave thought. I have often gone forth to the lambing with the shepherds, toiled all day in the brown moors, and at night dropped straight off to sleep as I sat in my chair at meat. Then there was the salmon fishing in the winter, when the blood ran hot at the flare of the torches and the shimmer of the spears, and I, a forlorn young fool, shivered in my skin as the keen wind blew down the water. There was the swing and crackle of the stones when the haughlands of Manor were flooded, and a dozen brown-faced men came to the curling and the air rang with shouts and laughter. I have mind, too, of fierce days of snow when men looked solemn and the world was so quiet that I whistled to keep me from despondency, and the kitchen at Barns was like a place in an inn with famishing men and dripping garments. Then Tweed would be buried under some great drift and its kindly flow sorely missed by man and beast. But best I remember the loosening of winter, when the rains from the moors sent down the river roaring red, and the vale was one pageant of delicate greenery and turbid brown torrent.

Often I would take my books and go into the heart of the hills for days and nights. This my father scarce liked, but he never hindered me. It was glorious to kindle a fire in the neuk of a glen, broil trout, and make my supper under the vault of the pure sky. Sweet, too, at noonday to lie beside the wellhead of some lonely burn, and think of many things that can never be set down and are scarce remembered. But these were but dreams, and this is not their chronicle; so it behoves me to shut my ear to vagrom memories.

To Dawyck I went the more often the older I grew. For Marjory Veitch had grown into a beautiful, lissom girl, with the same old litheness of body and gaiety of spirit. She was my comrade in countless escapades, and though I have travelled the world since then I have never found a readier or a braver. But with the years she grew more maidenly, and I dared less to lead her into mad ventures. Nay, I who had played with her in the woods and fished and raced with her as with some other lad, began to feel a foolish awe in her presence, and worshipped her from afar. The fairy learning of her childhood was but the index of a wistfulness and delicacy of nature which, to my grosser spirit, seemed something to uncover one's head before. I have loved her dearly all my life, but I have never more than half understood her; which is a good gift of God to most men, for the confounding of vanity.

To her a great sorrow had come. For when she was scarce thirteen, her father, the laird of Dawyck, who had been ever of a home-keeping nature, died from a fall while hunting on the brow of Scrape. He had been her childhood's companion, and she mourned for him as sorely as ever human being mourned for another. Michael, her only brother, was far abroad in a regiment of the Scots French Guards, so she was left alone in the great house with no other company than the servants and a cross-grained aunt who heard but one word in twenty. For this reason I rode over the oftener to comfort her loneliness.

CHAPTER III

THE SPATE IN TWEED

The year 1683 was with us the driest year in any man's memory. From the end of April to the end of July we had scarce a shower. The hay harvest was ruined beyond repair, and man and beast were sick with the sultry days. It was on the last Monday of July that I, wearied with wandering listlessly about the house, bethought myself of riding to Peebles to see the great match at bowls which is played every year for the silver horn. I had no expectation of a keen game, for the green was sure to be wellnigh ruined with the sun, and men had lost spirit in such weather. But the faintest interest is better than purposeless idleness, so I roused myself from languor and set out.

I saddled Maisie the younger, for this is a family name among our horses, and rode down by the Tweed side to the town. The river ran in the midst of a great bed of sunbaked gravel—a little trickle that a man might step across. I do not know where the fish had gone, but they, too, seemed scared by the heat, for not a trout plashed to relieve the hot silence. When I came to the Manor pool I stood still in wonder, for there for the first time in my life I saw the stream dry. Manor, which is in winter a roaring torrent and at other times a clear, full stream, had not a drop of running water in its bed: naught but a few stagnant pools green with slime. It was a grateful change to escape from the sun into the coolness of the Neidpath woods; but even there a change was seen, for the ferns hung their fronds wearily and the moss had lost all its greenness. When once more I came out to the sun, its beating on my face was so fierce that it almost burned, and I was glad when I came to the town and the shade of tree and dwelling.

The bowling green of Peebles, which is one of the best in the country, lies at the west end of the High Street at the back of the Castle Hill. It looks down on Tweed and Peebles Water, where they meet at the Cuddie's Pool, and thence over a wide stretch of landscape to the high hills. The turf had been kept with constant waterings, but, notwithstanding, it looked grey and withered. Here I found half the menfolk of Peebles assembled, and many from the villages near, to see the match which is the greatest event of the month. Each player wore a riband of a special colour. Most of them had stripped off their coats and jerkins to give their arms free play, and some of the best were busied in taking counsel with their friends as to the lie of the green. The landlord of the Cross Keys was there with a great red favour stuck in his hat, looking, as I thought, too fat and rubicund a man to have a steady eye. Near him was Peter Crustcrackit, the tailor, a little wiry man with legs bent from sitting cross-legged, thin active hands, and keen eyes well used to the sewing of fine work. Then there were carters and shepherds, stout fellows with bronzed faces and great

17

brawny chests, and the miller of the Wauk-mill, who was reported the best bowl-player in the town. Some of the folk had come down like myself merely to watch; and among them I saw Andrew Greenlees, the surgeon, who had tended me that time I went over the cauld. A motley crowd of the odds and ends of the place hung around or sat on the low wall—poachers and black-fishers and all the riff-raff of the town.

The jack was set, the order of the game arranged, and the play commenced. A long man from the Quair Water began, and sent his bowl curling up the green not four inches from the mark.

"Weel dune for Quair Water," said one. "They're nane sae blind thereaways."

Then a flesher's lad came and sent a shot close on the heels of the other and lay by his side.

At this, there were loud cries of "Weel dune, Coo's Blether," which was a name they had for him; and the fellow grew red and withdrew to the back.

Next came a little nervous man, who looked entreatingly at the bystanders as if to bespeak their consideration. "Jock Look-up, my dear," said a man solemnly, "compose your anxious mind, for thae auld wizened airms o' yours 'll no send it half-road." The little man sighed and played his bowl: it was even as the other had said, for his shot was adjudged a *hogg* and put off the green.

Then many others played till the green was crowded at one end with the balls. They played in rinks, and interest fell off for some little time till it came to the turn of the two acknowledged champions, Master Crustcrackit and the miller, to play against one another. Then the onlookers crowded round once more.

The miller sent a long swinging shot which touched the jack and carried it some inches onward. Then a bowl from the tailor curled round and lay between them and the former mark. Now arose a great dispute (for the players of Peebles had a way of their own, and to understand their rules required no ordinary share of brains) as to the propriety of Master Crustcrackit's shot, some alleging that he had played off the cloth, others defending. The miller grew furiously warm.

"Ye wee, sneck-drawin' tailor-body, wad ye set up your bit feckless face against a man o' place and siller?"

"Haud your tongue, miller," cried one. "Ye've nae cause to speak ill o' the way God made a man."

Master Crustcrackit, however, needed no defender. He was ready in a second.

"And what dae ye ca' yoursel' but a great, Godforsaken dad o' a man, wi' a wame like Braid Law and a mouth like the bottomless pit for yill and beef and a' manner o' carnal bakemeats. You to speak abune your breath to me," and he hopped round his antagonist like an enraged fighting cock.

What the miller would have said no one may guess, had not a middle-aged man, who had been sitting on a settle placidly smoking a long white pipe, come up to see what was the dispute. He was dressed in a long black coat, with small-clothes of black, and broad silver-buckled shoon. The plain white cravat around his neck marked him for a minister.

"William Laverlaw and you, Peter Crustcrackit, as the minister of this parish, I command ye to be silent. I will have no disturbance on this public green. Nay, for I will adjudge your difference myself."

All were silent in a second, and a hush of interest fell on the place.

"But that canna be," grumbled the miller, "for ye're nae great hand at the bowls."

The minister stared sternly at the speaker, who sank at once into an aggrieved quiet. "As God has appointed me the spiritual guide of this unworthy town, so also has He made me your master in secular affairs. I will settle your disputes and none other. And, sir, if you or any other dare gainsay me, then I shall feel justified in leaving argument for force, and the man who offends I shall fling into the Cuddie's Pool for the clearing of his brain and the benefit of his soul." He spoke in a slow, methodical tone, rolling the words over his tongue. Then I remembered the many stories I had heard of this man's autocratic rule over the folk of the good town of Peebles; how he, alien alike to Whig and prelatist, went on his steadfast path caring for no man and snapping his fingers at the mandates of authority. And indeed in the quiet fierce face and weighty jaws there was something which debarred men from meddling with their owner.

Such was his influence on the people that none dared oppose him, and he gave his decision, which seemed to me to be a just and fair one. After this they fell to their play once more.

Meantime I had been looking on at the sport from the vantage ground of the low wall which looked down on the river. I had debated a question of farriery with the surgeon, who was also something of a horse doctor; and called out greetings to the different players, according as I favoured their colours. Then when the game no longer amused me, I had fallen to looking over the country down to the edge of the water where the small thatched cottages were yellow in the heat, and away up the broad empty channel of Tweed. The cauld, where salmon leap in the spring and autumn, and which is the greatest cauld on the river unless it be the one at Melrose, might have been crossed dryshod. I began to hate the weariful, everlasting glare and sigh for the clouds once more, and the soft turf and the hazy skyline. Now it was so heavily oppressive that a man could scarce draw a free breath. The players dripped with sweat and looked nigh exhausted, and for myself the sulphurous air weighed on me like a mount of lead and confused such wits as I had.

Even as I looked I saw a strange thing on the river bank which chained my languid curiosity. For down the haugh, swinging along at a great pace, came a man, the like of whom I had seldom seen. He ran at a steady trot more like a horse than a human creature, with his arms set close by his sides and without bonnet or shoes. His head swung from side to side as with excessive weariness, and even at that distance I could see how he panted. In a trice he was over Peebles Water and had ascended the bank to the bowling green, cleared the low dyke, and stood gaping before us. Now I saw him plainer, and I have rarely seen a stranger sight. He seemed to have come a great distance, but no sweat stood on his brow, only a dun copper colour marking the effect of the hot sun. His breeches were utterly ragged and in places showed his long supple limbs. A shock of black hair

20

covered his head and shaded his swarthy face. His eyes were wild and keen as a hawk's, and his tongue hung out of his mouth like a dog's in a chase. Every man stopped his play and looked at the queer newcomer. A whisper went round the place that it was that "fule callant frae Brochtoun," but this brought no news to me.

The man stood still for maybe three minutes with his eyes fixed on the ground as if to recover breath. Then he looked up with dazed glances, like one wakening from sleep. He stared at me, then at the players, and burst into his tale, speaking in a high, excited voice.

"I hae run frae Drummeller to bring ye word. Quick, and get the folk out o' the waterside hooses or the feck o' the toun 'll be soomin' to Berwick in an 'oor."

No one spoke, but all stared as if they took him for a madman.

"There's been an awfu' storm up i' the muirs," he went on, panting, "and Tweed's comin' doun like a millrace. The herd o' Powmood tellt me, and I got twae 'oors start o't and cam off here what I could rin. Get the folk out o' the waterside hooses when I bid ye, wi' a' their gear and plenishing, or there'll be no sae muckle as a groat's worth left by nicht. Up wi' ye and haste, for there's nae time to lose. I heard the roar o' the water miles off, louder than ony thunderstorm and mair terrible than an army wi' banners. Quick, ye doited bodies, if ye dinna want to hae mourning and lamentation i' the toun o' Peebles."

At this, as you may believe, a great change passed over all. Some made no words about it, but rushed into the town to give the alarm; others stared stupidly as if waiting for more news; while some were disposed to treat the whole matter as a hoax. This enraged the newsbearer beyond telling. Springing up, he pointed to the western sky, and far off we saw a thick blackness creeping up the skyline. "If ye'll no believe me," said he, "will ye believe the finger o' God?" The word and the sight convinced the most distrusting.

Now Tweed, unlike all other rivers of my knowledge, rises terribly at the first rain and travels slowly, so that Tweedsmuir may be under five feet of water and Peebles high and dry. This makes the whole valley a place of exceeding danger in sultry weather, for no man knows when a thunderstorm may break in the hills and send the stream down a raging torrent. This, too, makes it possible to hear word of a flood before it comes, and by God's grace to provide against it.

The green was soon deserted. I rushed down to the waterside houses, which were in the nearest peril, and in shorter time than it takes to tell we had the people out and as much of their belongings as were worth the saving; then we hastened to the low-lying cottages on Tweed Green and did likewise. Some of the folk seemed willing to resist, because, as they said, "Whae kenned but that the body micht be a leear and they werena to hae a' this wark for naething?" For the great floods were but a tradition, and only the old men had seen the ruin which a spate could work. Nevertheless, even these were convinced by a threatening sky and a few words from the newsbearer's trenchant tongue. Soon the High Street and the wynds were thick with household belongings, and the Castle Hill was crowded with folk to see the coming of the flood.

By this time the grim line of black had grown over half the sky, and down fell great drops of rain into the white, sunbaked channel. It was strange to watch these mighty splashes falling into the little stagnant pools and the runlets of flowing water. And still the close, thick heat hung over all, and men looked at the dawnings of the storm with sweat running over their brows. With the rain came a mist—a white ghastly haze which obliterated the hills and came down nigh to the stream. A sound, too, grew upon our ears, at first far away and dim, but increasing till it became a dull hollow thunder, varied with a strange crackling swishing noise which made a moan eerie to listen to. Then all of a sudden the full blast of the thing came upon us. Men held their breaths as the wind and rain choked them and drove them back. It was scarce possible to see ahead, but the outlines of the gorge of Neidpath fleeted through the drift, whence the river issued. Every man turned his eyes thither and strained them to pierce the gloom.

Suddenly round the corner of the hill appeared a great yellow wave crested with white foam and filling the whole space. Down

22

it came roaring and hissing, mowing the pines by the waterside as a reaper mows down hay with a scythe. Then with a mighty bound it broke from the hill barriers and spread over the haugh. Now the sound was like the bubbling of a pot ere it boils. We watched it in terror and admiration, as it swept on its awful course. In a trice it was at the cauld, and the cauld disappeared under a whirl of foam; now it was on the houses, and the walls went in like nutshells and the rubble was borne onward. A cry got up of "the bridge", and all hung in wonder as it neared the old stonework, the first barrier to the torrent's course, the brave bridge of Peebles. It flung itself on it with fiendish violence, but the stout masonwork stood firm, and the boiling tide went on through the narrow arches, leaving the bridge standing unshaken, as it had stood against many a flood. As we looked, we one and all broke into a cheer in honour of the old masons who had made so trusty a piece of stone.

I found myself in the crowd of spectators standing next to the man who had brought the tidings. He had recovered his breath and was watching the sight with a look half of interest and half of vexation. When all was past and only the turbid river remained, he shook himself like a dog and made to elbow his way out. "I maun be awa'," he said, speaking to himself, "and a sair job I'll hae gettin' ower Lyne Water." When I heard him I turned round and confronted him. There was something so pleasing about his face, his keen eyes and alert head, that I could not forbear from offering him my hand, and telling him of my admiration for his deed. I was still but a boy and he was clearly some years my elder, so I made the advance, I doubt not, with a certain shyness and hesitancy. He looked at me sharply and smiled.

"Ye're the young laird o' Barns," said he; "I ken ye weel though ye maybe are no acquaint wi' me. I'm muckle honoured, sir, and gin ye'll come Brochtoun-ways sometime and speir for Nicol Plenderleith, he'll tak ye to burns that were never fished afore and hills that never heard the sound o' a shot."

I thanked him, and watched him slipping through the crowd till he was lost to view. This was my first meeting with Nicol

Plenderleith, of whose ways and doings this tale will have much to say. The glamour of the strange fellow was still upon me as I set myself to make my road home. I am almost ashamed to tell of my misfortunes; for after crossing the bridge and riding to Manor Water, I found that this stream likewise had risen and had not left a bridge in its whole course. So I had to go up as far as St. Gordians' Cross before I could win over it, and did not reach Barns till after midnight, where I found my father half-crazy with concern and Tam Todd making ready to go and seek me.

CHAPTER IV

I GO TO THE COLLEGE AT GLASGOW

By this time I had grown a great stalwart lad, little above the middle height, but broad and sinewy. I had made progress in all manly sports and could fling the hammer almost as far as the Manor blacksmith, while in leaping and running I had few rivals among lads of my age. Also I was no bad swordsman, but could stand my own against all the wiles of Tam Todd, and once even disarmed him, to his own unspeakable disgust. In my studies, which I pursued as diligently as I could, with no teachers and not over many books, I had made some little advance, having read through most of the Greek tragedians and advanced some distance in the study of Plato; while in the Latin tongue I had become such an adept that I could both read and write it with ease.

When I had reached the mature age of eighteen, who should come up into our parts but my famous relative, Master Gilbert Burnet, the preacher at St. Clement's in London, of whom I have already spoken. He was making a journey to Edinburgh and had turned out of his way to revive an old acquaintance. My father was overjoyed to see him, and treated him to the best the house could produce. He stayed with us two days, and I remember him still as he sat in a great armchair opposite my father, with his broad velvet cap and grey, peaked beard, and weighty brows. Yet when he willed, though for ordinary a silent man, he could talk as gaily and wittily as any town gallant; so much indeed that my father, who was somewhat hard to please, declared him the best companion he ever remembered.

Before he left, Master Burnet examined me on my progress in polite learning, and finding me well advanced, he would have it that I should be sent forthwith to Glasgow College. He exacted a promise from my father to see to this, and left behind him, when he departed, letters of introduction to many of the folk there, for he himself had, at one time, been professor of divinity in the place. As for myself, I was nothing loath to go and see places beyond Tweeddale and add to my stock of learning; for about this time a great enthusiasm for letters had seized me (which I suppose happens at some time or other to most men), and I conceived my proper vocation in life to be that of the scholar. I have found in an old manuscript book a list of the titles of imaginary works, editions, poems, treatises, all with my unworthy name subscribed as the author. So it was settled that I should ride to Glasgow and take lodgings in the town for the sake of the college classes.

I set out one November morning, riding Maisie alone, for no student was allowed to have a servant, nor any one below the degree of Master of Arts. The air was keen and frosty, and I rode in high fettle by the towns of Biggar and Lanark to the valley of the Clyde. I lay all night at Crossford in the house of a distant relative. Thence the next day I rode to Hamilton, and in the evening came to the bridge of the Clyde at Glasgow. Then I presented myself to the Principal and Regents of the college and was duly admitted, putting on the red gown, the badge of the student class, than which I believe there is no more hideous habiliment.

The college in those days was poor enough, having been wellnigh ruined by the extortions of Lord Middleton and his drunken crew; and it had not yet benefited by the rich donations of the Reverend Zachary Boyd of the Barony Kirk. Still, the standard of learning in the place was extraordinarily high, especially in dialectic and philosophy—a standard which had been set by the famous Andrew Melville when he was a professor in the place. I have heard disputations there in the evenings between the schoolmen and the new philosophers, the like of which could scarcely be got from the length and breadth of the land.

Across the High Street were the college gardens and green pleasant orchards where the professors were wont to walk and the scholars to have their games. Through the middle ran the clear Molendinar Burn, so called by the old Romans, and here I loved to watch the trout and young salmon leaping. There was a severe rule against scholars fishing in the stream, and I was fain to content myself with the sight. For soon a violent fit of homesickness seized me, and I longed for the rush of Tweed and the pleasant sweep of Manor; so it was one of my greatest consolations to look at this water and fancy myself far away from the town. One other lad who came from Perthshire used to come and stand with me and tell me tales of his fishing exploits; and I did likewise with him till we became great companions. Many afternoons I spent here, sometimes with a book and sometimes without one; in the fine weather I would lie on the grass and dream, and in rough, boisterous winter days I loved to watch the Molendinar, flooded and angry, fling its red waters against the old stones of the bridge.

No one of us was permitted to carry arms of any kind, so I had to sell my sword on my first coming to the town. This was a great hardship to me, for whereas when I carried a weapon I had some sense of my own importance, now I felt no better than the rest of the unarmed crowd about me. Yet it was a wise precaution, for in other places where scholars are allowed to strut like cavaliers there are fights and duels all the day long, so that the place looks less like an abode of the Muses than a disorderly tavern. Nevertheless, there were many manly exercises to be had, for in the greens in the garden we had trials of skill at archery and golf and other games of the kind. At the first mentioned I soon became a great master, for I had a keen eye from much living among woods and hills, and soon there was no one who could come near me at the play. As for golf, I utterly failed to excel; and indeed it seems to me that golf is like the divine art of poetry, the gift for which is implanted in man at his birth or not at all. Be that as it may, I never struck a golf ball fairly in my life, and I misdoubt I never shall.

As for my studies, for which I came to the place, I think I made great progress. For after my first fit of homesickness was over, I fell in with the ways of the college and acquired such a liking for the pursuit of learning that I felt more convinced than ever that Providence had made me for a scholar. In my classes I won the commendation of both professors; especially in the class of dialectic, where an analysis of Aristotle's method was highly praised by Master Sandeman, the professor. This fine scholar and accomplished gentleman helped me in many ways, and for nigh two months, when he was sick of the fever, I lectured to his class in his stead. We were all obliged to talk in the Latin tongue, and at first my speech was stiff and awkward enough but by-and-by I fell into the way of it and learned to patter it as glibly as a Spanish monk.

It may be of interest to those of my house that I should give some account of my progress in the several studies, to show that our family is not wholly one of soldiers. In Greek I studied above others the works of Plato, delighting especially in his *Phaedo*, which I had almost by heart; Aristotle likewise, though I read but little of him in his own tongue. I completed a translation of the first part of Plato's *Republic* into Latin, which Master Sandeman was pleased to say was nigh as elegant as George Buchanan's. Also I was privileged to discover certain notable emendations in the text of this work, which I sent in manuscript to the famous Schookius of Groningen, who incorporated them in his edition then in preparation, but after the fashion of Dutchmen sent me no thanks.

As regards philosophy, which I hold the most divine of all studies, I was in my first year a most earnest Platonic; nay, I went farther than the master himself, as is the way of little minds when they seek to comprehend a great one. In those days I went about in sober attire and strove in all things to order my life according to the rule of philosophy, seeking to free myself from all

27

disturbing outside powers and live the life of pure contemplation. I looked back with unutterable contempt on my past as a turbid and confused medley, nor did I seek anything better in life than quiet and leisure for thought and study. In such a condition I spent the first month of my stay at Glasgow.

Then the Platonic fit left me and I was all for Aristotle and the Peripatetics. Here, at last, thought I, have I got the *siccum lumen*, which Heraclitus spoke of; and his distinct and subtle reasoning seemed to me to be above doubt. And indeed I have never wondered at the schoolmen and others who looked upon Aristotle as having reached the height of human wisdom, for his method is so all-embracing and satisfying that it breeds wonder in the heart of any man; and it affords so sure a bottom for thought that men perforce become Aristotelians.

In the midsummer months I went down to Tweeddale again, where I astonished my father and all in the place with my new learning, and also grieved them. For I had no love for fishing or shooting; I would scarce ride two miles for the pleasure of it; my father's tales, in which I delighted before, had grown tiresome; and I had no liking for anything save bending over books. When I went to Dawyck to see Marjory, she knew not what had come over me, I was so full of whims and fancies. "O John," she said, "your face is as white as a woman's, and you have such a horrible cloak. Go and get another at once, and not shame your friends." Yet even Marjory had little power over me, for I heeded her not, though aforetime I would have ridden post-haste to Peebles and got me a new suit, and painted my face if I had thought that thereby I would pleasure her.

When the autumn came again I returned to college more inclined than ever for the life of a scholar. I fell to my studies with renewed zeal, and would doubtless have killed myself with work had I not been nearly killed with the fever, which made me more careful of my health. And now, like the weathercock I was, my beliefs shifted yet again. For studying the schoolmen, who were the great upholders of Aristotle, I found in them so many contradictions and phantasies which they fathered on their master that, after reading the diatribes of Peter Ramus and others against him, I was almost persuaded that I had been grievously misled. Then, at last, I saw that the fault lay not in Aristotle but in his followers, who sought to find in him things that were beyond the compass of his thought. So by degrees I came round toward the new philosophy, which a party in the college upheld. They swore by the great names of Bacon and Galileo and the other natural philosophers, but I hesitated to follow them, for they seemed to me to disdain all mental philosophy, which I hold is the greater study. I was of this way of thinking when I fell in one day with an English book, a translation of a work by a Frenchman, one Renatus Descartes, published in London in the year 1649. It gave an account of the progress in philosophy of this man, who followed no school, but, clearing his mind of all presuppositions, instituted a method for himself. It marked for me the turning point; for I gave in my allegiance without hesitation to this philosopher, and ever since I have held by his system with some modifications. It is needless for me to enter further into my philosophy, for I have by me a written exposition of the works of this Descartes with my own additions, which I intend, if God so please, to give soon to the world.

For two years I abode at the college, thinking that I was destined by nature for a studious life, and harbouring thoughts of going to the university of Saumur to complete my studies. I thought that my spirit was chastened to a fit degree, and so no doubt it was, for those who had feared me at first on account of my heavy fist and straightforward ways, now openly scoffed at me without fear of punishment. Indeed, one went so far one day as to jostle me off the causeway, and I made no return, but went on as if nothing had happened, deeming it beneath a wise man to be distracted by mundane trifles. Yet, mind you, in all this there was nothing Christian or like unto the meekness of our Master, as I have seen in some men; but rather an absurd attempt to imitate those who would have lived very differently had their lot been cast in our hot and turbid days.

How all this was changed and I veered round of a sudden to the opposite I must hasten to tell. One April day, towards the close of my second year, I was going up the High Street toward the Cathedral with a great parcel of books beneath my arm, when I heard a shouting and a jingling, and a troop of horse came down the street. I stood back into the shelter of a doorway, for soldiers were wont to bear little love to scholars, and I did not care to risk their rough jests. From this place I watched their progress, and a gallant sight it was. Some twenty men in buff jerkins and steel headpieces rode with a clatter of bridles and clank of swords. I marked their fierce sun-brown faces and their daredevil eyes as they looked haughtily down on the crowd as on lower beings. And especially I marked their leader. He sat a fine bay horse with ease and grace; his plumed hat set off his high-coloured face and long brown curls worn in the fashion of the day; and as he rode he bowed to the people with large condescension. He was past in a second, but not before I had recognized the face and figure of my cousin Gilbert.

I stood for some minutes staring before me while the echoes of the horses' hooves died away down the street. This, I thought, is the destiny of my cousin, only four years my elder, a soldier a gentleman, a great man in his place; while I am but a nameless scholar, dreaming away my manhood in the pursuits of a dotard. I was so overwhelmed with confusion that I stood gaping with a legion of thoughts and opposing feeling running through my brain. Then all the spirit of my family rose within me. By Heaven, I would make an end of this; I would get me home without delay; I would fling my books into the Clyde; I would go to the wars; I would be a great cavalier, and, by the Lord, I would keep up the name of the house! I was astonished myself at the sudden change in my feelings, for in the space of some ten minutes a whole age had passed from me, and I had grown from a boy to some measure of manhood. I came out from the close-mouth with my head in the air and defiance against all the world in my eye.

Before I had gone five paces I met the lad who had jostled me aforetime, a big fellow of a raw-boned Ayrshire house, and before he could speak I had him by the arm and had pulled him across the way into the college gardens. There I found a quiet green place, and plucking off my coat I said, "Now, Master Dalrymple, you and I have a small account to settle." With that we fell to with our fists, and in the space of a quarter of an hour I had beaten him so grievously that he was fain to cry mercy. I let him go, and with much whimpering he slunk away.

Then I went into the town and bought myself a new blade and a fine suit of clothes—all with the greatest gusto and lightness of heart. I went to the inn where Maisie was stabled, and bade them have her ready for me at the college gate in an hour. Then I bade goodbye to all my friends, but especially to Master Sandeman, from whom I was loath to part. I did not fling my books into the Clyde as at first I proposed, but left injunctions that they were to be sent by the carrier. So, having paid all my debts, for my father had kept me well appointed with money, I waved a long farewell and set out for my own country.

CHAPTER V

COUSINLY AFFECTION

It was near midday before I started, so that night I got no farther than the town of Hamilton, but lay at the inn there. The next morning I left betimes, thinking to reach Barns in the afternoon. As I rode along the green sward by the side of Clyde, the larks were singing in the sky and the trout were plashing in the waters, and all the world was gay. The apple orchards sent their blossom across the road, and my hat brushed it down in showers on my horse and myself, so that we rode in a mail of pink and white. I plucked a little branch and set it in my hat, and sang all the songs I knew as I cantered along. I cried good-day to every man, and flung money to the little children who shouted as I passed, so that I believe if there had been many more boys on the road I would have reached Tweeddale a beggar. At Crossford, where the Nethan meets the Clyde, I met a man who had been to the fishing and had caught a big salmon-trout; and as I looked, my old love for the sport awoke within me, and I longed to feel a rod in my hand. It was good to be alive, to taste the fresh air, to feel the sun and wind, and I cried a plague on all close lecture-rooms and

31

musty books.

At Lanark I had a rare dinner at the hostel there. The inn had excellent fare, as I knew of old, so I rode up to the door and demanded its best. It was blessed to see a man obey your words after for many months being a servant of others. I had a dish of well-fed trout and a piece of prime mutton and as good claret, I think, as I have ever tasted. Then I rode over Lanark Moor to Hyndford and through the moor of Carmichael and under the great shadow of Tintock. Here the smell of burning heather came to greet my nostrils, and so dear and homelike did it seem that I could have wept for very pleasure. The whaups and snipe were making a fine to-do on the bent, and the black-faced sheep grazed in peace. At the top of the knowe above Symington I halted, for there before my eyes were the blue hills of Tweeddale. There was Trehenna and the hills above Broughton, and Drummelzier Law and Glenstivon Dod, and nearer, the great Caerdon; and beyond all a long blue back which I knew could be none other than the hill of Scrape which shadowed Dawyck and my lady.

I came to Barns at three o'clock in the afternoon, somewhat stiff from my ride, but elated with my home-coming. It was with strange feelings that I rode up the long avenue of beeches, every one of which I could have told blindfold. The cattle looked over the palings at me as if glad to see me return. Maisie cocked up her ears at the hares in the grass, and sniffed the hill air as if she had been in a prison for many days. And when I came to the bend of the road and saw the weather-beaten tower, my heart gave a great leap within me, for we Tweeddale men dearly love our own countryside, doubtless by reason of its exceeding beauty.

As I rode up Tam Todd came out from the back, and seeing me, let fall the water which he was carrying and ran to my side.

"Eh, Maister John," said he, "I'm blithe to see ye back, sae braw and genty-like. My airm's fair like timmer wi' stiffness for want o' the backsword play, and the troots in Tweed are turned as thick as peas for want o' you to haul them oot; and twae mornings last week there were deer keekin' in at the front door as tame as kittlins. There's muckle need o' ye at hame."

He would have gone on in this strain for an hour had I not cut him short by asking for my father.

"Middlin', just middlin'. He misses ye sair. He'll scarce gang outdoors noo, but he'll be a' richt gin he sees ye again. Oh, and I've something mair to tell ye. That wanchancy cousin o' yours, Maister Gilbert, cam yestreen, and he'll be bidin' till the deil kens when. I'se warrant he's at meat wi' the auld maister the noo, for he cam in frae the hills geyan hungry."

Now at this intelligence I was not overpleased. My cousin was a great man and a gentleman, but never at any time over friendly to me, and I knew that to my father he was like salt in the mouth. I blamed the ill-luck which had sent him to Barns on the very day of my home-coming. I needs must be on my dignity in his company, for he was quick to find matter for laughter, and it was hard that he should come at the time when I longed so eagerly for the free ways of the house. However, there was no help for it, I reflected, and went in.

In the passage I met Jean Morran, my old nurse, who had heard the sound of voices, and came out to see who the newcomer might be. "Maister John, Maister John, and is't yoursel'? It's a glad day for the house o' Barns when ye come back"; and when I gave her the shawl-pin I had brought her from Glasgow, she had scarce any words to thank me with. So, knowing that my father would be in the dining-hall with his guest, I opened the door and walked in unbidden.

My father sat at the head of the long oak table which had been scoured to a light brown and shone like polished stone. Claret, his favourite drink, was in a tankard by his elbow, and many wines decked the board. Lower down sat my cousin, gallantly dressed in the fashion of the times, with a coat of fine Spanish leather and small-clothes of some rich dark stuff. His plumed hat and riding cloak of purple velvet lay on the settle at his side. His brown hair fell over his collar and shoulders and well set off his strong, brown face. He sat after the fashion of a soldier, on the side of his chair half turned away from the table, and every now and then he would cast a piece of meat to Pierce, my old hound, who lay stretched by the fireplace.

My father turned round as I entered, and when he saw me his

face glowed with pleasure. Had we been alone we should have met otherwise, but it is not meet to show one's feelings before a stranger, even though that stranger be one of the family. He contented himself with looking eagerly upon me and bidding me welcome in a shaking voice. I marked with grief that his eye did not seem so keen and brave as before, and that he was scarce able to rise from his chair.

My cousin half arose, and made me a grand bow in his courtly fashion.

"Welcome, my dear cousin," said he. "I am glad to see that your studies have had little effect on your face." (I was flushed with hard riding.) "You look as if you had just come from a campaign. But fall to. Here are prime fish which I can commend; and venison, also good, though I have had better. Here, too, is wine, and I drink to your success, my learned cousin;" and he filled his glass and drank it at a gulp. He spoke in a half-bantering tone, though his words were kindly. I answered him briskly.

"I had little thought to find you here, Gilbert, but I am right glad to see you. You are prospering mightily, I hear, and will soon be forgetting your poor cousins of Barns;" and after a few more words I set myself to give my father a history of my doings at Glasgow College. Again, had we been alone, I should have told him my causes for leaving and my wishes for my after-life, but since my cousin was present, who had ever a sharp tongue, I judged it better to say nothing.

I told my father all that I could think of, and then asked how he had fared in my absence, for I had had but few letters, and what of note had happened at Barns.

"Ay, John," he said, "I'm an old man. I fear that my life here will be short. I scarce can get outside without Tam Todd to lean on, and I have little sleep o' nights. And, John, I could wish that you would bide at home now, for I like to see you beside me, and you'll have learned all the folk of Glasgow have to teach you. I once wished you a soldier, but I am glad now that I let the thing blow by, for I would have cared little to have you coming here but once in the six months, for a flying visit."

"Nay, uncle," said my cousin, "you do not put the matter

34

fairly. For myself, I believe there is none busier in Scotland than I, but, Gad, I have always time to slip home to Eaglesham for a day or more. But my father would care little though he never saw me but once in the year, for each time I go back I get a long sermon on my conduct, with my expenses for the year as a text, till I am fairly driven out of the house for peace."

At this my father laughed. "Ay, ay," said he, "that's like my brother Gilbert. He was always a hard man at the siller. Man, I mind when we were both the terrors o' the place, but all the while not a thing would he do, if it meant the loss of a bodle. Pity but I had taken after him in that, and John would have been better supplied today."

"Oh," I answered, "I have all I need and more."

Hereupon my cousin spoke with a sneer in his voice. "A groat is enough for a scholar, but the soldier must have a crown. Your scholar, as doubtless John can tell, is content if he have a sad-coloured suit, some musty books, and a stoup of bad wine; but your fine gentleman must have his horses and servants, and dress himself like his quality for all the maids to stare at, and have plenty of loose silver to fling to the gaping crowd; and he is a poor fellow indeed if he do not eat and drink the best that each tavern can give. As for me, I would as soon be a clown in the fields as a scholar, with apologies to my cousin;" and he made me another of his mocking bows.

I answered as gently as I could that gentrice did not consist in daintiness of eating and drinking or boisterous display, and that in my opinion nothing gave so fine a flavour to gentility as a tincture of letters; but my father changed the conversation by asking Gilbert what he had been after that day.

" 'Faith, it would be hard to say." said he. "I got a gun from that long-legged, sour-faced groom and went up the big hill above the trees to have a shot at something. I killed a couple of hares and sprung an old muirfowl; but the day grew warm and I thought that the wood would make a pleasant shade, so I e'en turned my steps there and went to sleep below a great oak, and dreamed that I ran a man through the bowels for challenging my courage. It was an ill-omened dream, and I expected to meet with some mishap to account for it ere I got back; but I saw nothing except a lovely girl plucking primroses by the waterside. Zounds, Jock, what a fool you must be never to have found out this beauty! She had hair like gold and eyes like sapphires. I've seen many a good-looking wench, but never one like her."

"And what did you do?" I asked, with my heart beating wildly.

"Do?" he laughed. "Your scholar would have passed in silence and written odes to her as Venus or Helen for months; whereas I took off my bonnet and made haste to enter into polite conversation. But this girl would have none of me; she's a rose, I warrant, with a pretty setting of thorns. She tripped away, and when I made to follow her, became Madame Fine-airs at once, and declared that her servants were within easy reach, so I had better have a care of my conduct."

My father shot a sharp glance at me, and addressed my cousin. "The maid would be Marjory Veitch, old Sir John's daughter, at Dawyck. He, poor man, has gone to his account, and her brother is abroad, so the poor girl is lonely enough in that great house. John and she have been friends from the time they were children. She has come here, too, and a pretty, modest lass she is, though she favours her mother rather than her father's folk."

At this intelligence my cousin whistled long and low. "So, so," said he, "my scholar has an eye in his head, has he? And Dawyck is not far off, and—well, no wonder you do not care for the military profession. Though, let me tell you, it is as well for the course of true love that there are few cavaliers in this countryside, else Mistress Marjory might have higher notions."

I answered nothing, for, though I loved Marjory well, and thought that she loved me, I had never spoken to her on the matter; for from childhood we had been comrades and friends. So I did not care to reply on a matter which I regarded as so delicate and uncertain.

My cousin was a man who grew sorely vexed by receiving no answer from the object of his wit; and, perhaps on this account, he went further than he meant in his irritation. "Nay, John," he went on, "you're but a sorry fellow at the best, with your tags from the Latin, and your poor spirit. I am one of the meanest of his Majesty's soldiers, but I can outride you, I can beat you at swordplay, at mark-shooting, at all manly sports. I can hold my head before the highest in the land; I can make the vulgar bow before me to the ground. There are no parts of a gentleman's equipment in which I am not your better."

Now, had we been alone, I should not have scrupled to fling the lie in his teeth, and offer to settle the matter on the spot. But I did not wish to excite my father in his feeble health, so I made no reply beyond saying that events would show the better man. My father, however, took it upon himself to defend me. "Peace, Gilbert," he said. "I will not have my son spoken thus of in my own house. He has as much spirit as you, I'll warrant, though he is less fond of blowing his own trumpet." I saw with annoyance that my father plainly thought my conduct cowardly, and would have been better pleased had I struck my cousin then and there. But I knew how cruelly excited he would be by the matter, and, in his weakness, I feared the result. Also, the man was our guest, and my cousin.

When we rose from supper I assisted my father in walking to his chair by the fire; for, though the weather was mild and springlike, his blood was so impoverished that he felt the cold keenly. Then my cousin and myself strolled out of doors to the green lawn, below which Tweed ran low and silvery clear. I felt anger against him, yet not so much as I would have felt towards another man, had he used the same words; for I knew Gilbert to be of an absurd boasting nature, which made him say more evil than he had in his heart. Still my honour, or pride (call it what you please), was wounded, and I cast about me for some way to heal it.

"Gilbert," I said, "we have both done much work today, so we are both about equally wearied."

"Maybe," said he.

"But your horse is fresh, and a good one, as I know; and you are a good horseman, as you say yourself. You had much to say about my poor horsemanship at supper. Will you try a race with me?"

He looked at me scornfully for a minute. "Nay there is little honour to be got from that. You know the ground, and your horse, for all I know, may be swifter than mine. It was not of horses I spoke, but of the riders."

"In the race which I offer you," I answered, "we will both start fair. Do you see yon rift in the hill beyond Scrape? It is the Red Syke, a long dark hole in the side of the hill. I have never ridden there, for the ground is rough and boggy, and I have never heard of a horseman there since Montrose's rising. Will you dare to ride with me to yonder place and back."

At this my cousin's face changed a little, for he had no liking for breaking his neck on the wild hills. And now, when I look back on the proposal, it seems a mad, foolhardy one in very truth. But then we were both young and spirited, and reckless of our lives.

"Mount and ride," said he. "I'll be there and back before you are half-road, unless, indeed, I have to carry you home."

Together we went round to the stables, and I saddled a black horse of my father's, for Maisie had already travelled far that day. The Weasel, we called him, for he was long and thin in the flanks, with a small head, and a pointed muzzle. He was viciously ill-tempered, and would allow no groom to saddle him; but before I had gone to Glasgow I had mounted and ridden him bareback up and down the channel of Tweed till he was dead beat, and I half drowned and shaken almost to pieces. Ever since this escapade he had allowed me to do what I liked with him; and, though I did not find him as pleasant to ride as the incomparable Maisie, yet I knew his great strength and fleetness. My cousin's horse was a good cavalry charger, strong, but, as I thought, somewhat too heavy in the legs for great endurance.

We mounted and rode together out among the trees to the fields which bordered on the hills. I was sore in the back when I started, but, after the first half-mile, my sprightliness returned and I felt fit to ride over Broad Law. My cousin was in an ill mood, for the sport was not to his taste, though he felt bound in honour to justify his words.

The spur of Scrape which we came to was called by the country people the Deid Wife, for there an Irishwoman, the wife of one of Montrose's Camp followers, had been killed by the folk of the place after the rout at Philiphaugh. We had much ado to keep our horses from slipping back, for the loose stones which covered the face of the hill gave a feeble foothold. The Weasel took the brae like a deer, but my cousin's heavy horse laboured and panted sorely ere it reached the top. Before us stretched the long upland moors, boggy, and cleft with deep ravines with Scrape on the right, and straight in front, six miles beyond, the great broad crest of Dollar Law. Here we separated, my cousin riding forward, while I thought the road to the left would be the surer. Clear before us lay the Red Syke, an ugly gash, into which the setting sun was beginning to cast his beams.

And now I found myself in a most perilous position. The Weasel's feet were light and tender, and he stumbled among the stones and tall heather till I had sore work to keep my seat. My cousin's horse was of a heavier make, and I could see it galloping gallantly over the broken ground. I cheered my steed with words, and patted his neck, and kept a tight hand on the rein. Sometimes we slipped among the shingle and sometimes stumbled over rocks half hid in brackens. Then we passed into a surer place among short, burned heather. The dry twigs gave forth a strange creaking sound as the horses' feet trod on them, and puffs of grey dust and ashes, the sign of the burning, rose at every step. Then, beyond this, we came to a long stretch of crisp mountain grass, pleasant for both horse and rider. We splashed through little tumbling burns, and waded through pools left by the spring rains. But, of a sudden, the ground grew softer, and even the Weasel's light weight could not pass in safety. At one time, indeed, I reined him back just on the brink of a treacherous well-eye, from which neither of us would have returned. I cast a glance at my cousin, who was still ahead; his heavy charger was floundering wearily, and he lashed it as if his life were at stake. Then we passed the green bog and came to a great peat-moss, full of hags, where the shepherds had been casting peats. Here the riding was more difficult, for the holes whence the peats had come were often some five feet deep, and it was no easy matter to get a horse out of that treacherous black mud. The Weasel did gallantly, and only once did I dismount, when his hind feet were too deeply sunk to permit him to leap. Beyond me I saw my cousin, riding swiftly, for the middle of the moss, as it chanced, was the firmest and evenest place. We were now scarce a hundred yards from the ravine of the Red Syke, and, even as I looked, I saw him reach it, rest a second to give his horse breathing space, and then turn on his homeward way.

I came to the place a minute after, and having compassion on my brave horse, I dismounted, and eased him of my weight for a little. Then I got on his back again and set off. Gilbert I saw before me, riding, as I thought, in the worst part, and with a fury that must tell sooner or later on his heavy steed. I had scarce been a moment in the saddle, when, so strange are the ways of horses, the Weasel became aware, for the first time, of the other in front. Before, it had been a toil for him, now it became a pleasure, a race which it lay with his honour to win. He cocked up his wicked black ears, put down his head, and I felt the long legs gathering beneath me. I cried aloud with delight, for now I knew that no horse in Tweeddale could hope to match him when the mood was on him. He flew over the hags as if he had been in a paddock; he leaped among the hard parts of the green bog, from tussock to tussock, as skilfully as if he had known nothing but mosses all his days. We came up with Gilbert at the edge of the rough ground, lashing his horse, with his face flushed and his teeth set. We passed him like the wind, and were galloping among the rocks and brackens, while he was painfully picking his steps. A merciful Providence must have watched over the Weasel's path that day, for never horse ran so recklessly. Among slippery boulders and cruel jagged rocks and treacherous shingle he ran like a hare. I grew exultant, laughed, and patted his neck. The sun was setting behind us, and we rode in a broad patch of yellow light. In a trice we were on the brow of the Deid Wife. Down we went, now slipping yards at a time, now doubling along the side; sometimes I was almost over the horse's head, sometimes all but off at the tail; there was never, since the two daft lairds rode Horsehope Craig, such a madcap ride. I scarce know how I reached the foot in safety: but reach it I did, and rode merrily among the trees till I came to the green meadow lands about the house of Barns. Here I dismounted and waited for my cousin, for I did not care to have the serving-men laugh at him riding in after me.

I waited a good half-hour before he appeared. A sorry sight he presented. His breeches and jerkin had more than one rent in them; his hat was gone; and his face was flushed crimson with effort. His horse had bleeding knees, and its shoulders shook pitifully.

"Pardon me, Gilbert," I said in a fit of repentance; "it was a foolish thing in me to lead you such a senseless road. I might have known that your horse was too heavy for the work. It was no fault of yours that you did not come home before me. I trust that we may forget our quarrels, and live in friendship, as kinsmen should."

"Friendship be damned," he cried in a mighty rage.

CHAPTER VI

HOW MASTER GILBERT BURNET PLAYED
A GAME AND WAS CHECKMATED

That night I was too wearied and sore in body to sleep. My mind also was troubled, for I had made an enemy of my cousin, who, as I knew, was not of a nature to forgive readily. His words about Marjory had put me into a ferment of anxiety. Here was my love, bound to me by no promise, at the mercy of all the gallants of the countryside. Who was I to call myself her lover, when as yet no word of love had passed between us? Yet, in my inmost heart, I knew that I might get the promise any day I chose. Then thoughts of my cousin came to trouble me. I feared him no more than a fly in matters betwixt man and man; but might he not take it into his head to make love to the mistress of Dawyck? and maids dearly love a dashing cavalier. At length, after much stormy indecision, I made up my mind. I would ride to Dawyck next morn and get my lady's word, and so forestall Gilbert or any other.

I woke about six o'clock; and, looking out from the narrow window, for Barns had been built three hundred years before, I saw that the sky was cloudless and blue, and the morning as clear as could be seen in spring. I hastily dressed, and, getting some slight breakfast from Jean Morran, saddled Maisie, who was now as active as ever, and rode out among the trees. I feared to come to Dawyck too early, so I forded Tweed below the island, and took the road up the farther bank by Lyne and Stobo. All the world was bright; an early lark sang high in the heaven; merles and thrushes were making fine music among the low trees by the river. The haze was lifting off the great Manor Water hills; the Red Syke, the scene of the last night's escapade, looked very distant in the morning light; and far beyond all Dollar Law and the high hills about Manorhead were flushed with sunlight on their broad foreheads. A great gladness rose in me when I looked at the hills, for they were the hills of my own country; I knew every glen and corrie, every water and little burn. Before me the Lyne Water hills were green as grass with no patch of heather, and to the left, the mighty form of Scrape, half clothed in forest, lay quiet and sunlit. I know of no fairer sight on earth; and this I say, after having travelled in other countries, and seen something of their wonders; for to my mind there is a grace, a wild loveliness, in Tweedside, like a flower garden on the edge of a moorland, which is wholly its own.

I crossed Lyne Water by the new bridge, just finished in the year before, and entered the wood of Dawyck. For this great forest stretches on both sides of Tweed, though it is greater on the side on which stands the house. In the place where I rode it was thinner, and the trees smaller, and indeed around the little village of Stobo there lies an open part of some fields' width. At the little inn there, I had a morning's draught of mulled ale, for I was somewhat cold with riding in the spring air. Then I forded Tweed at a place called the Cow Ford, and, riding through a wide avenue of lime trees, came in sight of the grey towers of Dawyck.

I kept well round to the back, for I did not care that the serving-folk should see me and spread tales over all the countryside. I knew that Marjory's window looked sharp down on a patch of green lawn, bordered by lime trees, so I rode into the shadow and dismounted. I whistled thrice in a way which I had, and which Marjory had learned to know long before, when we were children, and I used to come and beguile her out for long trampings among the hills. Today it had no effect, for the singing of birds drowned my notes, so I had nothing left but to throw bits of bark against her window. This rude expedient met with more success than it deserved, for in a minute I saw her face behind the glass. She smiled gladly when she saw me, and disappeared, only to appear again in the little door beside the lilacs. She had no hat, so her bright hair hung loose over her neck and was blown about by the morning winds. Her cheeks were pink and white, like apple blossom, and her lithe form was clad in a dress of blue velvet, plainly adorned as for a country maiden. A spray of lilac was in her breast, and she carried a bunch of sweet-smelling stuff in her hands.

She came gladly towards me, her eyes dancing with pleasure. "How soon you have returned! And how brave you look," said she, with many more pretty and undeserved compliments.

"Ay, Marjory," I answered, "I have come back to Tweeddale, for I have had enough of Glasgow College and books, and I was wearying for the hills and Tweed and a sight of your face. There are no maidens who come near to you with all their finery. You are as fair as the spring lilies in the garden at Barns."

"O John," she laughed, "where did you learn to pay fine compliments? You will soon be as expert at the trade as any of them. I met a man yesterday in the woods who spoke like you, though with a more practised air; but I bade him keep his fine words for his fine ladies, for they suited ill with the hills and a plain country maid."

At this, I must suppose that my brows grew dark, for she went on laughingly.

"Nay, you are not jealous? It ill becomes a scholar and a philosopher as you are, Master John, to think so much of an idle word. Confess, sir, that you are jealous. Why, you are as bad as

43

a lady in a play."

I could not make out her mood, which was a new one to me—a mocking pleasant raillery, which I took for the rightful punishment of my past follies.

"I am not jealous," I said, "for jealousy is feeling which needs an object ere it can exist. No man may be jealous, unless he has something to be jealous about."

"John, John," she cried, and shook her head prettily, "you are incorrigible. I had thought you had learned manners in the town, and behold, you are worse than when you went away. You come here, and your first word to me is that I am nothing."

"God knows," I said, "I would fain be jealous, and yet—" I became awkward and nervous, for I felt that my mission was not prospering, and that I was becoming entangled in a maze of meaningless speech. The shortest and plainest way is still the best, in love as in all things.

But I was not to be let off, and she finished my sentence for me. "If only you could find a worthy object for your feeling, you mean," she said. "Very well, sir, since I am so little valued in your eyes, we will speak no more on the matter."

"Marjory," I said, coming to the matter at once, "you and I have been old comrades. We have fished and walked together, we have climbed the hills and ridden in the meadows. I have done your bidding for many years."

"True, John," she said, with an accent of grudging reminiscence, "you have dragged me into many a pretty pickle. I have torn my dress on rough rocks and soaked my shoes in bogs, all in your company. Surely we have had a brave time together."

"You met a man in the wood yesterday who would fain have made love to you. That man was my cousin Gilbert."

"Oh," she replied in a tone of mock solemnity and amused wonder, for I had blurted out my last words like the last dying confession of some prisoner. "Verily you are honoured in your cousinship, John."

"It is against him and such as him that I would protect you," I said.

"Nay," she cried, with an affected remonstrance, "I will have

44

no fighting between cousins on my account. I will even defend myself, as Alison did when the miller made love to her."

"O Marjory," I burst out, "will you not give me this right to defend you? We have been old companions, but it was only yesterday that I knew how dearly I loved you. I have had more cares since yesternight than ever in my life. We have been comrades in childhood; let us be comrades on the rough paths of the world."

I spoke earnestly, and her face, which had been filled with mockery, changed gently to something akin to tenderness.

"How little you know of women!" she cried. "I have loved you for years, thinking of you at all times, and now you come today, speaking as if you had scarce seen me before. Surely I will bear you company in life, as I have been your comrade at its beginning."

What followed I need scarce tell, since it is but part of the old comedy of life, which our grandfathers and grandmothers played before us, and mayhap our grandchildren will be playing even now when our back is turned. Under the spring sky among the lilies we plighted our troth for the years, and I entered from careless youth into the dim region of manhood.

With a great joy in my heart I rode home. I took the high way over the shoulder of Scrape, for I knew that few folk ever went that road, and I wished to be alone. The birds were singing, the fresh clean air was blowing on my face, and the primroses and wind-flowers made a gay carpet under my horse's feet. All the earth seemed to partake in my gladness. It was a good world, I thought, full of true hearts, fair faces, and much good; and though I have seen wickedness and sorrow in my day, I am still of the same way of thinking. It is a brave world; a royal world for brave-hearted men.

When I came to Barns I found that my cousin had gone out an hour since and left my father greatly wondering at my absence. He sat in the chair by the fireplace, looking more withered and old than I had ever seen him. My heart smote me for not staying at his side, and so I sat down by him and told him many things of my doings in Glasgow, and how I desired above all things to see the world, having had my fill of books and colleges. Then I told him what he had long guessed, of my love for Marjory Veitch and the promise which she had given me. He heard me in silence, but when he spoke, his words were cheerful, for he had long liked the lass. He made no refusal, too, to the rest of my plans. "You shall go and see the world, John," he said, "and take my blessing with you. It ill becomes a young mettlesome lad in these stirring times to lounge at home, when he might be wearing a steel breastplate in the King's Guards, or trying the manners of twenty nations. Though I could wish you to bide at home, for I am an old broken man with few pleasures, and I love the sight of your face."

"Nay, I will never leave you," I said, "an you wish it. I am young yet and a boy's road is a long road. Time enough for all."

After this I went out to see if the Weasel had come to any mishap in the last night's ride. I found him as stout as ever, so I saddled him and rode away by the green haugh lands up the valley of the Manor, for I longed for motion and air to relieve my spirit; and coming home in the afternoon, I found my cousin returned and sitting with my father in the dining-hall.

He glanced sharply at me when I entered, and I saw by his looks that he was in no good temper. His heavy face was flushed and his shaggy eyebrows were lowered more than their wont.

"Where have you been, Gilbert?" I asked. "I found you gone when I came back in the morning."

"I took my horse down to Peebles to the farrier. His knees were sorely hurt last night on your infernal hills."

Now I knew that this was a lie, for I had looked at his horse before I went out in the morning and his wounds were so slight that it would have been mere folly to take him to a farrier; and Gilbert, I well knew, was not the man to be in error where horses were concerned. So I judged that he had ridden in the contrary direction, and one to Dawyck, and, as I inferred from his sour looks, met with no good reception there. I could afford to be generous; I felt a sort of half-pity for his discomfiture, and forbore to ask him any further questions.

We sat down to supper, he and I and my father, in a sober

frame of mind. I was full of my own thoughts, which were of the pleasantest; my cousin was plainly angry with something or other; and my father, in his weakness dimly perceiving that all was not right, set himself to mend matters by engaging him in talk.

"You're a good shot with the musket, they tell me, Gibbie," he said, using the old name which he had called him by when he first came to Barns as a boy, "and I was thinking that it would be a ploy for you and John to go down the water to Traquair, where Captain Keith's horse are lying. He is an old friend of mine, and would be blithe to see any of my kin. They tell me he has great trials of skill in all exercises, and that he has gathered half the gentry in the place about him."

"John," said my cousin in a scornful voice, "John is too busily employed at Dawyck to care much for anything else. A flighty maid is a sore burden on any man."

"I would have you learn, Master Gilbert," I said angrily, "to speak in a better way of myself and my friends. You may be a very great gentleman elsewhere, but you seem to leave your gentility behind when you come here."

Now my cousin and I were of such opposite natures that I took most things seriously, while he found matter for a jest in all—yet not in full good-nature, but with a touch of satire.

"Even a barn-door cock will defend his own roost. How one sees the truth of proverbs!"

And then he added that which I will not set down, but which brought my father and myself to our feet with flashing eyes and quivering lips. I would have spoken, but my father motioned me to be silent.

"Gilbert," he said, his voice shaking with age and anger, "you will leave this house the morn. I will have no scoundrelly fellow of your kidney here. You are no true nephew of mine, and God pity the father that begat you."

My cousin smiled disdainfully and rose from his chair. "Surely I will go and at once when my hospitable uncle bids me. The entertainment in this damned hole is not so good as to keep me long. As for you, Cousin John," and he eyed me malignantly, "you and I will meet some day where there are no dotards and wenches to come between us. Then I promise you some sport. Till then, farewell. I will down to Peebles tonight, and trouble you no more." With a wave of his hand he was gone, and five minutes later we heard his horse's hooves clatter over the stones of the yard.

When he was gone his conduct came back to my father with a rush, and he fell to upbraiding himself for his breach of hospitality and family honour. He would have me call Gilbert back, and when I showed him how futile it was, fell into low spirits and repented in great bitterness.

Now the worst of this day's business remains to be told. For when I looked at my father some time after I found him sunk in his chair with his face as pale as death. With the help of Jean Morran and Tam Todd I got him to bed, from which he never rose, but passed peacefully away in the fear of God two days later. The heat into which he had been thrown was the direct cause, and though I could not very well lay the thing to my cousin's charge when the man was already so far down the vale of years, yet in my heart I set it against him. Indeed, from this day I date my antagonism to the man, which before had been a mere boyish rivalry.

I stayed with my father to the end. Just before he died he bade me come near and gave me his blessing, bidding me be a better gentleman than he had been. We did not bury him in the Kirk of Lyne, for he had always said he never could abide to lie within walls, but on a green flat above Tweed, where the echo of the river and the crying of moor birds are never absent from his grave.

CHAPTER VII

THE PEGASUS INN AT PEEBLES AND HOW A
STRANGER RETURNED FROM THE WARS

Of my doings for some months after my father's death I must tell hastily. I fell heir to the lands of Barns, and being of age entered at once into my possession. The place remained the same as in my father's time, the same servants, and the same ways about the house. I lived simply as I had always lived, spending my days in seeing to the land, in field sports, and some little study, for I had not altogether forsaken the Muses. But all the time I felt as one who is kept at home against his will, being conscious of a restlessness and an inclination to travel which was new to me, but which I doubt not is common to all young men at this time of life. I talked much with Tam Todd of the lands which he had visited, and heard of the Dutch towns with their strange shipping, their canals and orderly houses, and of the rough Norlanders, clad in the skins of wild animals, who came down to the Swedish markets to trade; of the soldiery of Germany and France and the Scots who had gone over there to push their fortunes with their swords; and, what I loved best, of the salt sea with its boundless waste of waters and wild tales of shipwreck. Formerly I had been wont often to bid Tam sharply to hold his peace when he entered on one of his interminable narrations; but now I sat and drank in every word like a thirsty man. It was the winter time, when the roads were often snowed up and all the folk of the place gathered in the great kitchen at nights round the fire; so it was the time for stories and we had our fill of them.

One blustering day, the first Monday, I think, after the New Year, when the ice was beginning to melt from the burns and a wet, cold wind from the north-west was blowing, I rode down to Peebles to settle some matters about money with Saunders Blackett, who had managed my father's affairs and was now entrusted with mine. All things were done to my satisfaction; so bethinking myself that the way to Barns was cold and long and that it was yet early in the afternoon, being scarce four o'clock, I found myself thinking pleasantly of the warm inn-parlour of the Pegasus, so thither I went.

The Pegasus or "Peg" Inn stands at the corner of the Northgate and the High Street, a black-gabled building, once the town house of the Govans of Cardrona, and still retaining marks of its gentility in the arms carved above the door. A great sign flapped in the wind, bearing on a white ground a gorgeous representation of a winged horse soaring through clouds. The landlord at this time was one Horsbrock, a portly, well-looking man, who claimed to be kin to the Horsbrocks of that ilk and held his chin two inches higher in consequence. The place was famed in all the country round for good wine and comfort.

I stabled my horse, and, bidding the host bring me a bottle of Rhenish (so fine a thing it is to have succeeded to lands and money), I went into the low-ceilinged room where the company sat. It was panelled in a darkish wood, and hung round with old weapons—halberds and falchions and what not—which glimmered brightly in the firelight. A narrow window gave it light, but now it sufficed only to show the grey winter dusk coming swiftly on. Around the fire sat some few of the men of Peebles, warming themselves and discussing the landlord's ale and the characters of their neighbours.

They rose to give me welcome when I entered, for my name and family were well known in the countryside.

"It's awfu' weather for man and beast, Laird," said an old man with a bent back, but still hale and hearty in the face. "A snawy winter I can abide, and a cauld yin, but drizzlin', dreepin', seepin' weather wi' a wind that taks the heart out o' ye is mair than my patience can stand."

"You have little need to speak, you folk," I said, "living in a well-paved town with stones beneath your feet and nothing more to do than go round a street corner all day. Up at Barns, with Tweed swirling in at the yard gate, and the stables flowing like a linn, and the wind playing cantrips day and night in and out of the windows, you might talk."

"Ay, but, good sir," put in a thin voice which came from a little man I had seen at the bowling green, "ye may thank the Lord for a roof abune your heids and dry claes to put on, when sae many godly folks are hiding like pelicans in the wilderness among the high hills and deep mosses. I bless the Lord that my faither, that sant o' the Kirk, is not living in thae evil times. He was a man o' a truly great spirit, and had he been alive, I'se warrant he wad hae been awa to join them. He was aye strong on his conscience. 'John Look-up,' so the godless called him. 'John Look-up,' said my mother, 'ye'll ne'er be pleased till we're a' joltin' in a cairt to the Grassmarket o' Edinburgh. And a braw sicht ye'll be, hanging there like a hoodie-craw wi' a' your bairns side ye.' Ay, these were often her words, for she had a sarcastic tongue."

"Jock Look-up, my man," said another, "I kenned your faither a' his days, and he was na the man to hang. He lookit up and he lookit a' ways. He was yin whae could baith watch and pray. Gin ye were mair like him, ye wad be a mair thrivin' man."

"Aboot the hill-folk," said the old man who had first spoken, drinking his ale and turning up the measure to see that no more was left, "did ye ever hear o' my son Francie and what happened to him when he gaed awa to Moffat wi' 'oo'? He gaed ower by Traquair and keepit the road till he got to Moffat, for he had a horse that wasna ower sure o' its feet on the hills. But when he had it a' sellt, whae does he meet in wi' but Wull Hislop the travelling packman, whae's sair needing a beast. So Francie sells him his horse and comes aff hame walking ower the muirs. He gaed up Moffat Water and ower the muckle hill they ca' Corriefragauns, and got on nane sae bad till he cam to the awfu' craigs abune Loch Skene. He was walking briskly, thinking o' hame and the siller in his pouch and how he wad win to Peebles that nicht, when he saw afore him the awfu'est sicht that ever he had seen. It was a man o' maybe the same heicht as himsel', wi' a heid o' red hair, and nae claes to speak o', but just a kind o' clout about his middle. He began to speak in an outlandish voice, and Francie kenned at yince that he maun be yin o' thae Hieland deevils brocht doun to hunt up the Whigs. He was for Francie's money, and he oot wi' a big knife and flashed it up and doun. But this was no to Francie's liking. 'Put that doun, ye ill-looking deevil,' says he, 'ye'll find I'm nane o' your hill folk, but an honest man frae Peebles wi' a nieve as hard as your heid's saft, and if ye dinna let me by, I'll put ye in the loch as sure as my name's Francie Trummle.' The body understood him brawly, and wi' a grunt slunk aff among the heather, and Francie had nae mair bother wi' him. But oh, it's an awfu' thing to think o' men o' your ain blood hunted and killed by thae foreign craturs. It maks me half-mindit to turn Whig mysel'."

"Dinna fash yoursel', Maister Trummle," said a younger man, a farmer by his looks, "ye're better bidin' in peace and quiet at hame. The Lord never meant folk to gang among hills and peat bogs, unless after sheep. It's clean against the order o' things. But there's yae thing that reconciles me to this Whig hunting. They're maistly wast country folk, and wast country folk are an ill lot, aye shoving their nebs where they're no wantit. There's no many Whigs in Tweeddale. Na, na, they're ower canny."

Master Turnbull made as if he would have answered, when a clatter of feet was heard in the passage, and the door opened. Two men entered, one a great swarthy fellow well known for his poaching escapades when the salmon came up the water, and the other, Peter Crustcrackit the tailor. They did not enter in company, for Peter swaggered in with as gallant an air as two bent legs and a small body could permit, while the other slunk in with a half-apologetic look, glancing keenly round to see who were the other occupants of the room.

"The 'Peg' is honoured with company tonight, I see," said Peter, making a bow to me. " 'Tis the finest gathering that I remember: the Laird o' Barns, worthy Maister Trumbull, myself, and my honoured freend, Maister Simon Doolittle."

The black fisher lifted his face from the ale which the landlord had brought. "Your guid health, gentlemen. I'm prood o' your company, though I'm no just fit for't, since I'm no half an 'oor oot o' the Dookit Pool."

All eyes were turned to the speaker, and we saw that his clothes hung limp and wet.

"And pray, how did you get there, Maister Doolittle? Was't by the working o' Providence, or the wiles o' sinfu' man?"

52

"A mixture o' baith. I took a bit daunder up Tweed to the Castle Rock to see how the water was rinnin'. It's been raither grumly for fishin' o' late. Ye a' ken the rocks that they're no exactly the sort o' place that a man would choose for dancin' a reel in tackety boots. Well, I was admiring the works o' God as manifested in a big, deep, swirlin' hole, when afore ever I kenned I was admirin' the hole frae the middle o't. I was gey near chokit wi' Tweed water, but I wabbled a bit, and syne grippit a birk and held on."

There was a pause, and he took a draught of ale.

"Weel, I roared as loud as I could, and the auld runt whae bides i' the Castle heard me. He cam doun and askit me what was wrang. 'Wrang,' says I. 'If ye dinna ca' ten feet o' water and you no able to soom, wrang, I just wis ye were here yoursel.' So he gangs cannily back and brings anither man to look at me; and the twae thocht for a while, and then each grippit an airm and after a gey wammlin' I got oot. I was angry at their delay, for I couldna hae held on muckle langer, so I kickit them baith an' cam aff here. I've muckle need o' yill, for I feel as if I had eaten ten pund o' snaw."

"Come nearer the fire, Simon," said one. "Ye're a muckle-tried man."

"I'm a' that," said the brown-faced poacher and relapsed into silence.

The lights were now lit in the dwellings of Peebles, as we could see by the glimmer through the windows; but in our room no lamp was needed, for the bright firelight was sufficient for a man to read a little book by. The great shadows danced on the wall, bent and crooked into a thousand phantasms; and the men by the fire nodded and spoke little. Then the old man Turnbull began an argument with the tailor about some clothes in which he said he had been cheated; and Peter Crustcrackit, never a quiet-tempered man, was rejoining with vigour. I heard only fragments of their talk, being taken up in dreaming of my future course, and when I should go to see the world.

The mild-mannered man, him they called John Look-up, was sleeping in his chair, and his jug of ale which he had emptied hung limply in his hand. In a little it fell to the floor and rolled beneath his chair; but the sleeper never stirred. The poacher sat shrouded in vapour, which the heat of the fire had brought out of his wet garments, and a mingled smell of damp cloth and burning wood filled the room. The discordant voices of the tailor and his antagonist rose and fell, now sinking to a mumbled whisper, and now rising to sharp recrimination. By-and-by they came to an end of their dispute, and silence reigned undisturbed; and I verily believe that in five minutes we should all have been sound asleep, had not something occurred to rouse us.

This was no less than the entrance of another guest. The door was flung open and a man entered, swaggering with a great air and bearing into the slumbrous place a breath of the outer world. He was the finest man I had ever seen, two inches and more taller than myself, who am not short, and clean made as a greyhound. His face was tanned a deep brown, and bare save for a yellow moustache on his upper lip. His hair hung long and fine over his shoulders, setting off the erect poise of his head. He had removed his cloak and hat, and showed a dress of the height of fashion; his cravat was of delicate foreign lace, and the sash around his middle of the finest silk. But what I marked especially were his features—the thin, straight nose, the well-bred chin, and the clear eyes; but for a certain weakness in the jaw I should have called it the handsomest face I had ever seen. More, it was a face that was familiar to me. I had seen the like of it before; but where I could not tell, and I cudgelled my brains to think of it.

"Ah, my faith," said the stranger, speaking with a foreign accent, "what have we here? A room full of sleepy citizens. Or drunk, egad! drunk, I believe."

And he walked over to where Peter Crustcrackit sat nodding, and stared in his face. Now the noise wakened the rest; and Peter also, who sitting up with a stupid air thought that he was still in his shop, and cried hurriedly, "What d'ye lack, sir? Silks or satins or plain kersey," and ran into a recital of his wares.

The newcomer looked at him with an amused smile. "It is not difficult to tell your profession, my friend. The ninth of a man."

Then he surveyed the rest of us in turn with his restless eyes,

54

until his look fell upon me. He must have marked something about my appearance distinct from the others, for he bowed and addressed me politely.

"You are not one of these fellows, I think. May I ask the favour of your name? I have been long absent from this country and have forgot faces."

"You are welcome to it," said I. "They call me John Burnet— of Barns," I added, using my new-found title.

He crossed to my side in an instant and held out his hand. "Your hand, Master John. You and I should be well known to each other, for we shall be near neighbours. You may have heard of Michael Veitch of Dawyck, him that was soldiering abroad. I am that same, returned like the prodigal from far countries."

Now I knew where I had seen the face before. It was but a coarse and manly counterpart of Marjory's, though I fancied that hers was still the braver and stronger, if all were told.

"I have often heard of you," I said, "and I am glad to be the first to bid you welcome to your own countryside. These are some men of the town, honest fellows, who come here for their evening ale."

"Your health, gentlemen," he cried, bowing to the company. "Landlord, bring ale and a bottle of your best Burgundy till I pledge these honest fellows."

"Eh, sirs," I heard Peter Crustcrackit mutter under his breath, "sic an invasion o' gentles. The Northgate o' Peebles micht be the High Street o' Embro', for a' the braw folk that are coming tae't. I maun think aboot shifting my shop."

It would be well on for eight o'clock ere Master Veitch and I left the Pegasus to ride homeward. The night was quieter and milder, and overhead a patch of clear sky showed the stars. He had with him two serving-men who carried his belongings, but they rode some little distance behind. He was full of questions about Dawyck and his kinsfolk there, and the countryside around; so I must needs tell him something of what had passed between Marjory and myself. He seemed not ill-pleased. "What," he cried, "little Marjory, who was scarce higher than my knee when I left! To think that she should have grown into a woman already! And you say she is pretty?"

Which question gave me much opportunity for such talk as one must use when he feels the littleness of words.

Then he must ask me about myself, of my father, of whose death he was ignorant, and what I purposed to do. "For I doubt," said he, "that you will have but a dull time of it at Barns in that great desolate house. It little befits an active man to pine at home like a mouse in a cell."

So from one thing to another, he had me to tell him of all my desires, of how I longed above all things to travel and see the world; and he spoke to me in such a fashion that ere we had come to the ford of Tweed my intention was fixed to ride out like the Spanish Don to see what might befall me.

CHAPTER VIII

I TAKE LEAVE OF MY FRIENDS

The next month was, I think, the busiest in my life. For from the evening of my meeting with Michael Veitch my mind was firmly made up to go to travel abroad, and with this determination came all the countless troubles which a man must meet before he can leave his home. I was busy night and day, now down at Peebles, now riding up Manor and all over the Barns lands, seeing that all things were in right order ere my departure. I got together the money I desired, and with drafts on the Dutch bankers, which the lawyer folk in Edinburgh got for me, I was in no danger of falling into poverty abroad.

On Tam Todd I laid the management of all things in my absence; and Tam, much impressed by his responsibility, though it was a task which he had really undertaken long before in the later years of my father's life, went about his work with a serious, preoccupied air, as of Atlas with the world on his shoulders. I had much ado in getting ready my baggage for the journey, for I wished to take little, being confident that I could buy all things needful abroad. Jean Morran, on the other hand, would have had me take half the plenishing of the house of Barns, from linen sheets to fresh-kirned butter; for I could not persuade her to think otherwise than that I was going into a desolate land among heathen savages.

Then I had to visit many folk up and down Tweed to take farewell; and I had so many letters given me to men of standing abroad that, if I had delivered them all, I should have done little else. One I valued more than any other—a letter written by Master Gilbert Burnet, of London, to a professor in the university of Leyden—which I hoped would bring me into the company of scholars. For I had changed my original intention of going to the wars, first, because I found on examination that, in my inmost heart, I had that hankering after learning which would never be sated save by a life with some facilities for study; second, because now that I was the sole member of the house, it behoved me to bide on the land and see to it, and any such thing as soldiering would keep me away for too great a time. I sent, too, to the College Library at Glasgow for all the books on the Low Countries to be had, and spent much profitable time reading of the history of the place, and how the land lay.

During these days I was much in the company of the new master of Dawyck, and a most delectable comrade I found him. He had a vast stock of tales and jests, collected in his travels, with which he would amuse his friends; he was something of a scholar, and could talk learnedly when he chose; and he was expert at all outdoor sports, pressing me hard at the swordplay, in which I prided myself on my skill. He was of a free, generous nature, and singularly courteous to all, high and low, rich and poor alike. Yet, with all these excellencies, there was much that I liked ill about him, for he was over-fond of resorting to the taverns at Peebles, where he would muddle his wits in the company of his inferiors. His life at Dawyck was none of the most regular, though, indeed, I have little cause to blame him, being none so good myself; though the vice of over-indulging in wine was one that Providence always mercifully kept me from.

He came perhaps every third day to Barns to ride with me in the haugh, and he would abide to supper time, or even overnight, making me fear for Marjory's peace of mind. To his sister he was most dutiful and kind, and I was glad to think that now the days might be more pleasant for her with her brother in the house. And it pleased me to think that when I went abroad, my lady would be left in no bad keeping.

The days, the short January days, passed quickly over my head, and, almost ere I knew, the time had come for my departure. And now, when the hour came so nigh, I felt some pain at the thought of leaving home and my beloved countryside for unknown places; though, to tell the truth, such thoughts were not ill to dispel by the contemplation of the pleasures in prospect. Yet it was with mingled feelings that I rode over to Dawyck on a sharp Monday afternoon to bid Marjory farewell.

I found her in the low, dim room, looking to the west, where she was wont to sit in winter. A great fire crackled cheerily on the hearth, and many little devices about the place showed a woman's hand. Holly, with scarlet berries, put colour into the sombre walls, and Marjory herself, brighter than any flower, made the firelight dull in the contrast; so fair she looked, as she greeted me, with her bright hair and unfathomable eyes.

"I have come to see you for the last time, Marjory," I said; "tomorrow I set out on my travels."

"I am vexed that you are going away," and she looked at me sadly; "it will be lonely in Tweeddale without you."

"My dear lass, I will not be long. Two years at the longest, and then I will be home to you, and travel no more. What say you, Marjory?"

"Your will be done, John. Yet I would I could have gone with you."

"I would you could, my dear," I said. "But that might scarce be. You would not like, I think, to sail on rough seas, or bide among towns and colleges. You love the woods too well."

"Wherever you were," said she, with her eyes drooped, "I would be content to be."

"But, Marjory lass," I spoke up cheerfully, for I feared to make her sad, "you would not like me to stay at home, when the world is so wide, and so many brave things to be seen."

"No, no. I have no love for folks who bide in the house like children. I would have you go and do gallantly, and come home full of fine tales. But where do you mean to go, and how will you pass your time?"

"Oh," said I, "I go first to Rotterdam, where I may reside for a while. Then I purpose to visit the college at Leyden, to study; for I would fain spend some portion of my time profitably. After that I know not what I will do, but be sure that I will be home within the two years. For, though I am blithe to set out, I doubt not that I will be blither to come back again."

"I trust you may not learn in those faraway places to look down on Tweeddale and the simple folks here. I doubt you may, John; for you are not a steadfast man," and at this she laughed and I blushed, for I thought of my conduct at Glasgow.

"Nay, nay," I answered; "I love you all too well for that. Though the Emperor of Cathay were to offer me all his treasure to bide away, I would come back. I would rather be a shepherd in Tweeddale than a noble in Spain."

"Brave words, John," she cried, "brave words! See you hold to them."

Then after that we fell to discussing Michael and his ways of amusing himself; and I bade Marjory tell her brother to look in now and then at Barns to see how Tam Todd fared. Also I bade her tell him that it was my wish that he should hunt and fish over my lands as much as he pleased. "And see you keep him in order," I added, laughing, "lest he slip off to the wars again."

"O John," she said, with a frightened look, "do not speak so. That is what I fear above all things, for he is restless even here, and must ever be wandering from one place to another."

"Tut, my dear," I said; "Michael, be sure, is too honest a man to leave you again, when I am off, once I have left you in his care. Have no fear for him. But we are getting as dull as owls, and it is many days since I heard your voice. I pray you sing me a song, as you used to do in the old days. 'Twill be long ere I hear another."

She rose and went without a word to her harpsichord and struck a few notes. Now Marjory had a most wonderful voice, more like a linnet's than aught else, and she sang the old ballads very sweetly. But today she chose none of them, but a brisk martial song, which pleased me marvellously well. I will set down the words as she sang them, for I have hummed them many a time to myself:

> "Oh, if my love were sailor-bred,
>   And fared afar from home,
> In perilous lands, by shoal and sands,
>   If he were sworn to roam,
> Then, oh, I'd hie me to a ship,
>   And sail upon the sea,
> And keep his side in wind and tide
>   To bear him company.
>
> "And if he were a soldier gay,
>   And tarried from the town,
> And sought in wars, through death and scars
>   To win for him renown,
> I'd place his colours in my breast,
>   And ride by moor and lea,
> And win his side, there to abide
>   And bear him company.
>
> "For sooth a maid, all unafraid,
>   Should by her lover be,
> With wile and art to cheer his heart,
>   And bear him company."

"A fine promise, Marjory," I cried, "and some day I may claim its fulfilment. But who taught you the song?"

"Who but the Travelling Packman, or maybe the Wandering Jew!" she said laughingly; and I knew this was the way of answer she used when she would not tell me anything. So, to this day, I know not whence she got the catch.

Then we parted, not without tears on her part, and blank misgivings on my own. For the vexed question came to disturb me, whether it was not mere self-gratification on my side thus to travel, and whether my more honourable place was not at home. But I banished the thoughts, for I knew how futile they were, and comforted my brave lass as best I could.

"Fare thee well, my love," I cried, as I mounted my horse, "and God defend you till I come again;" and, whenever I looked back, till I had passed the great avenue, I saw the glimmer of Marjory's dress, and felt pricked in the conscience for leaving her.

CHAPTER IX

I RIDE OUT ON MY TRAVELS
AND FIND A COMPANION

It was on a fine sharp morning, early in February, that I finally bade goodbye to the folk at Barns and forded Tweed and rode out into the world. There was a snell feel in the air which fired my blood, and made me fit for anything which Providence might send. I was to ride Maisie as far as Leith, where I was to leave her with a man at the Harbour Walk, who would send her back to Tweeddale; for I knew it would be a hard thing to get passage for a horse in the small ships which sailed between our land and the Low Countries at that time of year.

At the Lyne Water ford, Michael Veitch was waiting for me. He waved his hat cheerfully, and cried, "Good luck to you, John, and see that you bide not too long away." I told him of a few things which I wished him to see to, and then left him, riding up the little burn which comes down between the Meldon hills, and whither lies the road to Eddleston Water. When I was out of sight of him, I seemed to have left all my home behind me, and I grew almost sorrowful. At the top of the ridge I halted and looked back. There was Barns among its bare trees and frosted meadows, with Tweed winding past, and, beyond, a silvery glint of the Manor coming down from its blue, cold hills. There was Scrape, with its long slopes clad in firs, and the grey house of Dawyck nestling at its foot. I saw the thin smoke curling up from the little village of Lyne, and Lyne Kirk standing on its whin-covered brae, and the bonny holms of Lyne Water, where I had often taken great baskets of trout. I must have stayed there gazing for half an hour; and, whenever I looked on the brown moors and woods, where I had wandered in boyhood, I felt sorrowful, whether I would or no.

"But away with such thoughts," I said, steeling my heart. "There's many a fine thing awaiting me, and, after all, I will be back in a year or two to the place and the folk that I love." So I went own to the village of Eddleston whistling the "Cavalier's Rant," and firmly shutting my mind against thoughts of home. I scarce delayed in Eddleston, but pushed on up the valley, expecting to get dinner at the inn at Leadburn, which stands at the watershed, just where the county of Edinburgh touches our shire on Tweeddale. The way, which is a paradise in summer, was rugged and cold at this season. The banks of the stream were crusted with ice, and every now and then, as I passed, I raised a string of wild duck, who fled noisily to the high wilderness.

I came to Leadburn about eleven o'clock in the forenoon, somewhat cold in body, but brisk and comforted in spirit. I had Maisie stabled and myself went into the hostel and bade them get ready dinner. The inn is the most villainous, bleak place that I have ever seen, and I who write this have seen many. The rooms are damp and mouldy, and the chimney-stacks threaten hourly to come down about the heads of the inmates. It stands in the middle of a black peat-bog, which stretches nigh to the Pentland Hills; and if there be a more forsaken countryside on earth I do not know it. The landlord, nevertheless, was an active, civil man, not spoiled by his surroundings; and he fetched me an excellent dinner—a brace of wild fowl and a piece of salted beef, washed down with very tolerable wine.

I had just finished, and was dallying a little before ordering my horse, when the most discordant noise arose in the inn yard; and, going to the window, I beheld two strong serving-men pulling a collie by a rope tied around the animal's neck. It was a fine, shaggy, black-and-white dog, and I know not what it could have done to merit such treatment. But its captors had not an easy task, for it struggled and thrawed at the rope, and snarled savagely, and every now and then made desperate sallies upon the hinderparts of its leaders. They cursed it, not unnaturally, for an ill-conditioned whelp, and some of the idlers, who are usually found about an inn, flung stones or beat it with sticks from behind. Now I hate, above all things, to see a beast suffer, no matter how it may have deserved it; so I had it in my mind to go down and put a stop to the cruelty, when some one else came before me.

This was a very long, thin man, with a shock of black hair and a sunburnt face, attired in a disorder of different clothes—a fine though tarnished coat, stout, serviceable small-clothes, and the coarsest of shoes and stockings. He darted forward like a hawk from a corner of the yard, and, ere I could guess his intentions, had caught the rope and let the dog go free. The beast ran howling to seek shelter, and its preserver stood up to face the disappointed rascals. They glared at him fiercely, and were on the point of rushing on him, had not something in his demeanour deterred them.

"Oh," said he, in a scornful voice, "ye're fine folk, you Leidburn folk. Braw and kindly folk. Graund at hangin' dowgs and tormentin' dumb beasts, but like a wheen skelpit puppies when ye see a man."

"Ye meddlin' deevil," said one, "whae askit ye to come here? The dowg was an ill, useless beast, and it was time it was hangit."

"And what d'ye ca' yoursel?" said the stranger. "I ken ye fine, Tam Tiddup, for a thievin', idle vaigabond, and if every useless beast was hangit, there wadna be yin o' ye here."

This made them grumble, and a stone was thrown, but still something in the easy, dauntless air of their enemy kept them back.

"But I'm no the man to let a dowg gang free wi'oot giein' some kind o' return. Ye're a' brave men, dour warlike men, and I've nae doot unco keen o' a fecht. Is there no some kind o' green bit hereaways whaur I could hae a fling wi' yin o' ye? I'll try ye a' in turn, but no to mak ill-feelin', I'll tak the biggest yin first. Will ye come, ye muckle hash?" he said suddenly, addressing the tallest of the number.

Now the man addressed had clearly no stomach for fight, but he was tall and stout, and stood in fear of the ridicule of his companions, and further, he doubtless thought that he would have an easy victory over the lean stranger, so he accepted with as good a show of readiness as he could muster.

63

"Come on, ye flee-up-i'-the-air, and I'll see if I canna pit thae fushionless airms o' yours oot o' joint."

I heard them appoint a flat place beside the burn, just on the edge of the bog, and watched them trooping out of the yard. The rabble went first, with a great semblance of valour, and the brown-faced stranger, with a sardonic grin on his countenance, stepped jauntily behind. Now I dearly love a fight, but yet I scarce thought fit to go and look on with the rest; so I had Maisie saddled, and rode after them, that I might look like some chance passer-by stopping to witness the encounter.

When I came up to the place, there were already some thirty men collected. It was a green spot by the side of the Hawes burn, with the frost not lifted from the grass; and in the burn itself the ice lay thick, for it flows sluggishly like all bogland waters. The place was beaten down as if folk were used to go there, and here the men made a ring about their champion, some helping him to unbuckle his belt, some giving advice about how to close with his adversary. The adversary himself stood waiting their pleasure with the most unconcerned air, whistling "The Green Holms o' Linton," and stamping his feet on the ground to keep himself warm.

In a little the two were ready, and stood facing each other on the cold moor. A whistling wind came in short blasts from the hills, and made their ears tingle, and mine also; till I wished that I were one of the two to have some chance of warming my blood. But when once the fight began, I thought little more of the cold.

The countryman gripped the stranger round the middle and tugged desperately to throw him. Up and down, backwards and forwards they went, kicking up in their struggle pieces of turf and little stones. Once they were all but in the water, but the stranger, seeing his peril, made a bold leap back and dragged the other with him. And now I feared that it was going to go hard with the succourer of distressed dogs; for his unwieldy opponent was pressing so heavily upon him that I expected every moment to see him go down. Once I caught sight of his face, and, to my surprise, it was calm as ever; the very straw he had been chewing before being still between his teeth.

Now the fight took another turn; for my friend, by an adroit movement, slipped below the other's arms, flung himself backwards, just as I have seen a tumbler do at a fair at Peebles, and before the other knew his design, stood smiling before him. The man's astonishment was so great that he stood staring, and if the stranger had used his advantage, he might have thrown him there and then. By-and-by he recovered and came on, swearing and wrathful. "Ye've slippit awa' yince, ye ether, but I'll see that ye'll no dae't again;" and with his sluggish blood roused to some heat, he flung himself on his foe, who received him much as a complacent maid receives the caresses of a traveller. The fellow thought his victory certain, and put out all his strength; but now, of a sudden, my friend woke up. He twisted his long arms round his adversary, and a mighty struggle began. The great, fat-bellied man was swaying to and fro like a basket on a pack-horse; his face grew purple and pale at the lips, and his body grew limper and weaker. I expected to see a good fight, but I was disappointed; for before I knew, they were on the edge of the pool, tottered a second, and then, with a mighty crunching and splashing, bounded through the thin ice into the frosty water.

A brown face, with draggled, black hair, followed closely by a red and round one, appeared above the surface, and two dripping human beings dragged themselves to the bank. The teeth of both chattered like a smith's shop, but in the mouth of one I espied a yellowish thing, sorely bitten and crumbled. It was the piece of straw. A loud shout greeted their appearance, and much laughter. The one slunk away with his comrades in no very high fettle, leaving the other shaking himself like a water-dog on the grass.

I found the stranger looking up at me, as I sat my horse, with a glance half quizzical and half deprecatory. The water ran down his odd clothes and formed in pools in the bare places of the ground. He shivered in the cold wind, and removed little fragments of ice from his coat. Then he spoke.

"Ye'll be the Laird o' Barns settin' oot on your traivels?"

"Good Lord! What do you know of my business?" I asked, and, as I looked at him, I knew that I had seen the face before.

65

Of a sudden he lifted his arm to rub his eyebrows, and the motion brought back to me at once a vision of excited players and a dry, parched land, and a man perplexedly seeking to convince them of something; and I remembered him for the man who had brought the news to Peebles of the rising of Tweed.

"I know you," I said. "You are the man who came down with news of the great flood. But what do you here?"

"Bide a wee and I'll tell ye. Ye'll mind that ye tellt me if ever I was in need o' onything, to come your way. Weel, I've been up Tweed, and doun Tweed, and ower the hills, and up the hills, till there's nae mair places left for me to gang. So I heard o' your gaun ower the seas, and I took it into my heid that I wad like to gang tae. So here I am, at your service."

The fellow's boldness all but took my breath away. "What, in Heaven's name, would I take you with me for?" I asked. "I doubt we would suit each other ill."

"Na, na, you and me wad gree fine. I've heard tell o' ye, Laird, though ye've heard little o' me, and by a' accoonts we're just made for each ither."

Now if any other had spoken to me in this tone I should have made short work of him; but I was pleased with this man's conduct in the affair just past, and, besides, I felt I owed something to my promise.

"But," said I, "going to Holland is not like going to Peebles fair, and who is to pay your passage, man?"

"Oh," said he, "I maun e'en be your body-servant, so to speak."

"I have little need of a body-servant. I am used to shifting for myself. But to speak to the purpose, what use could you be to me?"

"What use?" the man repeated. "Eh, sir, ye ken little o' Nicol Plenderleith to talk that gait. A' the folk o' Brochtoun and Tweedsmuir, and awa' ower by Clyde Water ken that there's no his match for rinnin' and speelin' and shootin' wi' the musket; I'll find my way oot o' a hole when a'body else 'ill bide in't. But fie on me to be blawin' my ain trumpet at siccan a speed. But tak me wi' ye, and if I'm no a' I say, ye can cry me for a gowk at the Cross o' Peebles."

Now I know not what possessed me, who am usually of a sober, prudent nature, to listen to this man; but something in his brown, eager face held me captive, and his powerful make filled me with admiration. He was honest and kindly—I had had good evidence of both; and his bravery was beyond doubting. I thought how such a man might be of use to me in a foreign land, both as company and protection. I had taken a liking to the fellow, and, with our family, such likings go for much. Nevertheless, I was almost surprised at myself when I said—

"I like the look of you, Nicol Plenderleith, and am half-minded to take you with me as my servant."

"I thank ye kindly, Laird. I kenned ye wad dae't. I cam to meet ye here wi' my best claes for that very reason."

"You rascal," I cried, half laughing at his confidence, and half angry at his audacity. "I've a good mind to leave you behind after all. You talk as if you were master of all the countryside. But come along; we will see if the landlord has not a more decent suit of clothes for your back if you are going into my service. I will have no coughing, catarrhy fellows about me."

"Hech," muttered my attendant, following, "ye micht as well expect a heron to get the cauld frae wadin' in the water as Nicol Plenderleith. Howbeit, your will be done, sir."

From the landlord at the inn I bought a suit of homespun clothes, which, by good fortune, fitted Nicol; and left his soaked garments as part payment. Clad decently, he looked a stalwart man, though somewhat bent in the back, and with a strange craning forward of the neck, acquired, I think, from much wandering among hills. I hired a horse to take him to Edinburgh, and the two of us rode out of the yard, followed by the parting courtesies of the host.

Of our journey to Edinburgh I have little else to tell. We came to the town in the afternoon, and went through the streets to the port of Leith, after leaving our horses at the place arranged for. I was grieved to part from Maisie, for I had ridden her from boyhood, and she had come to know my ways wondrous well. We found a vessel to sail the next morn for Rotterdam, and bargained with the captain for our passage. When all had been settled, and we had looked our fill upon the harbour and the craft, and felt the salt of the sea on our lips, we betook ourselves to an inn, *The Three Herrings*, which fronted the quay, and there abode for the night.

BOOK II

THE LOW COUNTRIES

CHAPTER I

OF MY VOYAGE TO THE LOW COUNTRIES

WE were aboard on the next morning by a little after daybreak, for the captain had forewarned me the night before that he purposed to catch the morning tide. To one inland bred, the harbour of Leith was a sight to whet the curiosity. There were vessels of all kinds and sizes—little fishing smacks with brown, home-made sails, from Fife or the Lothian coast towns; great seagoing ships, many with strange foreign names on their sides, and full of a great bustle of lading and unlading. There was such a concourse of men, too, as made the place like a continuous horse fair. Half a dozen different tongues jabbered in my ear, of which I knew not one word, save of the French, which I could make a fair shape to speak, having learned it from Tam Todd, along with much else of good and bad. There were men in red cowls like Ayrshire weavers, and men in fur hats from the North, and dark-skinned fellows, too, from the Indies, and all this motley crew would be running up and down jabbering and shrilling like a pack of hounds. And every now and then across the uproar would come the deep voice of a Scots skipper, swearing and hectoring as if the world and all that is in it were his peculiar possession.

But when we had cleared the Roads of Leith, and were making fair way down the firth, with a good north-westerly breeze behind us, then there was a sight worth the seeing. For behind lay Leith, with its black masts and tall houses, and at the back again Edinburgh, with its castle looming up grim and solemn, and farther still, the Pentlands, ridged like a saw, running far to the westward. In front I marked the low shore of Fife, with the twin Lomonds, which you can see by climbing Caerdon, or Dollar Law, or any one of the high Tweedside hills. The channel was as blue as a summer sky, with a wintry clearness and a swell which was scarce great enough to break into billows. The *Kern*, for so the vessel was called, had all her sail set, and bounded gallantly on her way. It was a cheerful sight, what with the sails filling to the wind, and men passing hither and thither at work with the cordage, and the running seas keeping pace with the vessel. The morning fires were being lit in the little villages of Fife, and I could see the smoke curling upwards in a haze from every bay and neuk.

But soon the firth was behind us, and we passed between the Bass Rock and the May, out into the open sea. This I scarcely found so much to my liking. I was inland bred, and somewhat delicate in my senses, so, soon I came to loathe the odour of fish and cookery and sea-water, which was everywhere in the vessel. Then the breeze increased to a stiff wind, and the *Kern* leaped and rocked among great rolling billows. At first the movement was almost pleasing, being like the motion of a horse's gallop in a smooth field. And this leads me to think that if a boat were but small enough, so as to be more proportionate to the body of man, the rocking of it would be as pleasing as the rise and fall of a horse's stride. But in a great cumbrous ship, where man is but a little creature, it soon grows wearisome. We stood well out to sea, so I could but mark the bolder features of the land. Even these I soon lost sight of, for the whole earth and air began to dance woefully before my eyes. I felt a dreadful sinking, and a cold sweat began to break on my brow. I had heard of the seasickness, but I could not believe that it was this. This was something ten times worse, some deadly plague which Heaven had sent to stay me on my wanderings.

I leaned over the side of the ship in a very disconsolate frame of mind. If this was all I was to get on my journey, I had better have stayed at home. I was landward bred and knew naught of boats, save one which Tam Todd had made as a ferry across the Tweed, and which was indeed more like a meal-chest than aught else. In it we were wont to paddle across when we were fearful of wetting our shoon. But this rolling, boisterous ship and turgid seas were strange to me, and I fear I fell monstrous sick.

Nicol Plenderleith had disappeared almost as soon as he came aboard, and I saw him deep in converse with the sailors. When we had cleared the Forth he came back to me, as I leaned disconsolately against the bulwarks, and asked me how I did. His lean, brown face was not a whit changed by the rocking of the ship; indeed, if he had been astraddle the Saddleback in a gale he would not have been perturbed. When he saw my plight he ran below and brought brandy.

"Here, sir, take some o' this. It's tasty at a' times, but it's mair than tasty the noo, it's halesome."

"Nicol," I groaned, "if I never get home again, I look to you to tell the folk in Tweeddale. It's terrible to die here of this villainous sickness, for I shall certainly die if it continues. Will it never cease?"

"I've been speirin' at the captain and by a' accounts we're no at the warst o't. He says it's juist like the backs o' Leith. If ye win by the Fisherraw ye'll meet your death i' the Kettle Wynd, and if by any chance ye're no killed there, ye'll be dune for i' the Walk. He was speaking o' the stinks o' the place and no the folk, for they're peaceable eneuch, puir bodies. 'Weel,' says he, 'it's the same here. It's ill for some folk to win by the Forth, but it's waur i' the open sea, and when it comes to the Dutch waters, it's fair awfu'.' I wis, Laird, ye maunna dee."

This was poor consolation, and had I not formed some guess of my servant's manners, I should have been downhearted enough; but there was a roguish twinkle in his eye, and, even as he spoke, his mouth broadened to a grin. I heard him humming the lines of an old ditty which I supposed to have some reference to my state:

> "Tam o' the Linn and a' his bairns
> Fell into the fire in ilk ither's airms.
> 'Eh,' quoth the binmost, 'I have a het skin.'
> 'It's hetter below,' quo' Tam o' the Linn."

But, sure enough, the captain's prophecy did not come true. For in a little the waves grew calmer, and my sickness left me. 'Tis true that soon we entered troubled waters once more, but I was fortified with experience and some measure of brandy, and so could laugh defiance at the power of the sea.

The wind throughout our course was fair in our favour, so we made the journey in shorter time than I had dared to hope for. On the morning of the third day a dense mist shut us in so that the captain was much confused and angered. But on the wind's rising, the fog rolled back, and we went on our way once more. Early in the afternoon we sighted the mouth of the Maas, and the tall lines of shipping, which told of the entrance to Rotterdam. You may imagine that all this was very strange to me, who had lived only among hills and rough woods, and had seen the sea but once, and that afar off. 'Twas a perpetual wonder to see the great sails moved up and down according to the airt of the wind, and the little helm guiding the great ship. As I have said, I soon got over all sickness, and was as hale as ever, so that on the last two days of the voyage I ever look back as upon a time of great pleasure.

But if my wonder was great in the open seas, 'twas still greater once we had entered the Dutch river. It was so unlike my own land that the homesickness which travellers tell of had almost taken hold of me. There were all manner of ships—some little coasting vessels, others huge merchantmen which brought home the wares of the Indies and Americas. There was such a jabbering, too, in Dutch, of which tongue I knew naught, that I longed to hear one good, intelligible word of Scots, for which cause I kept my servant near me. By-and-by we neared the quay, and saw the merchants' red storehouses standing in long line, and the streets of the city running back from the river. Here we came to an anchor. Our journey was over, and I had to bid farewell to captain and vessel and go ashore.

It is not to be expected that I should seek to describe what is known to nigh every one in these days, when a man thinks nothing of crossing to France or Holland on any pretext or in any weather. From such, therefore, by word of mouth, let he who desires it seek information; for myself, I have enough to do to write down the main acts of my life.

One thing I noted—that the air was somewhat soft and damp, lacking, to my mind, the acid strength of the air of Tweeddale, or even of the Lothians. But all the streets were clean swept and orderly; the folk well-groomed and well-looking; and the trees by the riverside gave a pleasant surprise to one accustomed to the grim, grey, narrow streets of the North. I made my way by the help of an inquisitive Scots tongue and the French language to a decent hostelry in the Groote Markt, just opposite the statue (but lately erected) of the great Erasmus. This pleased me much, for to be near even the poor bronze figure of so great a man seemed to lend to the place an air of learning. I employed myself profitably in reading the Latin inscriptions; the others I could make no more of than the rudest ploughboy in Scotland.

Both Nicol and I were up betimes in the morning, that we might get the coach for Leyden, which started almost from the door of our inn. I solemnly set down my testimony that the ale in that same house is the most villainous in the world, for it made us both dismal and oppressed, a trouble which did not leave us till we had taken our seats in the diligence and the horses were starting.

Of the events of that day's journey how shall I tell? Leyden is a day's length from Rotterdam to the north, through a land flat as a girdle-cake. The horses were lumbering, sleepy brutes, and the driver scarce any better, for every now and again he would let them come to the walk for long distances, and then, suddenly awaking to the fact that he must get to his destination before night get up and shout wildly, and feebly flick their backs with his whip. I had much ado to keep Nicol from trying to take the reins from his hands; and certainly, if that firebrand had once taken them, we should have awakened the quiet countryside, and, God helping us, might even have awakened the driver. I knew nothing of the country, and heard but vaguely the names shouted out by the guard of the coach; yet, somehow or other, the name of Ryswick clung to my memory, and I remembered it well when, long after, at that place the treaty was signed which closed the war. But at that time the great duke was plain Master Churchill, and there was no thought of war between our land and France. The place was so new to my eyes that I rebelled against its persistent flatness and dull, dead watercourses; but soon I came to acknowledge a kind of prettiness in it, though 'twas of a kind far removed from the wild loveliness of Tweedside. The well-ordered strips of trees, the poplars like sentinels around the homesteads, the red-roofed homesteads themselves, with their ricks and stables, had a homely and habitable look, and such of the folk as we saw by the roadside were as sleek and stolid as their land. I could not think of the place as a nursery of high and heroical virtues, but rather of the minor moralities of good sense and good nature.

It was late in the afternoon when we came to Leyden, and rattled down the rough street to the market-place, which was the stopping-place of the coach. This was a town more comely and conformable to my eye than the greater city of Rotterdam. For here the streets were not so even, the houses not so trim, and the whole showing a greater semblance of age. There were many streams and canals crossed by broad, low bridges. It was a time of great mildness for the season of the year. The place had all that air of battered age and historic worth which I have observed in our own city of Edinburgh. Even as I looked on it my mind was full of memories of that terrible siege, when the folk of Leyden held out so stoutly against the black Spaniards, till their king overthrew the dykes and saved the town by flooding the land.

It was my first concern to secure lodgings, since I purposed to spend no little portion of my time here for the next two years; and, as I had been directed by my kinsman, Dr. Gilbert Burnet, I sought the house of one Cornelius Vanderdecker, who abode in a little alley off the Breedestraat. Arrived there, I found that the said Cornelius had been in a better world for some fifteen months, but that his widow, a tranquil Dutchwoman, with a temper as long as a Dutch canal, was most willing to lodge me and treat me to the best which the house could afford. We speedily made a bargain in bad French, and Nicol and I were installed in rooms in the back part of the house overlooking a long garden, which ended in one of the streams of water which I have spoken of. It was somewhat desolate at that time, but I could see that in summer, when the straight trees were in leaf, the trim flower-beds and the close-cropped lawn would make the place exceeding pretty. I was glad of it, for I am country-bred and dearly do I love the greenery and the sight of flowers.

I delayed till the next morning, when I had got the soil of travel from my clothes and myself once more into some semblance of sprightliness, ere I went to the college to present my letters and begin my schooling. So after the morning meal, I attired myself in befitting dress and put Nicol into raiment suiting his rank and company; and set out with a light heart to that great and imposing institution, which has been the star of Europe in philosophy and all other matters of learning. I own that it was with feelings of some trepidation that I approached the place. Here had dwelt Grotius and Salmasius and the incomparable Scaliger. Here they had studied and written their immortal books; the very place was still redolent of their memories. Here, too, unless my memory deceived me, had dwelt the Frenchman, Renatus Descartes, who had first opened a way for me from the chaos of the schoolmen to the rectitude of true philosophy. I scarcely dared to enrol my unworthy name in the halls of such illustrious spirits. But I thought on my name and race, and plucked up heart thereupon to knock stoutly at the gates. A short, stout man opened to me, clad in a porter's gown, not unlike the bedellus in the faraway college of Glasgow, but carrying in his hand a black staff, and at his belt a large bunch of keys. It came upon me to address him in French, but remembering that this was a place of learning, I concluded that Latin was the more fitting tongue, so in Latin I spoke.

"I am a stranger," I said, "from Scotland, bearing letters for Master Sandvoort and Master Quellinus of this place. I pray you to see if they can grant me an audience."

He faced round sharply, as if this were the most ordinary errand in his life, and went limping across the inner courtyard till he disappeared from view behind a massive column. He returned shortly and delivered his message in a very tolerable imitation of the language of Cæsar.

"Their worships, Master Sandvoort and Master Quellinus, are free from business for the present, and will see you in their chambers." So bidding Nicol stay in the courtyard, lest he should shame me before these grave seniors (though 'twas unlikely enough, seeing they knew no Scots), I followed the hobbling

77

porter through the broad quadrangle, up a long staircase adorned with many statues set in niches in the wall, to a landing whence opened many doors. At one of them my guide knocked softly, and a harsh voice bade us enter. "This is Master Sandvoort," he whispered in my ear, "and I trust he be not in one of his tantrums. See ye speak him fair, sir."

I found myself in a high-panelled room, filled with books, and with a table in front of a fireplace, whereat a man sat writing. He wore a skullcap of purple velvet, and the ordinary black gown of the doctor. His face was thin and hard, with lines across the brow and the heaviness below the eyes which all have who study overmuch. His hair was turning to grey, but his short, pointed beard was still black. He had very shaggy eyebrows, under which his sharp eyes shone like the points of a needle. Such was Master Herman Sandvoort, professor of the Latin language in the ancient college of Leyden.

His first question to me was in the Latin.

"What tongue do you speak?"

I answered that I was conversant with the English, the French, and the Latin.

"Your letters, pray," he asked in French, and I took them from my pocket and gave them to him.

"Ah," he cried, reading aloud, "you desire to study in this university, and improve your acquaintance with certain branches of letters and philosophy. So be it. My fee is five crowns for attendance at my lectures. I will not abate one tittle of it. I will have no more poor students come cringing and begging to be let off with two. So understand my terms, Master Burnette."

I was both angry and surprised. Who was this man to address me thus?

"I pray you to finish the letter," I said curtly.

He read on for a little while, then he lifted his head and looked at me with so comical an expression that I had almost laughed. Before, his face had been greedy and cold; now it was worse, for the greed was still there, but the coldness had vanished and left in its place a sickly look of servility.

"Pardon me, pardon me, good Master Burnette; I was in a

great mistake. I had thought that you were some commoner from the North, and, God knows, we have plenty of them. I pray you forget my words. The college is most honoured by your presence, the nephew, or is it the son, of the famous Doctor Burnette. Ah, where were my eyes—the lord of much land, so says the letter, in the valley of the Tweed. Be sure, sir, that you can command all the poor learning that I have at my disposal. And if you have not already found lodging, why, if you will come to my house, my wife and daughters will welcome you."

I thanked him coldly for his invitation, but refused it on the ground that I had already found an abode. Indeed, I had no wish to form the acquaintance of Vrow Sandvoort and her estimable daughters. He gave me much information about the hours of the lectures, the subjects which he proposed to treat of, and the method of treatment; nor would he let me depart before I had promised to dine at his house.

Outside the door I found the porter waiting for me. He led me across the hall to another door, the room of Master Quellinus, the professor of Greek.

Here I found a different reception. A rosy-cheeked little man, with a paunch as great as a well-fed ox, was sitting on a high chair, so that his feet barely touched the ground. He was whistling some ditty, and busily mending his finger nails with a little knife.

"Why, whom have we here?" he cried out when he saw me; "another scholar, and a great one. Why, man, what do you at the trade, when you might be carrying a musket or leading a troop of pikemen?"

I was tempted to answer him in his own way.

"And what do you," I asked, "at the trade, when you might be the chief cook to the French king, with power to poison the whole nobility?"

He laughed long and loudly. "Ah, you have me there, more's the pity. But what though I love my dinner? Did not Jacob the patriarch, and Esau, the mighty Esau, though I have little credit by the ensample? But come, tell me your name, for I begin to love thee. You have a shrewd wit, and a pleasing presence. You may go far."

I gave him my letters, and when he had read them, he came down from his perch and shook me by the hand.

"You are a Scot," he said. "I never knew any Scot but one, and he was hanged on a tree for robbing the Burgomaster's coach. I was a lad at school, and 'twas rare sport. So I have a kindly feeling for your nation, though may God send you a better fate than that one. But what do you seek to learn? Greek? Faugh, there is no Greek worth a straw, save Anacreon, and he is not a patch upon our moderns, on François Villon of Paris, whose soul God rest, and our brave Desportes. Philosophy? Bah! 'Tis all a monstrous fraud. I have sounded all the depths of it, and found them but shallows. Theology? Tush! You will learn more theology in an inn in the Morschstraat than in all the schools. Such are my beliefs. But God has compelled me for my sins to teach the Hellenic tongue to a perverse generation at the small sum of five crowns. We study the *Republic* of Plato, and I trust you may find some profit. You will dine with me. Nay, I will take no denial. Tonight, in my house, I will show you how a quail should be dressed. I have the very devil of a cook, a man who could dress a dry goatskin to your taste. And wine! I have the best that ever came from the Rhineside and escaped the maw of the swinish Teuton. You will come?"

I could only escape by promising, which I did with a good grace, for if there was little profit in Master Quellinus's company, there was much pleasure.

CHAPTER II

I VISIT MASTER PETER WISHART

The life at the college of Leyden was the most curious that one could well conceive; yet ere I had been there a week, I had begun heartily to like it. The students were drawn from the four corners of Europe: Swedes, great men with shaggy beards and invincible courage; neat-coated Germans, Dutchmen by the score, and not a few Frenchmen, who were the dandies of the place. We all gathered of a morning in the dusky lecture-hall, where hung the portraits of the great scholars of the past, and where in the cobwebbed rafters there abode such a weight of dust that a breeze coming through the high windows would stir it and make the place all but dark. Nor had I fault to find with the worthy professors, for I found soon that Master Sandvoort, though a miserly churl, had vast store of Latin, and would expound the works of Cornelius Tacitus in a fashion which I could not sufficiently admire. His colleague, too, who was the best of good fellows in the seclusion of his house, in his lecture-room was dignified and severe in deportment. You never saw such a change in a man. I went on the first morning expecting to find little but buffoonery; and lo! to my surprise, in walks my gentleman in a stately gown, holding his head like an archduke; and when he began to speak, it was with the gravest accents of precision. And I roundly affirm that no man ever made more good matter come out of Plato. He would show wherein he erred and wherein he was wiser than those who sought to refute him; he would weigh with the nicest judgment the *variæ lectiones* on each passage; and he would illustrate all things with the choicest citations. In truth, I got a great wealth of good scholarship and sound philosophy from my squire of bottle and pasty.

I was not the only Scot in Leyden, as I soon discovered; for forbye that I had letters to Master Peter Wishart, who taught philosophy in the college, there abode in the town Sir James Dalrymple, afterwards my Lord Stair, the great lawyer, and sometime a professor in my old college, whose nephew I had so cruelly beaten before I bade farewell to Glasgow. He was a man of a grave deportment, somewhat bent with study, and with the look of exceeding weight on his face which comes to one who has shared the counsel of princes. There were also not a few Scots lords of lesser fame and lesser fortune, pensioners, many of them, on a foreign king, exiles from home for good and evil causes. As one went down the Breedestraat of a morning he could hear much broad Scots spoke on the causeway, and find many fellow-countrymen in a state ill-befitting their rank. For poverty was ever the curse of our nation, and I found it bitter to see ignoble Flemings and Dutch burghers flaunting in their finery, while our poor gentlemen were threadbare. And these folk, too, were the noblest in the land, bearing the proudest names, descendants of warriors and statesmen—Halketts of Pitfirran, Prestons of Gorton, Stewarts, Hays, Sinclairs, Douglases, Hamiltons, and Grahams. It was their fathers and grandfathers who had won the day at Rijnemants, under Sir Robert Stuart, when, says Strada, "Nudi pugnant Scoti multi." They had fought to the death on the Kowenstyn dyke when Parma beleaguered Antwerp. And in all the later wars they took their share—Scotts of Buccleuch, Haigs of Bemersyde, Erskines, Grants, and Kilpatricks. In the Scots brigade in Holland had served John Graham of Claverhouse, as some will have it, the greatest soldier of our age. I saw nothing of him, for while I was in the Low Lands he was already riding in the western hills, shooting and hanging and dealing martial law to herds and weavers. But I saw often the gallant figure of that Colonel Hugh Mackay who met Claverhouse in that last awful fight in the Highland pass when the mountaineers swept on the lowlanders like a winter storm, and who marched to his death long after on the field of Steenkirk, and fell with the words on his lips, "The will of the Lord be done." This valiant soldier had made the Scots brigade into some semblance of that doughty regiment which Lord Reay commanded under the great Gustavus. He had driven out all the foreign admixture, and, by keeping it to Scotsmen of gentle blood, rendered it wellnigh invincible. But the pay was poor, and they who entered it did so for the sake of honour and for no notions of gain.

But though it cheers me yet to tell of such fellows, and though it pleased me vastly to meet them in that distant land, it is not of such that I must write. As I have said, forbye attending the two classes of Greek and Latin, I resorted to the lectures of Master Wishart, who hailed from Fife, and had taught philosophy with much success among the Hollanders for some twenty years. He was well acquainted with my family, so what does he do but bid me to his house at Alphen one Saturday in the front of March. For he did not abide in Leyden, never having loved the ways of a town, but in the little village of Alphen, some seven miles to the north-east.

I accepted his bidding, for I had come there for no other cause than to meet and converse with men of learning and wisdom; so I bade Nicol have ready the two horses, which I had bought, at eleven o'clock in the forenoon. One of the twain was a bay mare, delicately stepping, with white pasterns and a patch of white on her forehead. The other was the heavier, reserved for Nicol and what baggage I might seek to carry, black and deep-chested, and more sedate than his comrade.

It was a clear, mild day when we set out, with no trace of frost, and but little cold. The roads were dry underfoot, and the horses stepped merrily, for they were fresh from long living indoors. The fields on either side were still bleak, but the sowers were abroad, scattering the seeds of the future harvest. The waters that we passed were alive with wildfowl, which had wintered in the sea marshes, and were now coming up to breed among the flags and rushes of the inland lakes. The tender green was sprouting on the trees, the early lark sang above the furrows, and the whole earth was full of the earnest of spring.

Alphen is a straggling line of houses by a canal. They are all well-sized, and even with some pretension to gentility, with long gardens sloping to the water and shady coverts of trees. Master Wishart's stood in the extreme end, apart from the rest, low-built, with a doorway with stuccoed pilasters. It was a place very pleasant to look upon, and, save for its flatness, I could have found it in my heart to choose it for a habitation. But I am hill-bred, and must have rough, craggy land near me, else I weary of the finest dwelling. Master Wishart dwelt here, since he had ever a passion for the growing of rare flowers, and could indulge it better here than in the town of Leyden. He was used to drive in every second day in his great coach, for he lectured but three times a week.

A serving-man took my horse from me, and, along with Nicol, led them to the stable, having directed me where, in the garden, I should find my host. I opened a gate in a quickset hedge, and entered upon the most beautiful pleasure-ground that I had ever beheld. A wide, well-ordered lawn stretched straightly down to the very brink of the canal, and though, as was natural at that season of the year, the grass had not come to its proper greenness, yet it gave promise of great smoothness and verdure. To the side of this again there ran a belt of low wood, between which and the house was a green all laid out into flower beds, bright even at that early time with hyacinths and jonquils. Below this the low wood began again, and continued to the borders of the garden, full of the most delightsome alleys and shady walks. From one of these I heard voices, and going in that direction, I came of a sudden to a handsome arbour, at the side of which flowered the winter jasmine, and around the door of which, so mild was the day, some half-dozen men were sitting.

My host, Master Wishart, was a short, spare man, with a long face adorned with a well-trimmed beard. He had the most monstrous heavy brows that I had ever seen, greater even than those of our Master Sandeman, of whom the students were wont to say that his eyebrows were heather besoms. His eyes twinkled merrily when he spoke, and but for his great forehead no one might have guessed that he stood in the presence of one of the most noted of our schoolmen.

He rose and greeted me heartily, bidding me all welcome to Alphen, saying that he loved to see the sight of a Scots face, for was he not an exile here like the Jews by the waters of Babylon? "This is Master John Burnet of Barns," said he, presenting me to a very grave and comely man some ten years my senior, "who has come all the way from Tweedside to drink at our Pierian spring." The other greeted me, looked kindly at me for a second, and then asked me some question of my family; and finding that a second cousin of his own on his mother's side had once married one of my race, immediately became very gracious, and condescended to tell me his opinions of the land, which were none so good. He was, as I did not know till later, Sir William Crichtoun of Bourhope: that Sir William who in after times was slain in the rout at Cromdale when the forces of Buchan and Cannon were caught unawares on the hillside.

I had leisure now to look around me at the others, and a

motley group they were. There was Quentin Markelboch, the famous physician of Leyden, who had been pointed out to me in the street some days before, a little, round-bellied man with an eye of wondrous shrewdness. There was likewise Master Jardinius, who had lectured on philosophy at one time in the college, but had now grown too old for aught save sitting in the sun and drinking Schiedam—which, as some said, was no great pity. But the one I most marked was a little, fiery-eyed, nervous man, Pieter van Mieris by name, own cousin to the painter, and one who lived for nothing else than to fight abstruse metaphysical quarrels in defence of religion, which he believed to be in great peril from men of learning, and, but for his exertions on its behalf, to be unable to exist. It was he who first addressed me.

"I have heard that the true religion is wondrous pure in your land, Master Burnet, and that men yet worship God in simple fashion, and believe in Him without subtleties. Is that so, may I beg of you to tell me?"

"Ay," I answered, "doubtless they do, when they worship Him at all."

"Then the most pernicious heresy of the pervert Arminius has not yet penetrated to your shores, I trust, nor Pelagianism, which, of old, was the devil's wile for simple souls?"

"I have never heard of their names," I answered bluntly. "We folk in Scotland keep to our own ways, and like little to import aught foreign, be it heresy or strong ale."

"Then," said my inquisitor triumphantly, "you are not yet tainted with that most vile and pernicious heresy of all, with which one Baruch Spinoza, of accursed memory, has tainted this land?"

I roused myself at the name, for this was one I had heard often within the past few weeks, and I had a great desire to find out for myself the truth of his philosophy.

"I am ashamed to confess," I said, "that I have read none of his writings, that I scarcely know his name. But I would be enlightened in the matter."

"Far be it from me," said the little man earnestly, "to corrupt the heart of any man with so pernicious a doctrine. Rather close thy ears, young man, when you hear any one speak his name, and pray to God to keep you from danger. 'Tis the falsest admixture of the Jewish heresy with the scum of ancient philosophy, the vain imaginings of man stirred up by the Evil One. He who made it is dead, and gone to his account, but I would that the worthy magistrates had seen fit to gibbet him for a warning to all the fickle and light-minded. Faugh! I cannot bear to pollute my mouth with his name."

And here a new voice spoke.

"The man of whom you speak was so great that little minds are unable to comprehend him. He is dead, and has doubtless long since learned the truth which he sought so earnestly in life. I am a stranger, and I little thought to hear any Hollander speak ill of Baruch Spinoza, for though God, in His mercy, has given many good gifts to this land, He has never given a greater than him. I am no follower of his, as they who know me will bear witness, but I firmly believe that when men have grown wiser and see more clearly, his name will shine as one of the lights of our time, brighter, may be, even than the great Cartesius."

The speaker was but newly come, and had been talking with my host when he heard the declamation of Master van Mieris. I turned to look at him and found a tall, comely man, delicately featured, but with a chin as grim as a marshal's. He stood amid the crowd of us with such an easy carriage of dignity and breeding that one and all looked at him in admiration. His broad, high brow was marked with many lines, as if he had schemed and meditated much. He was dressed in the pink of the fashion, and in his gestures and tones I fancied I discerned something courtierlike, as of a man who had travelled and seen much of courts and kingships. He spoke so modestly, and withal so wisely, that the unhappy Pieter looked woefully crestfallen, and would not utter another word.

A minute later, finding Master Wishart at hand, I plucked him by the sleeve.

"Tell me, who is that man there, the one who spoke?"

"Ah," said he, "you do not know him, perhaps you do not know his name; but be sure that when you are old you will look back upon this day with pleasure, and thank Providence for bringing you within sight of such a man. That is the great Gottfried Leibnitz, who has been dwelling for a short space in London, and now goes to Hanover as Duke Frederick's councillor."

But just at this moment all thoughts of philosophy and philosophers were banished from my mind by the sudden arrival of a new guest. This was no other than the worthy professor of Greek, Master Quellinus, who came in arrayed in the coarsest clothes, with a gigantic basket suspended over his shoulders by a strap, and a rod like a weaver's beam in his hand. In truth the little man presented a curious sight. For the great rod would not stay balanced on his shoulders but must ever slip upward and seriously endanger the equipoise of its owner. His boots were very wide and splashed with mud, and round the broad-brimmed hat which he wore I discerned many lengths of horsehair. My heart warmed to the man, for I perceived he was a fellow fisherman, and, in that strange place, it was the next best thing to being a fellow Scot.

He greeted us with great joviality. "A good day to you, my masters," he cried; "and God send you the ease which you love. Here have I been bearing the heat and burden of the day, all in order that lazy folk should have carp to eat when they wish it. Gad, I am tired and wet and dirty, this last beyond expression. For Heaven's sake, Master Wishart, take me where I may clean myself."

The host led the fisherman away, and soon he returned, spruce and smiling once more. He sat down heavily on a seat beside me. "Now, Master Burnet," says he, "you must not think it unworthy of a learned Grecian to follow the sport of the angle, for did not the most famous of their writers praise it, not to speak of the example of the Apostles?"

I tried hard to think if this were true.

"Homer, at any rate," I urged, "had no great opinion of fish and their catchers, though that was the worse for Homer, for I am an angler myself, and can understand your likings."

"Then I will have your hand on it," said he "and may Homer

87

go to the devil. But Theocritus and Oppian, ay, even Plato, mention it without disrespect, and does not Horace himself say 'Piscemur'? Surely we have authority."

But this was all the taste I had of my preceptor's conversation, for he had been walking all day in miry ways, and his limbs were tired; nor was I surprised to see his head soon sink forward on his breast, and in a trice he was sleeping the sleep of the just and labouring man.

And now we were joined by a newcomer, no less than Mistress Kate Wishart, as pretty a lass as you will see in a day's journey. She had been nurtured by her father amid an aroma of learning and truly, for a maid, she was wondrous learned, and would dispute and cite instances with a fine grace and a skill which astonished all. To me, who am country-bred and a trifle over-fastidious, she seemed a thought pedantic and proud of her knowledge; but what is hateful in a hard-featured woman is to be pardoned in a fresh lass. Her father brought me to her and presented me, which she acknowledged with a curtsy which became her mightily; but I spoke not two words to her for the old man led me away down one of the alleys among the trees.

"Kate'll look after thae auld dotterels," said he, speaking in the broadest Scots. "I brocht her out that I micht get a word wi' ye my lane, for I'm fair deein' for news frae the auld country. First of a', how is Saunders Blackett at Peebles? Him and me were aince weel acquant." And when I had told him, he ran off into a string of inquiries about many folk whom I knew, and whom he once had known, which I answered according to my ability.

"And now," he says, "I've bidden twa-three o' the officers o' the Scots brigade to supper the nicht, so ye'll see some guid Scots physiogs after thae fosy Dutchmen. Ye'll maybe ken some o' them."

I thanked him for his consideration, and after I had answered his many questions, we returned to the others, whom I found busily arguing some point in divinity, with Mistress Kate very disgusted in their midst.

"Gang intil the house wi' my dochter, John," said Master Wishart, and, giving her my arm, I did as I was bid, while the others straggled after in twos and threes.

CHAPTER III

THE STORY OF A SUPPER PARTY

My first thought on entering the supper room was one of amazement. The owner of the house, whom I had taken to be a man of simple tastes, here proved himself to be a very caliph for magnificence. Many choice paintings looked down at us from the sides, richly framed, and fitting into recesses in the panelled walls. The floor was laid with bright-dyed rugs and carpets of Venetian stuff, and the chairs and couches were of finely carven wood. The whole was lit with a long line of waxen candles in silver sconces, which disputed the sovereignty with the departing daylight. But the choicest sight was the table, which was laden, nay heaped, with rich dishes and rare meats, while in the glass and metal flagons the wine danced and flamed. I was of country-bred habits, and the display at first all but took the breath from me; indeed, it was not a little time ere I could take my eyes from it and turn them on the assembled guests.

Those who had not been present in the garden were gathered at the lower end of the room, whither the master of the place betook himself to greet them. I marked two or three of the burgher folk by their dress, and well-filled bellies, contrasting strangely with the lean figure of a minister who stood among them clothed in some decent dark stuff, and wearing white bands ostentatiously. There were also some of the officers in the Scots regiment, at least of that portion of it which was then lying at Leyden. Their dress was sober compared with the richness of such soldiery as I had seen in my own land, but against the attire of the citizens it was gaudiness itself.

I found myself sitting close to the head of the table, on the right hand of my host, betwixt a portly doctor of laws and my worthy Master Quellinus. This latter was now all but recovered from his fatigue, having slept soundly in the arbour. He was in a high good humour at the sight of the many varied dishes before him, and cried out their merits to me in a loud, excited tone, which made my cheeks burn. "There," he cried "there is the dish I love above all others. 'Tis hashed venison with young herbs, and sour wine for a relish. Ah, I have already enjoyed it in anticipation. In a few seconds I shall have enjoyed it in reality. Therefore, I argue, I have gained two pleasures from it, whereas men of no imagination have but one. And, God bless my eyes! do I see a plate of stewed eels over there before that thick man in the brown coat? Pest! I fear he will devour them all himself, for he looks to have capacity and judgment. Plague take him, I am in a very torment of anxiety. Prithee, my good John, seek out a servant and bid him bring it over here." I know not how far he might have gone, had not all talking been put an end to by the minister arising and saying a lengthy Latin grace. In the midst of it I stole a glance at my neighbour, and his face wore so comical an expression of mingled disgust and eagerness that I could scarcely refrain from laughing. But all did not conduct themselves so well, for there was a great disputation going on among some of the regiment which much hindered the effect of the minister's Latin. Indeed, I believe had he spoken another dozen words, the patience of some would have gone altogether.

"Now," said Master Wishart from the head of the table, "I trust, gentlemen, that ye may find the entertainment to your liking. Fall to heartily, for this weather gives a keen edge to the appetite. *Occupet extremum scabies*, as Horatius hath it; which being translated into the vulgar idiom is 'Deil tak the hinmost.' Know you that proverb, John? Come, Master Quellinus, set to, man, ye've had a serious day's work, and our fleshy tabernacles will not subsist on nothing"—adding in an undertone to me, "though it's little pressing ye need, for to press ye to eat is like giving a shog to a cairt that's fa'in ower the Castle Rock."

I paid little heed to Master Quellinus's conversation, which ran chiefly on viands, or to that of my left-hand neighbour, whose mouth was too full for words. But I found great entertainment in watching the faces and listening to the speech of some of the other guests. The table was wide and the light dim, so that I had much ado to make out clearly those opposite me. I marked Mistress Kate, very daintily dressed, talking gaily to some one at

90

her side.

"To tell you the truth, my dear Mistress Kate, this land of yours is not very much to my liking. To be sure a soldier is contented wherever his duty calls him, but there is no fighting to be done, and the sport is not what I have found it elsewhere. I am in such a devilish strict place that Gad, I cannot have a game with a fat citizen without having to listen to a rigmarole of half an hour's duration on the next morning. There is so much psalm-singing in the place that an honest gentleman can scarcely raise a merry song without having his voice stopped by half a dozen sour-faced knaves. 'Faith, I wish I were back in my own land, where there is some work for a cavalier. There is but one thing that I should except"—and he bowed low to his neighbour—"the women, who are as beautiful as the menfolk are hideous. Though, in truth, I believe that the most lovely of them all is a countrywoman of my own"; and again he made her a fine bow.

The voice and the tone were strangely familiar but for the life of me, I could not give them a name. I could only note that the man was a big, squarely-made fellow, and that he seemed to be in a mind to make love to his host's daughter. She made some blushing reply to his compliments, and then, as luck would have it, a servant set a light between us, and the faces of both were revealed clearly to me.

I sat bolt upright in my chair with sheer astonishment. For there, dressed in the habiliments of the Scots regiment, and bearing himself with all his old braggadocio, sat my cousin Gilbert.

Then I remembered how I had heard that he had gone abroad to some foreign service, partly to escape the consequences of some scrapes into which he had fallen, partly to get rid of his many debts. And here he was, coming to the one place in Europe to which I had chosen to go, and meeting me at the one table which I had chosen to frequent. In that moment I felt as if the man before me were bound up in some sinister way with my own life.

Almost at the same instant he turned his eyes upon me, and we stared in each other's face. I saw him start, bend his head toward his companion and ask some question. I judged it to be some query about my name and doings, for the next moment he looked over to me and accosted me with a great semblance of hilarity.

"What," he cried. "Do I see my cousin John? I had not dared to hope for such a welcome meeting. How came you here?" And he asked me a string of questions.

I answered shortly and with no great cordiality, for I still remembered the doings in Tweeddale and my heart was still sore in the matter of my father's death. Forbye this, Gilbert spoke with not a little covert scorn in his tone, which I, who knew his ways well, was not slow to detect. It nettled me to think that I was once more to be made to endure the pleasantries of my cousin.

"And how goes all in Tweeddale, my dear cousin?" said he. "I condole with you on your father's death. Ah, he was a good man indeed and there are few like him nowadays. And how does Tam Todd, my friend, who has such a thick skull and merciless arm? And ah, I forgot! Pray forgive my neglect. How is fair Mistress Marjory, the coy maid who would have none of my courtesies?"

The amazing impudence of the fellow staggered me. It almost passed belief that he should speak thus of my father, whose death had lain so heavily at his door. This I might have pardoned; but that at a public table he should talk thus of my love irritated me beyond measure. I acted as I do always when thus angered— I gave him a short answer and fell into a state of moody disquietude.

Meanwhile my cousin, with all the gallantry in the world, kept whispering his flatteries into the pretty ears of Mistress Kate. This was ever Gilbert's way. He would make love to every tavern wench and kiss every village lass on his course. 'Twas a thing I never could do. I take no credit for the omission, for it is but the way God makes a man. Whenever I felt in the way to trying it, there was always Marjory's face to come before my eyes and make me think shame of myself.

As I sat and watched these twain I had no eyes for any other. The sight of Gilbert brought back to me all my boyhood in Tweedside, and a crowd of memories came surging in upon me. I fancied, too, that there was something of Marjory in the little graceful head at my cousin's elbow, and the musical, quick speech. I felt wretchedly jealous of him, God knows why; for the sight of him revived any old fragments which had long lain lurking in the corners of my mind; and as he chatted gaily to the woman at his side, I had mind of that evening at Barns when I, just returned from Glasgow college, first felt the lust of possession. I sat and moodily sipped my wine. Why had I ever left my own land and suffered my lady to be exposed to manifold perils? For with the first dawnings of jealousy and anger came a gnawing anxiety. I had never felt such a sickness for home before, and I cursed the man who had come to ruin my peace of mind. Yet my feeling toward my cousin was not that of hatred; indeed I could not refrain from a certain pity for the man, for I discerned in him much noble quality, and was he not of my own blood?

"Come now," I heard Mistress Kate simper; "I do not believe that tale of any one, and above all of him; for a soberer does not live. Fie, fie, Master Gilbert, I took you for a more generous man."

"On my faith, my dear, it is true," replied my cousin. "For all his docile looks, he is as fond of a game as the rest of us."

Now I guessed that my frolicsome cousin had been traducing me to the fair Kate, and I grew not a little hot. But his next word changed my heat into fierce anger. For my cousin continued—

"What saith the Latin poet?" and he quoted a couplet from Martial—a jest at the usual amusements of the seemingly decent man.

I know not where he got hold of it, for he was no scholar; but it was full of the exceeding grossness which is scarcely to be found outside that poet. He thought, I could guess, that the girl understood no Latin; but, as I knew, she had a special proficiency in that tongue. She understood the jest only too well. A deep blush grew over her face from her delicate throat to the very borders of her hair. 'Twas just in such a way that Marjory had looked when I first told her my love; 'twas in such a fashion she had bade me farewell. The thought of her raised a great storm of passion in my heart against any one who would dare thus to put a woman to shame. I strove hard to curb it, but I felt with each second that it would overmaster me.

"Well, John, what think you of my Latinity?" asked my cousin from over the table.

"I think, I think," I cried, "that you are a damned scurrilous fellow, a paillard, a hound; 'fore God, Gilbert, I will make you smart for this;" and, ere I well knew what I did, I had seized my glass and hurled it at his head.

It struck him on the cheek, scratching the skin, but doing little hurt.

In a trice he was on his feet with his hand at his sword. One half the table rose and stared at the two of us, while Master Wishart left the head and came rushing to the back of my chair. As for myself, I felt such desperate shame at my conduct that I knew not what to do. I had now made a fool of myself in downright earnest. I felt my cheek tingling and flaming, but I could do naught but look before me.

Then my cousin did a thing which gave him great honour, and completed my shame; for bridling his anger, as I saw, with a mighty effort, he said calmly, though his arms were quivering with rage—

"I would ask you to be more careful in your use of glasses. See, yours has flown right over to me and played havoc with my cheek. 'Faith, it is no light duty to sup opposite you, *mon ami*. But, indeed, gentlemen"—and he bowed to the company— " 'twas but an unfortunate mischance."

At this all sat down again, and scarce five minutes after Gilbert rose to leave, and with him the other gentlemen of his regiment. Master Wishart bade him sit down again, for the night was yet young, but my cousin would not be persuaded. He nodded carelessly to me, kissed his hand to pretty Mistress Kate, and swaggered out.

I sat dazed and meditative. I was raw to many things, but I knew well that Gilbert was not the man to sit down under such an affront. He had shielded me for his own reasons, of which I guessed that family pride was not the least; but he would seek a meeting with all dispatch. And, in truth I was not averse to it, for I had many accounts to settle with my dear cousin. I fell to thinking about the details of the matter. In all likelihood he would come on the Monday, for the Sabbath was a day of too strict propriety in this land, as in my own, to allow of the settling of any such business. Well, come when he might, I should be ready; and I rose from the table, for the sooner I was back in Leyden the better.

I took farewell of my host, and he could not refrain from whispering in my ear at parting: "Jock, Jock, my man, ye've made a bonny mess o't. Ye'll hae to fecht for it, and see ye dae't weel."

Nicol was waiting at the gate with the horses and together we turned on our homeward way.

CHAPTER IV

OUR ADVENTURE ON THE ALPHEN ROAD

We rode in silence for maybe half a mile, while I turned over the events of the evening in my mind and tried to find some way out of the difficulties in which, by my own folly, I found myself placed. Nicol looked steadfastly before him and said never a word. By-and-by I found the desire for some one to speak with so overpowering that I up and asked him if he had heard aught of the events of the evening.

"Ay, sir," said he, "I heard ye had some kind o' stramash, but that was a'. I trust ye're weel oot o't."

"Have you heard of my cousin Gilbert?" I asked.

"The wastland lad wha used to come aboot the Barns? Oh, aye! I've heard o' him."

"I flung a glass at his face tonight," said I.

"I hope, sir, that he flung anither at yoursel'?" he asked anxiously.

"No. He swallowed the insult and left soon after. He is not the man to let me off so easily."

"Whew," said Nicol, "but that's bad. Wad ye mind, Laird, if I rode on afore ye?"

"Why?" I asked.

"Cousins and sodger-folk are kittle cattle," said he. "I wadna wonder noo but that Maister Gilbert were ahint a dyke. I've heard tell o' some o' his pliskies in his ain land, and he's no the lad to let a midge stick in his throat."

I drew up my horse angrily.

"Nicol," I cried, "you are intolerable. My cousin is a gentleman of birth, and do you think he is the man to kill from a dykeside? Fie on you, you have the notions of a common roost-robber."

"Weel away then, my lord," cries he. "So be it; but I've little faith in your Gilberts for a' their gentrice. I ken their breed ower weel. But I maun ride afore ye, for there are some gey rough bits on the road, and I'm a wee bit mair sure in the saddle than yoursel', wi' a' respect to your lairdship."

So the wilful fellow must needs ride before me looking sharply to the right and left as though we were in far Muscovy instead of peaceful Holland.

As for me, I felt in no humour to listen to my servant's tales or do aught than think dolefully on my own matters. The sight of my cousin and of Mistress Kate had made me sore sick for home, and I could have found it in my heart once and again to take ship at the next sailing for Leith. But these thoughts I choked down, for I felt that they were unbecoming to any man. Yet I longed for Marjory as never lover longed for his mistress. Her bright hair was ever before my sight, and her last words on that February evening rang always in my head. I prayed to God to watch over her as I rode through the stiff poplars on the way to Leyden.

As for my quarrel, I cared not a straw for Gilbert and his ill-will, it having never been my nature to be timorous toward men. Nay, I looked forward to meeting him with no little pleasure, for it had long been an open question which of the twain was best at the swordplay.

"Maister John," said Nicol, suddenly turning round, "I saw twae men creeping roond thae scrunts o' trees. I wis they maunna be after ony ill." We were by this time nearing a bleak, inhospitable part of the land, where the road ran across a moor all covered with ferns and rushes and old trunks of trees.

"Ride on," said I; "if we turned for every man that crosses the path, we should never leave our own threshold."

He did as he was ordered, and our horses being put to the canter covered the ground gallantly, and our stirrup-chains clinked in the silent night.

Suddenly, to my amazement, I saw Nicol fling himself back in the saddle while his horse stumbled violently forward. It was one of the most ingenious feats of horsemanship that I have ever witnessed. The beast stood quivering, his ears erect with fright, while I rode alongside.

"For God's sake, sir, take care," Nicol cried. "There's some damned thing ower the road, and if I hadna been on the watch it wad hae been a' ower wi' yae guid man. Watch, for ye may get a shot in your belly any meenute."

Now, as it chanced, it was that lively canter which saved us, for the rogues who had set the trap had retired a good way, not expecting us so early. At the sound of the stumble they came rushing up from among the fern, and, ere I knew, a pistol shot cracked past my ears, and another and another.

Two went wide; one hit my horse on the ear and made him unmanageable, so that I sat there with my beast plunging and kicking, at the mercy of whosoever had a fourth pistol.

Nicol spoke not a word, but turning his horse dashed forward in the direction whence the shots had come. As it fell out, it was the best thing that any one could have done, for the robbers, not expecting any such assault, were preparing to fire again. As it was, the forefeet of the horse took one villain on the chest, knocking him senseless and wellnigh trampling the life out of him. A second gripped Nicol by the sleeve, and attempted to drag him from the saddle, which plan would doubtless have succeeded had not my servant, pulling the pistol (which was not loaded) from his holsters, presented it at the man's head with such effect that the fellow in fear of his life let go and fled across the moor.

By this time I had reduced my own animal to something like submission. I rode after Nicol, and came up just in time to see the third man of the band (there were but three, for doubtless they trusted to their trap for unhorsing if not stunning us) engaged in a desperate struggle. Nicol had him by the throat with one hand and was endeavouring to squeeze the breath out of him, while he in turn had his opponent by the other arm, which he was twisting cruelly. Had my servant been on foot the matter would soon have ended, for the throat fared badly which those long wiry hands once encircled; but being on horseback he dared not lean forward lest he should lose his seat. My appearance settled it; for the robber, freeing himself at one desperate leap, made off at the top of his speed, leaving his pistols behind him. There remained but the one whom Nicol's horse had deprived of his senses.

Unfortunately the blow had not been a very severe one, for he was not long in coming to himself. There was some water in a little stagnant pool near at hand which Nicol dashed in his face, and in a little the man opened his eyes and looked up.

At the sight of us he started, and the events of the past half-hour came back to his memory. Then a look of sullen, obstinate anger came into his face, and he lay still, waiting for events to take their course.

"Who are you?" I asked.

He made no answer.

I repeated the question several times, and still the man kept his silence.

"Ye donnert scoondrel," cried Nicol, "tell us whae ye are, or ye'll hang the morn on the gallows-hill at Leyden."

Still the fellow would not speak.

"Let's tie him up," said Nicol, "and I'll ride wi' him on the horse afore me. He'll get justice when we win to the toun."

But this was not my policy. I had other things to think of than bringing marauders to trial. A sudden thought struck me.

"I will try him another way," said I to Nicol. "Do you stand aside."

The man lay on the ground where my servant's horse had thrown him, with a belt round his legs, and his arms knotted together. I went up to him, and stood over.

"Do you know who I am?" I asked sternly, in as tragic a voice as I could assume.

The man stared sulkily, but did not speak.

"You fool," I cried, "do you think that thus you will circumvent me? Know that I am the great doctor, Joannes Burnetus of Lugdunum, skilled in all arts of earth and heaven, able to tell divinations and prophecies, learned in all magic and witchery. I know all that thou hast done since thy birth, and thy father and grandsire before thee, all the wickedness which shall entitle thee to eternal damnation in that place which the Devil is even now preparing for thee. Yea, I can tell thee the very death which thou shalt die—"

"Stop, stop," cried the fellow, "O most learned sir, spare me. I know thou knowest all things. I confess my sins, and oh, I promise you I shall mend my ways. Stop, I pray."

"There is still one ray of hope for thee," said I, "but I cannot give my word that thou shalt ever gain it, for thou hast advanced too far in sin already. But yet thou mayest escape, and there is but one way to set about it—namely, to tell me of all thy wickedness. I adjure thee, by the sacred sign *Tekel*, which the Chaldæans used of old; by *Men*, which was the sign of the Egyptians; by the *Eikon* of the Greeks; by the *Lar* of the Romans. I summon thee by the holy names of God, *Tetragrammaton, Adonay, Algramay, Saday, Sabaoth, Planaboth, Panthon, Craton, Neupmaton, Deus, Homo, Omnipotens*; by *Asmath*, the name of the Evil One, who is lord over thee and my slave—I summon thee to tell me all thy deeds."

The man was frightened past all telling. He tried to crawl to my knees, and began a recital of all manner of crimes and peccadilloes, from his boyhood till the present hour. I listened without interest.

"Had any Scot a part with thee in this night's work?" I asked.

"No, there was none. There were but Bol and Delvaux beside myself, both Dutch born and bred."

My mind was lightened. I never really believed my cousin to have had any part in such a matter, but I was glad to know it for truth.

"You may go now," I said, "go and repent, and may God blast thee with all His fire if thou turnest thy hand to evil again. By-the-by, thy name? I must have it from thy own lips."

"Jan Hamman, your lordship," said he.

"Well, God pity thee, Jan Hamman, if ever I lay my hand on thee again. Be off now."

He was off in a twinkling, running for his very life. Nicol and I remounted and rode onward, coming to Leyden at the hour of one on the Sabbath morning—a thing which I much regretted.

CHAPTER V

THE FIRST SUNDAY OF MARCH

I slept late on the next morning, so that it was near nine o'clock ere I was up and dressed. By the time that I broke my fast I had had some leisure to reflect upon the events of the preceding night and the consequences which should ensue. Nicol came to me as soon as the meal was over and together we sat down to consult.

"This is the Sabbath, your honour," said Nicol, "so ye may consider yourself free for the day at ony rate."

"Not so free," said I, for I knew my cousin Gilbert. "The men I've to deal with have no more respect for the Lord's day than you have for a Popish fast, so we must put that out of account."

"Weel, weel," said Nicol, "if that's sae it maun be sae. Will ye gang oot wi' him the day?"

"No," said I, "not that I am caring for the day, for you mind the proverb, 'The better the day the better the work,' but, being in a foreign land, I am loath to break with the customs of my own country. So we'll keep the Sabbath, Nicol, my lad, and let Gilbert whistle."

Now I would not have him who may read this narrative think from my conduct on this occasion that I was whiggishly inclined, for, indeed, I cared naught about such little matters. I would have a man use the Sabbath like any other day, saving that, as it seems to me, it is a day which may profitably be used for serious reading and meditation. But I was ever of an odd disposition, liking to be always in mind of Tweeddale and the folk there, so that I kept the Sabbath during my life abroad as strictly as a covenanting minister on the moors of Ayr.

"Weel, Laird, that means ye'll no see the body though he comes," said Nicol, "and, God help me, if ye dae that there'll be a terrible stramash at the street door. I'se warrant auld Mistress Vanderdecker'll get her ribs knockit in if she tries to keep them oot."

"They can make all the noise they please," said I hotly, "but if it comes to that the two of us are as good as their bit officers. I ask for nothing better than to take some of the pride out of Gilbert's friends with the flat of my sword. Then if they come today and are refused entrance, they will come tomorrow, and all will be well."

"Then what am I to dae? When the bodies come to the door, I'm to say, 'His lordship's compliments, but his lordship's busy keeping the Sabbath in his upper chamber, and if ye will come back the morn he'll look into your claims.' 'Faith, it's awfu' like auld Saunders Blackett, the lawyer at Peebles, when I gaed to him seeking the law o' the miller o' Rachan. It was about nine o'clock yae winter's nicht when I got there, and Saunders was at supper. He stappit his heid oot o' the window and, says he, 'Gang awa', my man, and come back the morn. I'm busy takin' the books.' But I saw by the een o' him that he was daein' nae siccan thing. 'Oh,' says I, 'if ye ca' kippered saumon and schnapps the books, I'm content. I'll just come in and help ye to tak' them tae.' But he says, verra angry, 'Go away, ye impious man, lest the judgment of Heaven light upon you. I've godly Maister Clovenclaws assisting me in the solemn ordinance.' 'Awa' wi your Clovenclaws,' says I; 'I've come ten mile to speak wi' ye, and I'll no gang hame wi'oot it.' But I was just thinkin' I would have to gang back after a', when a voice comes frae the inside, 'Saunders, ye limb o' the deil, whaur's the sugar?' I kenned Maister Clovenclaws' voice ower weel, so Saunders begins to think that it wadna dae to let it be telled a' ower the toun that him and the minister had been birling at the wine thegither. So 'Come in, Maister Plenderleith,' says he verra cannily, and in I gaed, and sic a nicht's drinking I never saw. I put Saunders in his bed, honest man, about twae o'clock i' the morning, and syne Clovenclaws and me gaed at it till daylicht. I wantit to see the body below the table afore I gaed, and he wantit to see me, so we sat at it till I was fain to drap for very decency's sake. So what does the man dae but lift me on his shouther and walk as straucht ower to the manse as if he were new oot o' his bed; and there he gied me some guid advice about no presumin' to contend wi' my superiors, and let me oot at a back door. 'Faith, it was an awfu' time."

"You will say to them that I am busy with other work, and that I will be glad to see them tomorrow about the matter they know of. Most like they will go away quietly, and if they do not it will be the worse for their own skins. You take my meaning?"

"I'll dae your orders, sir, to the letter." said Nicol, and I was well aware that he would.

I got my books out and set to work to read the gospel of John in Greek for my spiritual benefit, but I made little speed. This was mainly the fault of Nicol, who every few minutes came into the little room where I sat, on some feigned errand. I soon divined the reason, for the same chamber contained a window whence one might view the whole length of the narrow street wherein the house was situate, and even some little portion of the great Breedestraat at the head. It was plain that my servant was not a little concerned on my account.

"Are ye sure that your honour's guid wi' the small-swird?" he asked mournfully. "If this room were a wee bit braider and the day no what it is I micht gie ye a lesson."

I did not know whether to laugh or to be angry. "Why, you rascal," I cried, "do you know anything of these matters? There are many better swordsmen than I in the world, but I think I am more than a match for you."

"Weel," said Nicol modestly, "I've gien some folk a gey fricht wi' the swird, but let that be. I'll be blithe if ye get the better o' him, and a waefu' man I'll be if he kills ye. Lord, what'll I dae? I'll hae to become a sodger in this heathen land, or soom hame, whilk is a thing I am no capable o'." And he began to sing with a great affectation of grief—

"The craw killed the pussie O,
The craw killed the pussie O,
The wee bit kittlin' sat and grat
In Jennie's wee bit hoosie O."

—in which elegant rhyme the reader will observe that my cousin stood for the crow, I for the pussie, and my servant for the kittlin'.

I laughed; but it's not seemly to stand by while your own servant sings a song which compares you to a cat, so I straightway flung a Greek lexicon at his head, and bade him leave the room. I much regretted the act, for it was my only copy of the book, Master Struybroek's, and the best obtainable, and by the fall some leaves came out, and one, πολυπενθης to πολυπους has not been renewed to this day.

After Nicol had gone I amused myself by looking out of the window and watching the passers-by. Some sober Dutch citizens with Bibles beneath their arms and their goodly persons habited in decent black were striding solemnly to church, while their wives and children came more slowly behind. Others of the lighter sort were wandering aimlessly on no purpose but their own pleasure, but all I marked were dressed out in their finest clothes. What I noted most of all was the greater colour in the streets than we have in our own land. For there, you will see little but blacks and drabs and browns, while here the women were often gaily arrayed in bright tints which gave a pleasing look to the causeway.

I had not sat long when I noted two gentlemen coming down the alley from the Breedestraat, very finely clad, and with a great air of distinction in their faces. They kept the causeway in such a fashion that all whom they met had to get into the middle of the road to let them pass. I half guessed their errand, the more as the face of one of them seemed to me familiar, and I fancied that he had been one of the guests at the supper at Alphen. My guess was confirmed by their coming to a halt outside the door of my lodging and attentively considering the house. Meantime all their actions were plain to my view from the upper window.

One of them stepped forward and knocked loudly. Now I had bidden Nicol be ready to open to them and give my message. So

I was not surprised when I heard the street door opened and the voice of my servant accosting the men.

I know not what he said to them, but soon words grew high and I could see the other come forward to his comrade's side. By-and-by the door was slammed violently, and my servant came tearing upstairs. His face was flushed in wrath.

"O' a' the insolent scoondrels I ever met, thae twae are the foremost. They wadna believe me when I telled them ye were busy. 'Busy at what?' says the yin. 'What's your concern?' says I. 'If ye dinna let us up to see your maister in half a twinkling,' says the ither, 'by God we'll make ye.' 'Make me!' says I; 'come on and try it. If it wasna for your mithers' sake I wad tie your necks thegither.' "

"Nicol," I said, "bring these men up. It will be better to see them." My intention changed of a sudden, for I did not seek to carry my finicking too far.

"I was thinkin' sae, your honour," said Nicol, "but I didna like to say it."

So in a little the two gentlemen came up the stairs and into my room, where I waited to receive them.

"Gentlemen," said I, "I believe you have some matter to speak of with me."

"Why do you keep such scoundrelly servants, Master Burnet?" said one, whom I knew for Sir James Erskine of Tullo.

"Your business, gentlemen," I said, seeking to have done with them. They were slight men, whom I could have dropped out of the window; most unlike the kind of friends I should have thought my cousin Gilbert would have chosen.

"Well, if you will have our business," said the elder, speaking sulkily, "you are already aware of the unparalleled insult to which a gentleman of our regiment was subjected at your hands?"

"Oh yes," I said gaily, "I had forgotten. I broke Gilbert's head with a wine-glass. Does he want to ask my pardon?"

"You seem to take the matter easily, sir," said one severely. "Let me tell you that Master Gilbert Burnet demands that you meet him at once and give satisfaction with your sword."

"Right," I cried, "I am willing. At what hour shall it be? Shall we say seven o'clock tomorrow morning? That is settled then? I have no second and desire none. There is the length of my sword. Carry my compliments to my cousin, and tell him I shall be most pleased to chastise him at the hour we have named. And now, gentlemen, I have the honour to wish you a very good day," and I bowed them out of the room.

They were obviously surprised and angered by my careless reception of their message and themselves. With faces as flushed as a cock's-comb they went downstairs and into the street, and I marked that they never once looked back, but marched straight on with their heads in the air.

"Ye've gien thae lads a flee in their lug," said Nicol. "I wish ye may gie your cousin twae inches o' steel in his vitals the morn."

"Ah," said I, "that is a different matter. These folk were but dandified fools. My cousin is a man and a soldier."

The rest of the day I spent in walking by myself in the meadows beyond the college gardens, turning over many things in my mind. I had come to this land for study, and lo! ere I well knew how, I was involved in quarrels. I felt something of a feeling of shame in the matter, for the thing had been brought on mainly by my over-fiery temper. Yet when I pondered deeply I would not have the act undone, for a display of foolish passion was better in my eyes than the suffering of an insult to a lady to pass unregarded.

As for the fight on the morrow I did not know whether to await it with joy or shrinking. As I have said already, I longed to bring matters between the two of us to a head. There was much about him that I liked; he had many commendable virtues; and especially he belonged to my own house. But it seemed decreed that he should ever come across my path, and already there was more than one score laid up against him in my heart. I felt a strange foreboding of the man, as if he were my *antithesis*, which certain monkish philosophers believed to accompany every one in the world. He was so utterly different from me in all things; my vices he lacked and my virtues; his excellencies I wanted, and also, I trust, his faults. I felt as if the same place could not contain us.

If I conquered him, the upshot would be clear enough. He could not remain longer in Leyden. His reputation, which was a great one, would be gone, and he would doubtless change into some other regiment and retire from the land. If, again, he had the vantage of me, I had no reputation to lose, so I might remain where I pleased. So he fought with something of a disadvantage. It was possible that one or other might be killed; but I much doubted it, for we were both too practised swordsmen to butcher like common cut-throats. Nevertheless, I felt not a little uneasy, with a sort of restlessness to see the issue of it all—not fear, for though I have been afraid many times in my life it was never because of meeting a man in fair combat.

Toward evening I returned to my lodging and devoted the remainder of the day to the study of the books of Joshua and Judges for the comforting of my soul.

CHAPTER VI

THE FIRST MONDAY OF MARCH

Nicol wakened me before dawn and I made haste to get ready. I looked to see that my sword was in fit condition, for it was a stout cut-and-thrust blade of the kind which speedily takes the rust. Then having taken a draught of strong ale to brace my nerves for the encounter, I left the house and set off with my servant for the college gardens.

The morning was clear and fresh. The sun had not yet fully arisen, but it was light enough to see two hundred yards before me. A sharp wind fluttered my cloak, and sent a thrill of strength through me, for it minded me of the hill breezes which were wont to blow on the heights of Scrape. There was scarce any one stirring save a few drowsy burghers whom it behoved to be attending to their business in the early morn. I kept my cloak well over my face, for I did not relish the notion of being recognized by any one on my errand.

Now, from the college gardens there stretches down to the great canal a most beautiful pleasance, all set with flower beds and fountains. Beyond this again is a more rugged land—a grove with great patches of grass in it, and here it was that gentlemen of the Scots regiment were wont to settle their differences. The morning had been chosen as the time when it was less likely that some interloping busybody might interrupt us.

I cannot tell how I felt as I walked through the cool morning air among the young herbs and trees which still bore the dew upon them. It minded me so keenly of the mornings at home in Tweeddale, when I was used to rise before daylight and go far up Tweed with my rod, and bring back, if my luck were good, great baskets of trout. Now I was bound on a different errand. It was even possible that I might see my own land no more. But this thought I dismissed as unworthy of one who would be thought a cavalier.

In time we came to the spot which the others had fixed on. There I found my men already waiting me; my cousin stripped to his sark and small-clothes, with his blade glimmering as he felt its edge; his companions muffled up in heavy cloaks and keeping guard over Gilbert's stripped garments. They greeted me shortly as I came up, so without more ado I took off my coat and vest, and gave them into my servant's keeping. Then going up to my opponent I took his hand.

"Let there be no malice between us, Gilbert," said I. "I was rash maybe, but I am here to give account of my rashness."

"So be it, cousin," he said, as he took my hand coldly.

We both stepped back a pace and crossed swords, and in a trice we had fallen to.

My first thought, and I am not ashamed to confess it, when I felt my steel meet the steel of my foe, was one of arrant and tumultuous fear. I had never before crossed swords with any one in deadly hatred; and in my case the thing was the harder, for my feeling against my cousin was not so violent a passion as to make me heedless of aught else. Before me, behind the back of my antagonist, the thick underwood was already filled with the twittering of birds, and a great feeling of longing came upon me to get well through with the affair and escape death. For now a feeling which I had not reckoned with came to oppress me—the fear of death. Had my wits been more about me, I might have reflected that my cousin was too good a swordsman to kill me and lay himself open to many penalties. But my mind was in such a confusion that I could think of naught but an overwhelming danger.

Howbeit, in a little this fit passed, and once more I was myself. Gilbert, for what reason I know not, fenced swiftly and violently. Blow came upon blow till I scarce could keep my breath. I fell at once upon the defensive, and hazarded never a cut, but set all my powers to preserving my skin. And in truth this was no easy task, for he had acquired a villainous trick of passing suddenly from the leg-cut to the head-stroke, so that more than once I came not up to guard in time and had his sword almost among my hair. I could not guess what he meant by this strategy for I had ever believed that a man who began in a hot fit ended in a languor. He sought, I doubt not, speedily to put an end to the encounter by putting forth his greater strength, hoping to beat down my guard or bewilder me with the multiplicity of his flourishes.

Now this conduct of my opponent had an effect the very counter of what he proposed. I became completely at my ease; indeed, I swear I never felt more cool in my life. This has ever been the way with me, for I have always been at my cheerfulest in the extremest perils. Oftentimes when things went very sore with me, I was at a loss and saw no way of escape, but let them get a little worse and I was ready to meet them. So now I was on the watch to frustrate every movement, and since no man can fight rapidly and fight well, I kept him at bay till he deemed it prudent to give up this method.

But when he came down to slow, skilful fence I found my real danger. We were well matched, as had been proved in many a harmless encounter on the turf by the Tweed. I was something lighter, he somewhat stronger in the arm and firmer in the body; but taking us all in all we were as equal a pair as ever crossed swords. And now there was an utter silence; even the birds on the trees seemed to have ceased. The others no longer talked. The sharp clatter and ring of the swords had gone, and in its place was a deadly *swish—swish*, which every man who has heard it dreads, for it means that each stroke grazes the vitals. I would have given much in that hour for another inch to my arm. I put forth all my skill of fence. All that I had learned from Tam Todd, all that I had found out by my own wits was present to me; but try as I would, and I warrant you I tried my utmost, I could not overreach my opponent. Yet I fenced steadily, and if I made no progress, I did not yield my ground.

With Gilbert the case was otherwise. His play was the most brilliant I had ever seen, full of fantastic feints and flourishes such as is the French fashion. But I could not think that a man could last for ever in this style, since for one stroke of my arm there were two of his and much leaping from place to place. But beyond doubt he pressed me close. Again and again I felt his steel slipping under my guard, and it was only by a violent parry that I escaped. One stroke had cut open my sleeve and grazed my arm, but beyond this no one of us had suffered hurt.

But soon a thing which I had scarcely foreseen began to daunt me. I was placed facing the east, and the rising sun began to catch my eyes. The ground was my own choosing, so my ill-luck was my own and no fault of Gilbert's. But it soon began to interfere heavily with my play. I could only stand on guard. I dared not risk a bold stroke, lest, my eyes being dazzled by the light, I should miscalculate the distance. I own I began to feel a spasm of fear. More than one of my opponent's strokes came within perilous nearness. The ground too was not firm, and my foot slid once and again when I tried to advance. To add to it all there was Gilbert's face above the point of the swords, cold, scornful, and triumphant. I began to feel incredibly weak about the small of the back, and I suppose my arm must have wavered, for in guarding a shoulder-cut I dropped my point, and my enemy's blade scratched my left arm just above the elbow. I staggered back with the shock of the blow, and my cousin had a moment's breathing space. I was so obviously the loser in the game that Gilbert grew merry at my expense.

"Well, John," he cried, "does't hurt thee? My arm is

somewhat rougher than Marjory's."

There seems little enough in the words, yet I cannot tell how that taunt angered me. In the mouth of another I had not minded it, but I had a way of growing hot whenever I thought of my cousin and my lady in the same minute of time. It called to my mind a flood of bitter memories. In this encounter, at any rate, it was the saving of me. Once more I was myself, and now I had that overmastering passionate hate which I lacked before. When I crossed swords again I felt no doubt of the issue and desired only to hasten it. He on his part must have seen something in my eyes which he did not like, for he ceased his flourishes and fell on defence.

Then it was that the real combat of the day commenced. Before it had been little more than a trial of skill, now it was a deadly and determined battle. In my state of mind I would have killed my foe with a light heart, however much I might have sorrowed for it after. And now he began to see the folly of his conduct in the forepart of the fight. I was still fresh and stout of arm; he was a little weary and his self-confidence a little gone.

"By God, Gilbert, you will eat your words," I cried; and had at him with might and main.

I fenced as I had never fenced before, not rashly, but persistently, fiercely, cunningly. Every attempt of his I met and foiled. Again and again I was within an ace of putting an end to the thing, but for some trifling obstacle which hindered me. He now fought sullenly, with fear in his eyes, for he knew not what I purposed concerning him. I warrant he rued his taunt a hundred times in those brief minutes.

At last my opportunity came. He made a desperate lunge forward, swung half round and exposed his right arm. I thrust skilfully and true. Straight through cloth and skin went my blade, and almost ere I knew I had spitted him clean through the arm just above the elbow. The sword dropped from his helpless hand.

I had put forth too much strength, for as he stumbled back with the shock of the wound I could not check my course, but staggered heavily against him and together we rolled on the ground.

In a second I was on my feet and had drawn out my weapon. With lowered point I awaited his rising, for he was now powerless to continue.

"Well," said I, "have you had satisfaction?"

He rose to his feet with an ugly smile. "Sufficient for the present, cousin John," said he. "I own you have got the better of me this time. Hi, Stephen, will you lend me a kerchief to bind this cursed wound?"

One of his companions came up and saw to his wants. I made to go away, for there was no further need of my presence, but my cousin called me back.

"Farewell, John," he said. "Let us not part in anger, as before. Parting in anger, they say, means meeting in friendship. And, 'faith, I would rather part from you in all love and meet you next in wrath."

"Farewell," I said carelessly as I departed though I was amazed to hear a man with a pierced arm speak so lightly. Courage was not a quality which my cousin had to seek. So I left him in high good-humour with myself, much pleased at my own prowess, and sensible that all immediate annoyance from that quarter was at an end.

Little man knows what God hath prepared for him. Had it not been for his defeat, Gilbert had not left Holland, and my greater misfortunes had never happened. And yet at that hour I rejoiced that I had rid myself of a torment.

Nicol was awaiting me, and soon I was arrayed in my coat once more, for the air was shrewdly cold. My servant was pale as I had never seen him before, and it was clear that he had watched the combat with much foreboding.

"Eh, Maister John," he cried, "ye're a braw fechter. I never likit ye half as weel. I thocht a' was up whiles, but ye aye cam to yoursel' as sprig as a wull-cat. Ye're maybe a wee thing weak i' the heid cuts, though," he added. "I'll hae to see to ye. It's no what ye micht ca' profitable to be aye proddin' a man in the wame, for ye may prick him a' ower and him no muckle the waur. But a guid cleavin' slash on the harns is maist judeecious. It wad kill a stirk."

111

It was still early and we had breakfasted sparely, so we sought a tavern of good repute, The Three Crows, and made a hearty meal, washing it down with the best Rhenish. I was so mightily pleased with my victory, like a child with its toy, that I held my head a full inch higher, and would yield the causeway to no man. I do believe if M.Balagny or the great Lord Herbert had challenged me I would not have refused.

Some three days later I had sure tidings that my cousin had sailed for Leith, and was thought to have no design of returning.

CHAPTER VII

I SPEND MY DAYS IN IDLENESS

Summer came on the heels of spring, and the little strip of garden below my windows grew gay as the frock of a burgher's wife on a Sunday. There were great lines of tulips, purple and red and yellow, stately as kings, erect as a line of soldiers, which extended down the long border nigh to the edge of the water. The lawn was green and well trimmed, and shaded by the orderly trees. It was pleasant to sit here in the evenings, when Nicol would bring out the supper-table to the grass and we would drink our evening ale while the sun was making all the canal a strip of beaten gold. Many folk used to come of an evening, some of them come to the university on the same errand as myself, others, Scots gentlemen out of place and out of pocket, who sought to remedy both evils by paying court to the Stadtholder. Then we would talk of our own land and tell tales and crack jests till the garden rang with laughter. I could well wish those times back, if I could bring with them the *forte latus, nigros angusta fronte capillos, dulce loqui, ridere decorum.* But fie on me for such discontent! Hath not God given good gifts for age as well as youth—ay, perhaps in greater abundance?

I pursued my studies in the ancient literatures and philosophy with much diligence and profit. Nevertheless, there was much to turn my attention, and I doubt if I did not find the folk around me the more diverting objects of study. I lived in an air of theology and philosophy and statecraft, hearing discussions on these and kindred matters all the day long. There were many of my own countrymen in the place, who are notoriously the most contentious of mankind: so that I could scarcely walk down any street without hearing some violent disputation in my own tongue. As for the other people of the place, I found them both civil and hospitable.

The routine of my days was as regular as clockwork, for it was always part of my method to apportion my time equally among my duties. In the morning, immediately upon rising, I went to Master Sandvoort's lecture on the Latin tongue. Then I broke my fast in the little tavern, The Grey Goose, just at the south entrance to the college. It was a clean, well-fitted place, where was found the fattest landlord and the best ale in Holland. Then at the hour of ten in the forenoon I went to listen to the eloquence of Master Quellinus. Having returned thence to my lodging I was wont to spend the time till dinner in study. Thereafter I walked in the town, or resorted to the houses of my friends, or read in the garden till maybe four o'clock, when it was my custom to go to the dwelling of Sir William Crichtoun (him whom I have spoken of before), and there, in the company of such Scots gentlemen as pleased to come, to pass the time very pleasantly. From these meetings I had vast profit, for I learned something of the conduct of affairs and the ways of the world, in the knowledge of which I had still much to seek. Then home once more to study, and then to bed with a clear conscience and great drowsiness.

But there were several incidents which befell during this time, and which served to break the monotony of my life, which merit the telling. Firstly, towards the end of September who should come to visit me but my kinsman, Gilbert Burnet of Salisbury, a scholar shrewd and profound, a gentleman of excellent parts, and the devoutest Christian it had ever been my lot to fall in with. He was just returning from his journey to Italy, whereof he has written in his work, *Some Letters to T. H. R. B. concerning his Travels in Italy and Holland*. It was one afternoon as I sat in the arbour that Nicol came across the green followed by an elderly man of grave and comely appearance. It was to my great joy that I recognized my kinsman. He had alighted in Leyden that morning and proposed to abide there some days. I would have it that he should put up at my lodgings, and thither he came after many entreaties. During his stay in the city he visited many of the greater folk for his fame had already gone abroad, and he was welcome everywhere. He was a man of delightful converse, for had he not travelled in many lands and mixed with the most famous? He questioned me as to my progress in letters, and declared himself more than satisfied. "For, John," said he, "I have met many who had greater knowledge, but none of a more refined taste and excellent judgment. Did you decide on the profession of a scholar I think I could promise you a singular success. But indeed it is absurd to think of it, for you, as I take it, are a Burnet and a man of action, and one never to be satisfied with a life of study. I counsel you not to tarry too long in this foreign land, for your country hath sore need of men like you in her present distress." Then he fell to questioning me as to my opinions on matters political and religious. I told him that I was for the Church and the king to the death, but that I held that the one would be the better of a little moderation in its course, and that the other had fallen into indifferent hands. I told him that it grieved my heart to hear of my own countrymen pursued like partridges on the mountains by blackguard soldiers, and that when I did return, while deeming it my duty to take the part of the king in all things, I would also think it light to hinder to the best of my power the persecution. In this matter he applauded me. It pained him more than he could tell, said he, to think that the Church of his own land was in such an ill condition that it did not trust its friends. "What in Heaven's name is all this pother?" he cried. "Is a man to suffer because he thinks one way of worshipping his God better than another? Rather let us rejoice when he worships Him at all, whether it be at a dykeside or in the king's chapel." And indeed in this matter he was of my own way of thinking. When finally he took his leave it was to my great regret, for I found him a man of kindly and sober counsels.

Yet his visit had one result which I had little dreamed of, for it led me to show greater friendliness to such of the Scots Covenanters as were refugees in the town. I learned something of their real godliness and courage, and was enabled to do them many little services. In particular, such letters as they wished to write to their friends at home I transmitted under my own name and seal since all communication with Holland was highly suspected unless from a man of approved loyalty.

The other matter which I think worth noting was the acquaintance I formed with a Frenchman, one M. de Rohaine, a gentleman of birth, who was in great poverty and abode in a mean street off the Garen Markt. The way in which I first met him was curious. I was coming home late one evening from Master Swinton's house, and in passing through a little alley which leads from near the college to the Garen Markt, I was apprised of some disturbance by a loud noise of tumult. Pushing forward amid a crowd of apprentices and fellows of the baser sort, I saw a little man, maybe a tailor or cobbler from his appearance, with his back against a door and sore pressed by three ruffians, who kept crying out that now they would pay him for his miserly ways. The mob was clearly on their side, for it kept applauding whenever they struck or jostled him. I was just in the act of going forward to put an end to so unequal a combat, when a tall grave man thrust himself out of the throng and cried out in Dutch for them to let go. They answered with some taunt, and almost before I knew he had taken two of the three, one in either hand, and made their heads meet with a sounding crack. I was hugely delighted with the feat, and broke forward to offer my help, for it soon became clear that this champion would have to use all his wits to get out of the place. The three came at him swearing vehemently, and with evil looks in their eyes. He nodded to me as I took my stand at his side.

"Look after the red-beard, friend," he cried. "I will take the other two."

And then I found my hands full indeed, for my opponent was tough and active, and cared nothing for the rules of honourable warfare. In the end, however, my training got the mastery, and I pinked him very prettily in the right leg, and so put him out of the fight. Then I had time to turn to the others, and here I found my new-found comrade sore bested. He had an ugly cut on his forehead, whence a trickle of blood crawled over his face. But his foes were in a worse case still, and when word came at the moment that a body of the guard was coming they made off with all speed.

The man turned and offered me his hand.

"Let me thank you, sir, whoever you may be," said he. "I am the Sieur de Rohaine, at your service."

"And I am Master John Burnet of Barns in Scotland," said I.

"What," he cried, "a Scot!" And nothing would serve him but that I must come with him to his lodging and join him at supper. For, as it seemed, he himself had just come from Scotland and was full of memories of the land.

I found him a man according to my heart. When I spoke of his gallantry he but shrugged his shoulders. "Ah," said he, "it was ever my way to get into scrapes of that kind. Were I less ready to mix in others' business I had been a richer and happier man today," and he sighed.

From him I learned something more of the condition of my own land, and it was worse even than I had feared. M. de Rohaine had had many strange adventures in it, but he seemed to shrink from speaking of himself and his own affairs. There was in his eyes a look of fixed melancholy, as of one who had encountered much sorrow in his time and had little hope for more happiness in the world. Yet withal he was so gracious and noble in presence that I felt I was in the company of a man indeed.

If I were to tell all the benefit I derived from this man I should fill a volume and never reach the end of my tale. Suffice it to say that from him I learned many of the tricks of swordplay, so that soon I became as nigh perfect in the art as it was ever in my power to be. I learned too of other lands where he had been and wars which he had fought; and many tales which I have often told at home in Tweeddale I first heard from his lips. I was scarce ever out of his company, until one day he received a letter from a kinsman bidding him return on urgent necessity. He made his farewells to me with great regret, and on parting bade me count on his aid if I should ever need it. From that day to this I have never cast eyes on his face or heard tidings of him, but I herewith charge all folk of my family who may read this tale, if ever it be their fortune to meet with one of his name or race, that they befriend him to the best of their power, seeing that he did much kindness to me.

So the summer passed with one thing and another, till, ere I knew, winter was upon us. And I would have you know that winter in the Low Countries is very different from winter with us among the hills of Tweed. For here we have much mist and rain and a very great deal of snow; also the cold is of a kind hard to endure, since it is not of the masterful, overbearing kind, but raw and invidious. But there the frost begins in late autumn and keeps on well till early spring. Nor was there in my experience much haze or rain, but the weather throughout the months was dry and piercing. Little snow fell, beyond a sprinkling in the fore end of January. Every stream and pond, every loch and canal was hard and fast with ice, and that of the purest blue colour and the keenest temper I have ever seen. All the townsfolk turned out to disport themselves on the frozen water, having their feet shod with runners of steel wherewith they performed the most wondrous feats of activity. The peasant girls going to market with their farm produce were equipped with these same runners, and on them proceeded more quickly than if they had ridden on the high road.

Often too, during the winter, there were festivals on the ice, when the men arrayed in thick clothes and the women in their bravest furs came to amuse themselves at this pastime. I went once or twice as a spectator, and when I saw the ease and grace of the motion was straightway smitten with a monstrous desire to do likewise. So I bought a pair of runners and fitted them on my feet. I shall not dwell upon my immediate experiences, of which indeed I have no clear remembrance having spent the better part of that afternoon on the back of my head in great bodily discomfort. But in time I made myself master of the art, and soon was covering the ice as gaily as the best of them. I still remember the trick of the thing, and five years ago, when the floods in Tweed made a sea of the lower part of Manor valley, and the subsequent great frost made this sea as hard as the high road, I buckled on my runners and had great diversion, to the country folks' amazement.

In all this time I had had many letters from Marjory, letters writ in a cheerful, pleasant tone, praying indeed for my return, but in no wise complaining of my absence. They were full of news of the folk of Tweedside, how Tam Todd was faring at Barns, and what sport her brother Michael was having in the haughlands among the wild duck. I looked eagerly for the coming of those letters, for my heart was ever at Dawyck, and though I much enjoyed my sojourning in Holland, I was yet glad and willing for the time of departure to arrive. In January of the next year I received a bundle of news written in the gayest of spirits; but after that for three months or more I heard nothing. From this long silence I had much food for anxiety, for though I wrote, I am sure, some half-dozen times, no reply ever came. The uneasiness into which this put me cast something of a gloom over the latter part of the winter. I invented a hundred reasons to explain it. Marjory might be ill; the letters might have gone astray; perhaps she had naught to tell me. But I could not satisfy myself with these excuses, so I had e'en to wait the issue of events.

It was not till the month of April that I had news from my love, and what this was I shall hasten to tell.

CHAPTER VIII

THE COMING OF THE BRIG "SEAMAW"

It was the third day of April, a day so cool and mild that every one who could was in the open air, that I sat in the little strip of garden behind my lodging, reading the *Symposium* of Plato in the light of certain digests of Master Quellinus. The beds of hyacinth, yellow and blue and red, were flaunting before my eyes, and down by the water's edge the swallows were twittering and skimming. The soft spring wind fluttered the leaves of my book and stirred my hair, so that I found it hard indeed to keep my attention fixed. Some yards behind me Nicol sat cleaning a fishing-rod, for in the idle days he amused himself with trying his skill among the sleepy streams. He was whistling some bars of "Leezie Lindsay," and the tune, which I had often heard in Tweeddale, put me much in mind of home and inclined my heart violently to the place I had left. So soon I found my Plato lying listlessly on my lap, and my thoughts far away over sea.

Just now, I knew, would be the lambing time in the Tweed hills, and all the valleys would be filled with the noise of sheep. The shepherds, too, would be burning the bent, and the moors sending up wreaths of pungent smoke. I minded the smell so well that I almost fancied it was in my nostrils in place of the moist perfume of hyacinth and violet. At Barns, Tam Todd would be seeing to the young trees and fishing in the full streams. At Dawyck, Marjory would be early abroad, plucking the spring flowers and bringing in armfuls of apple blossom to deck the rooms. The thought of Marjory gave me sudden discomfort. I reflected for the thousandth time that I had heard nothing of her for months, and I fell to wondering greatly at her silence. By-and-by, what with thinking of home and of her and chafing at her neglect, I found myself in a very pretty state of discontentment.

It was just then that I heard a voice behind me, and turning round saw Nicol approaching in company with another. The stranger was a man of remarkable appearance. He was scarcely the middle height, but his breadth across the shoulders was so great that he seemed almost dwarfish. He had arms of extraordinary length, so long that they reached almost to his knees, like the Tartars in Muscovy that I have read of. His square, weather-beaten face was filled with much good-humour, and the two eyes which looked out from beneath his shaggy brows were clear and shrewd.

"This is Maister Silas Steen o' the brig *Seamaw*," said Nicol, making an introduction, "whae has come from Scotland this morning, and says he has letters wi' him for you." Having delivered himself, my servant retreated, and left the newcomer alone with me.

"You'll be Master John Burnet of Barns?" said he, looking at me sharply.

"The same, at your service," said I.

"It's just a bit letter for you," and he dived into his pocket and produced a packet.

I took it hastily, for I had some guess who was the writer. Nor was I wrong, for one glance at the superscription told me the truth. And this is how it ran:

> "*For Master John Burnet*
> *in the house of Mistress Vanderdecker*
> *near the Breedestraat, at Leyden.*

"DEAR JOHN,—I have not written thee for long, and I trust that thereby I have not given thee trouble. I am well and happy, when this leaves me, though desiring thy return. I trust your studies are to your satisfaction. Tam Todd, from the Barns, was over yestreen, and gave a good account of all things there."

Then came a pause, and the writing was resumed in a hurried, irregular hand.

"I am not free to write my will. O John, dear John, come back to me. I am so unhappy. I cannot survive without thee another day." (this latter word had been scored out and *month* put in its place.) "I am in dreadful perplexity. Come quick.

"MARJORY."

You may imagine into what state of mind the reading of this letter threw me. My lady was in trouble, that was enough for me, and she desired my aid. I guessed that the letter had been written stealthily and that some trouble had been found in its conveyance, for it bore the marks of much crumpling and haste. I could make no conjecture as to its meaning, and this doubt only the more increased my impatience.

"From whom did you get this?" I asked.

"From a great, thin, swart man, who brought it to me at Leith, and bade me deliver it. I came post haste from Rotterdam this day."

I ran over in my mind the serving-folk at Dawyck, and could think of none such. Then, like a flash, I remembered Tam Todd. This doubly increased my fears. If Marjory could get no porter for her message save one of my own servants, then the trouble must be at Dawyck itself.

I can find no words for the depths of my anxiety. To think of Marjory in sorrow and myself separated by leagues of land and sea wellnigh drove me distracted. There and then I resolved on my course.

"Your ship is at Rotterdam?" I asked.

"Yes," said the captain.

"When does she sail?"

"Tomorrow night, when the cargo is on board."

"I'll give you twenty pieces of gold if you'll sail tonight."

The captain shook his head. "It canna be done," he cried; "my freight is lace and schiedam, worth four times twenty pieces, and I canna have a voyage for naething."

"Listen," said I, "I am in terrible perplexity. I would give you a hundred, if I had them; but I promise you, if you bring me safely to the port of Leith, they shall be paid. Ride back to your vessel and ship all the stuff you can, and I will be with you at eleven o'clock this night, ready to sail."

The fellow shook his head, but said nothing.

"Man, man," I cried, "for God's sake, I implore you. It's a matter to me of desperate import. See, there are your twenty pieces, and I'll give you my bond for eighty, to be paid when we win to Leith."

"Tut, Master Burnet," said he, "I will not be taking your money. But I'm wae to see you in trouble. I'll take you over the nicht for the twenty pieces, and if I lose on the venture, you can make it up to me. It's safer carrying you and running straight for the pier, than carrying schiedam and dodging about the Bass. And I'm not a man that need count his pennies. Forbye, I see there's a lady in the case, and I deem it my duty to assist you."

121

I was at first astonished by the man's ready compliance, but when I saw that he was sincere, I thanked him to the best of my power. "Be sure I shall not forget this service, Captain Steen," said I; "and if it is ever in my power to serve you in return, you may count on me. You will take some refreshment before you go;" and, calling Nicol, I bade him see to the stranger's wants.

Meantime it behoved me to be up and doing if I was to sail that night. I knew not what to think of the news I had heard, for, as I thought upon the matter, it seemed so incredible that aught could have gone wrong that I began to set it all down to mere loneliness and a girl's humours. The strangeness of the letter I explained with all the sophistry of care. She did not wish to disturb me and bring me home before my time. This was what she meant when she said she was not free to write her will. But at the end her desolateness had overmastered her and she had finished with a piteous appeal. Even so I began to reason, and this casuistry put me in a more hopeful frame of mind. It was right that I should go home, but when I got there I should find no cause for fear. But there was much to be done in the town and the college ere I could take my departure. So when I had paid all the moneys that I owed, and bidden farewell to all my friends (among whom Sir William Crichtoun and Master Quellinus were greatly affected), I returned to my lodgings. There I found Nicol in great glee, preparing my baggage. He was whistling the "Lawlands of Holland," and every now and then he would stop to address himself. "Ye're gaun hame," I heard him saying, "ye're gaun hame to the hills and the bonny water o' Tweed, and guid kindly Scots folk, after thae frostit Hollanders, and fine tasty parritch and honest yill after the abominable meats and drinks o' this stawsome hole. And ye'd better watch your steps, Nicol Plenderleith, my man, I'm tellin' ye, and keep a calm sough, for there's a heap o' wark to be dune, and some o' it geyan wanchancy."

"Good advice, Nicol," said I, breaking in upon him; "see that you keep to it."

"Is that you, Maister John? Ye'll be clean high aboot gaun back. Ye'll hae seen a' that's to be seen here, for after a' it's no a great place. And ye maun mind and put a bottle o' French brandy in your valise, or you'll be awfu' oot on the sea. I think it's likely to be coorse on the water."

I took my servant's advice, and when all was done to my liking, I walked down to the college gate for one last look at the place. I was in a strange temper—partly glad, partly sad—and wholly excited. When I looked on the grey walls, breathing learning and repose, and thought of the wise men who had lived there, and the great books that had been written, and the high thoughts that had been born, I felt a keen pang of regret. For there was at all times in me much of the scholar's spirit, and I doubted whether it had not been better for me, better for all, had I chosen the life of study. I reflected how little my life would lie now in cloisters and lecture halls, in what difficulties I might soon be plunged and what troublous waters I might be cast upon. My own land was in a ferment, with every man's hand against his brother; my love might be in danger; of a surety it looked as if henceforward quiet and gentleness might be to seek in my life. I own that I looked forward to it without shrinking—nay, with a certain hopeful anticipation; but I confess also that I looked at the past and all that I was leaving with a certain regret. Indeed, I was born between two stools; for, while I could never be content to stay at home and spend my days among books, on the other hand the life of unlettered action was repugnant. Had it been possible, I should have gladly dwelt among wars and tumults with men who cared not for these things alone, and could return, when all violence was at an end, to books and study with a cheerful heart. But no man has the making of the world, and he must even fit himself to it as he finds it. Nor do I think it altogether evil to have many desires and even many regrets, for it keeps a man's spirit active, and urges him on to valiant effort. Of this I am sure, that contentment is the meanest of the virtues.

As I left the place there was a cool, grey haze over all the gardens and towers—mellow and soft and lucid. But to the north, where lay the sea, there was a broken sky, blue, with fitful clouds passing athwart. It seemed, as it were, the emblem of my life—the tranquil and the unsettled. Yet in the broken sky there was a promise of sunshine and brilliance, which was not in the even grey; and this heartened me.

So at four that evening we mounted horse and rode forth by the way we had come, and ere the hour of eleven were on the wharf at Rotterdam, sniffing the distant smell of the sea.

CHAPTER IX

AN ACCOUNT OF MY HOME-COMING

Captain Steen met me on deck and greeted me heartily. "There's a brisk wind from the sou'-east," said he, "which should speed us well"; and soon, amid creaking of cordage and flapping of sails, we dropped down the estuary and set our face seawards. There was something of a squall of rain which beat on us till we were fairly beyond the Dutch coast; but after that it drew down to the west, and when I awoke the next morn, the sky was blue and sunshiny, and the soft south wind whistled gaily in the rigging.

Of my voyage home I need not tell at length. On it I met with none of the mishaps which I had encountered before, so the brandy was wholly needless. Indeed, I found the greatest pleasure in the journey; the motion of the ship gave me delight, and it was fine to watch the great heaving deserts before and behind, when the sun beat on them at midday, or lay along them in lines of gold and crimson at the darkening. The captain I found a friendly, talkative man, and from him I had much news of the state of the land whither I was returning. Nor was it of such a sort as to elate me, for it seemed as if, in the short time I had been away, things had taken many steps to the devil. The truth of the matter, I fancy, was that when I left Tweeddale I was little more than a boy, with a boy's interests, but that now I had grown to some measure of manhood and serious reflection.

But my time during the days of our sailing was in the main taken up with thoughts of Marjory. The word I had got still rankled in my mind and I puzzled my brain with a thousand guesses as to its purport. But as the hours passed this thought grew less vexatious, for was not I on my way home, to see my love once more, to help her in perplexity, and, by God's help, to leave her side never again? So anxiety was changed by degrees to delight at the expectation of meeting her, and, as I leaned over the vessel's edge and looked at the foam curling back from the prow, I had many pleasing images in my fancy. I would soon be in Tweeddale again, and have Scrape and Dollar Law and Caerdon before my eyes, and hear the sing-song of Tweed running through the meadows. I thought of golden afternoons in the woods of Dawyck, or the holms of Lyne, of how the yellow light used to make the pools glow, and the humming of bees was mingled with the cry of snipe and the song of linnet. As I walked the deck there were many pictures of like nature before me. I thought of the winter expeditions at Barns, when I went out in the early morning to the snow-clad hills with my gun, with Jean Morran's dinner of cakes and beef tightly packed in my pocket; and how I was wont to come in at the evening, numb and frozen, with maybe a dozen white hares and duck over my shoulder, to the great fire-lit hall and supper. Every thought of home made it doubly dear to me. And more than all else, there was my lady awaiting me, looking for the sight of my horse's head at the long avenue of Dawyck.

Then I fell to thinking of the house of Barns, and of the many things which I should do were I home. There was much need of change in the rooms, which had scarce been touched for years. Also I figured to myself the study I should make, and the books which were to fill it. Then out of doors there was need of planting on the hillsides and thinning in the haughlands; and I swore I should have a new cauld made in Tweed, above the island, for the sake of the fishing.

We left Rotterdam on the evening of one day, and sailed throughout the day following; and since we had a fair wind and a stout ship, about noon on the next we rounded the Bass and entered the Forth. I was filled with great gladness to see my native land once more, and as for my servant, I could scarce prevail upon him to keep from flinging his hat into the sea or climbing to the masthead in the excess of his delight. The blue Lomonds of Fife, the long ridges of the Lammermoors, and the great battlements of the Pentlands were to me like honey in the mouth, so long had I been used to flat lands. And beyond them I saw the line of the Moorfoots, ending in Dundreich, which is a hill not five miles from the town of Peebles.

About three of the clock we entered Leith Roads and awaited the signals for admission. "The *Seamaw* lies at the wast harbour for usual," said the captain, "but there's something wrong thereaways the day, so we maun e'en run into the east." So, soon amid a throng of barques at anchor and small boats moving to and fro among them, we steered our course, and in a very little lay against the grey, sea-washed walls of the east quay. There we landed after bidding farewell to the captain; and as my feet touched the well-worn cobblestones, and I smelt the smell of tar and herrings, I knew my own land. The broad twang of the fishermen, the shrill yatter of the fishwives, the look of the black red-tiled houses, and the spires of the kirks—all was so Scots that it went straight to my heart, and it was with a cheerful spirit that, followed by my servant, I made for the inn of *The Three Herrings* where I purposed to sleep the night ere I rode to Tweeddale on the morrow. So much for man's devices: this was to be to me the last day of quiet life for many months. But as I briskly strode along the Harbour Walk, little I foresaw of the dangers and troubles which awaited my coming.

BOOK III

THE HILLMEN

CHAPTER I

THE PIER O' LEITH

WHEN I came to the door of *The Three Herrings*, I presented an imposing sight, with Nicol at my side and two sailors at my back with my baggage. The landlord, who was taking the afternoon air against the wall, made me a civil greeting, and placed his hostel at my service, opining that I was a stranger of consequence just come from abroad. So bidding my servant settle with the men, I followed my host upstairs to a room where a fire was burning. From below came the clink of glasses and the snatch of a song. The sun poured in at the open window; a girl in the street was singing the "Fishwives' Rant"; and all the world seemed in gay spirits.

An excellent supper was brought, on which I fell like a hawk, for the sea air had sharpened my hunger, and landward dishes are better than the meat of a ship. I bade the landlord let no one enter save my servant, for that I desired to be alone. Then I fell to summing up my moneys, and various calculations of a like nature, which it was proper to make on my return; and, finally, I pushed away my chair from the table, and, filling my glass, gave myself up to pleasing fancies.

It was near the darkening, as I saw from the window which opened on the backyard, and which at that hour was filled with the red glow of sunset. The chimneys on the tall houses rose like spikes into the still air, and somewhere in the place a bell was ringing for I know not what. Below in the room I heard many mingled voices, and a high imperious tone as of one accustomed to authority. I guessed that some body of soldiers was filling the taproom. I was in a fine, contented frame of mind, well pleased with the present, and looking cheerfully forward to the morrow. By-and-by I began to wish for Nicol's presence and to wonder at his long absence.

I was just approaching a state of irritation with my servant when the door was softly opened and the defaulter appeared. His face struck me with surprise, for, whereas for usual it was merry and careless, it was now filled with grave concernment. He closed the latch quietly behind him, and then slipped the bolt, locked the door, and pocketed the key.

I stared in silent amazement.

"If it comes to the warst," he said, "we can fecht for 't."

"What fooling is this?" said I. "Tell me at once, and have done with it."

"It's nae fooling, Laird, as ye'll be finding oot. Sit still, for I've a long story to tell ye." And, having first listened for a noise from below, he began his news, while I listened in much trepidation.

"I paid the men as ye tellt me, and syne I gaed doun to my cousin's shop i' the Rope Walk, just to speir if they were a' weel; and then I cam back to the inn, thinking to get a bit quiet gless a' by mysel' i' the chimley corner. But when I gaed into the room I fand it filled wi' muckle sodger folk, drinking and sweering like deevils. And the first man I clappit eyes on was yin Jock Cadder, whae was yince a freend o' mine, so sitting doun aside Jock, I fell into crack.

"Weel, I hadna been there mony meenutes when I hears a loud voice frae the ither end calling for a song. And anither voice answered, no sae loud, but weak and thin. I jumpit up in my seat, for the voices were weel kenned to me. And there I saw at the ither end o' the table your wanchancy cousin the Captain, sittin' glowrin' wi' his muckle een and playing wi' his gless. And aside him was nae ither than Maister Michael Veitch, him o' Dawyck, but no like what he used to be, but a' red aboot the een, and fosy aboot the face, like a man that's ower fond o' the bottle."

My heart leaped with a sudden terror at the news. What on earth was Marjory's brother doing on the Pier o' Leith in the company of my most bitter foe? A great sense of coming ill hung over me as Nicol went on.

"Weel, I was astonished; and speaking quiet in Jock Cadder's ear, I asks him what it meant, and what the twae were daein' here. And this is what I heard from him, for Jock never jaloused I had aught to dae wi' ye, but thocht I was aye the same auld hide-i'-the-heather I had been afore. 'When our Captain cam back

130

frae furrin pairts,' says he, 'he gangs off to Tweeddale, your ain countryside, for it seems there's a lassie there he's awfu' fond o'. She's the dochter o' auld Veitch o' Dawyck, rich, and, by a' accoont, terrible bonny. But she's trysted to the Captain's cousin, Burnet o' Barns, whae has been in Holland for mair nor a year. It's weel kenned that Gilbert Burnet, when he gets a ploy intil his heid, never stops till he wins his purpose; so he sets himsel' to mak love to the lass. And he couldna dae this unless he were weel in favour wi' her brother Michael, so he begins by winnin' him ower to his side. Noo Michael Veitch (that's him up there) was aye uncommon fond o' wine and yill o' a' description, so the Captain leads him on and on by drinkin' wi' him at a' times, till noo the man is fair helpless. But this wasna a', for if John Burnet cam hame and fund this gaun on, he would mak a rare camsteery, and, by a' accoont, he's a stieve dour chiel. So Gilbert, whae's high in favour wi' the Privy Council, gangs and tells them o' some daeings o' his cousin's abroad, o' some hobnobbing and plotting wi' rebels and outlawed folk, and sending treasonable letters to this land under his name; so he gets a warrant for the lad's arrest as sune as he sets foot on Scots earth—and a'body kens what that means, that he'll no be troubled muckle mair wi' his cousin in this warld. That's the reason we're doun here the day. We've had word that he's coming ower i' the *Seamaw*, whilk lies at the wast harbour. We've been sending doun word thae last 'oors, but she's no in there yet, and 'ill be noo till the morn.'

"That was what Jock Cadder tellt me, and I warrant I was in a fine fricht. It was clear the Captain had nae mind o' me, for he lookit twae or three times my way, and never changed his face. I slips oot the door wi'oot being noticed, and cam up here wi' a' speed to tell ye the tale. So, Laird, ye're in a close hole, and there's just some auld wooden planking atween you and the Tolbooth."

I cared little for the Tolbooth or anything else. One thing, and one alone, claimed all my attention. My whole soul was filled with a terror of anxiety, of mad jealousy, and desperate fear for my lady's sake. This was the cause of the letter, this the cause of her silence. I ground my teeth in helpless fury, and could have found it in my heart to rush down to Gilbert, and choke the life in his throat. I was so appalled by the monstrousness of the thing that I could scarce think. My own danger was nothing, but that Marjory should be the sport of ruffians—the thing overpowered me. It was too fearsome, too monstrous.

One thing was clear—that I must go to her at once. If Gilbert Burnet was on the Pier o' Leith, Marjory Veitch at Dawyck would be quit of his company. Were I once there I could see her, and, perchance, save her. I cannot write down my full trepidation. My fingers clutched at my coat, and I could scarce keep my teeth from chattering. It was no fright that did it, but an awful sickening anxiety preying on my vitals. But with an effort I choked down my unrest, and centred all my thoughts on the present. Were I only in Tweeddale I might yet find a way out of the trouble. But woe's me for the change in my prospects! I had come home thinking, in the pride of my heart, to be welcomed by all and to cut a great figure in my own countryside; and lo, I found myself an outlawed man, whose love was in peril, and whose own craig was none so sure. The sudden reversion all but turned my wits.

I walked to the window and looked down. The night was now dark, but below a glimmer from the taproom window lit the ground. It was a court paved with cobblestones from the beach, where stood one or two wagons, and at one end of which were the doors of a stable. Beyond that a sloping roof led to a high wall, at the back of which I guessed was a little wynd. Once I were there I might find my way through the back parts of Leith to the country, and borrow a horse and ride to Tweeddale. But all was hazardous and uncertain, and it seemed as if my chance of safety was small indeed. I could but try, and if I must perish, why then so it was fated to be.

"Nicol," said I, "bide here the night to keep off suspicion, and come on as soon as you can, for the days have come when I shall have much need of you."

"There's but ae thing to be dune, to tak to the hills, and if ye gang onywhere from the Cheviots to the Kells, Nicol Plenderleith 'ill be wi' ye, and ye need hae nae fear. I ken the hills as weel as auld Sawtan their maister. I'll e'en bide here, and if ever ye win to Dawyck, I'll no be lang ahint ye. Oh, if I could only gang wi' ye! But, by God, if ye suffer aught, there'll be some o' his Majesty's dragoons that'll dree their weird." My servant spoke fiercely, and I was much affected at the tenderness for me which it betokened.

"If I never see you again, Nicol, you'll watch over Marjory? Swear, man, swear by all that's sacred that you'll do my bidding."

"I swear by the Lord God Almighty that if ye come to ony scaith, I'll send the man that did it to Muckle Hell, and I'll see that nae ill comes ower Mistress Marjory. Keep an easy mind, Laird; I'll be as guid as my word."

Without more ado I opened the window and looked out. My servant's talk of taking to the hills seemed an over-soon recourse to desperate remedies. Could I but remove my sweetheart from the clutches of my rival, I trusted to prove my innocence and clear myself in the sight of all. So my thoughts were less despairing than Nicol's, and I embarked on my enterprise with good heart. I saw the ground like a pit of darkness lie stark beneath me. Very carefully I dropped, and, falling on my feet on the cobblestones, made such a clangour beneath the very taproom window that I thought the soldiers would have been out to grip me. As it was, I heard men rise and come to the window; and, crouching far into the lee of the sill, I heard them talk with one another. "Tut, tut, Jock," I heard one say, "it is nothing but a drunken cadger come to seek his horse. Let be and sit down again." When all was quiet I stole softly over to the other side, that I might scale the wall and reach the wynd, for I dared not pass through the open close into the Harbour Walk lest I should be spied and questioned by the soldiers who were ever lounging about.

But some fortunate impulse led me to open the stable door. A feebly-burning lantern hung on a peg, and there came from the stalls the noise of horses champing corn. They were the raw-boned hacks of the soldiers, sorry beasts, for the increase of the military in the land had led to a dearth of horses. But there was one noble animal at the right, slim of leg and deep of chest, with a head as shapely as a maiden's. I rushed hotly forward, for at the first glance I had known it for my own mare Maisie, the best in all Tweeddale. A fine anger took me again to think that my cousin had taken my steed for his own mount. I had sent it back to Barns, and, forsooth, he must have taken it thence in spite of the vigilant Tam Todd. But I was also glad, for I knew that once I had Maisie forth of the yard, and were on her back, and she on the highway, no animal ever foaled could come up with her. So I gave up all my designs on the wall, and fell to thinking how best I could get into the Harbour Walk.

There was but one way, and it was only a chance. But for me it was neck or nothing, my love or a tow in the Grassmarket; so I tossed my plumed hat, my sword, and my embroidered coat on a heap of hay, tore open my shirt at the neck, put a piece of straw between my lips, and soon was a very tolerable presentment of an ostler or farrier of some kind. So taking Maisie's bridle—and at my touch she thrilled so that I saw she had not forgotten me—I led her boldly across the court, straddling in my walk to counterfeit some fellow whose work was with horses. My heart beat wildly as I passed below the archway and confronted the knots of soldiers, who, sitting on a low bench or leaning against the wall, were engaged in loud talk and wrangling.

"Ho, you fellow, where are you going with the Captain's horse?" cried one. I knew by his tone that the man was a Southron, so I had little fear of detection.

"I'm gaun to tak it to the smiddy," said I in my broadest speech. "The Captain sent doun word to my maister, Robin Ratte, in the Flesh Wynd, that the beast was to be ta'en doun and shod new, for she was gaun far the neist day. So I cam up to bring it."

The man looked satisfied, but a question suggested itself to him.

"How knew you the one, if you were never here before?"

"It was the best beast i' the place," I said simply; and this so put his mind to rest that with a gratuitous curse, he turned round, and I was suffered to go on unmolested.

Down the Harbour Walk I led her, for I dared not mount lest some stray trooper recognized the mare and sought to interrogate me. Very quietly and circumspectly I went, imitating a stableman by my walk and carriage as I best knew how, till in ten minutes I came to the end, and, turning up the Fisherrow, came into Leith Walk and the borders of Edinburgh.

CHAPTER II

HOW I RODE TO THE SOUTH

The night was full of wind, light spring airs, which rustled and whistled down every street and brought a promise of the hills and the green country. The stars winked and sparkled above me, but I had no mind to them or aught else save a grey house in a wood, and a girl sitting there with a heavy heart. 'Faith, my own was heavy enough as I led Maisie through the West Vennel, shunning all but the darkest streets, for I knew not when I might be challenged and recognized, losing my way often, but nearing always to the outskirts of the town. Children brawled on the pavement, lights twinkled from window and doorway, the smell of supper came out of chink and cranny. But such things were not for me, and soon I was past all, and near the hamlet of Liberton and the highway to Tweeddale.

Now there was safety for me to mount, and it was blessed to feel the life between my knees and the touch of my mare's neck. By good luck I had found her saddled and bridled, as if some careless, rascally groom had left her untouched since her arrival. But I would have cared little had there been no equipment save a bridle-rope. I could guide a horse on the darkest night by the sway of my body, and it was not for nothing that I had scrambled bareback about the hills of Barns. Maisie took the road with long, supple strides, as light and graceful as a bird. The big mass of Pentland loomed black before me; then in a little it fell over to the right as we advanced on our way. The little wayside cottages went past like so many beehives; through hamlet and village we clattered, waking the echoes of the place, but tarrying not a moment, for the mare was mettlesome, and the rider had the best cause in the world for his speed.

Now this errand, which seems so light, was in truth the hardest and most perilous that could be found. For you are to remember that I was a man proscribed and all but outlawed, that any chance wayfarer might arrest me; and since in those troubled times any rider was suspected, what was a man to say if he saw one dressed in gentleman's apparel, riding a blood-horse, coatless and hatless? More, all the way to Peebles lay through dangerous land, for it was the road to the south-west and the Whigs of Galloway, and, since the Pentland Rising, that part had been none of the quietest. Also, it was my own country, where I was a well-kenned man, known to near every one, so what might have been my safety in other times was my danger in these. This, too, was the road which my cousin Gilbert had travelled from Barns, and well watched it was like to be if Gilbert had aught to do with the matter. But the motion of my mare was so free, the air so fine, the night so fair, and my own heart so passionate, that I declare I had forgotten all about danger, and would have ridden down the High Street of Edinburgh, if need had been, in my great absence of mind.

I was recalled to my senses by a sudden warning. A man on horseback sprang out from the shelter of a plantation, and gripped my bridle. I saw by the starlight the gleam of a pistol barrel in his hand.

"Stop, man, stop! there's nae sic great hurry. You and me 'ill hae some words. What hae ye in your pouches?"

Now I was unarmed, and the footpad before me was a man of considerable stature and girth. I had some remnants of sense left in me, and I foresaw that if I closed with him, besides the possibility of getting a bullet in my heart, the contest would take much time, and would have an uncertain ending. I was fairly at my wits' end what with hurry and vexation, when the thought struck me that the law and military which I dreaded were also the terror of such men as this. I made up my mind to throw myself on his mercy. Forbye, being a south-country man, the odds were great that my name would be known to him.

"I have no money," I said, "for I came off this night hot-speed, with a regiment of dragoons waiting behind me. I am the Laird of Barns, in Tweeddale, and this day an outlaw and a masterless man. So I pray you not to detain me, for there's nothing on me worth the picking. I have not a groat of silver, and, as you see, I ride in my shirt."

"Are ye the Laird o' Barns?" said the man, staring. "Man, I never kent it or I wadna ha' been sae unceevil as to stop ye. Be sure that I'm wi' ye, and sae are a' guid fellows that likena thae langnebbit dragoons and thae meddlesome brocks o' lawyers in Embro. Gang your ways for me. But stop, ye've nae airms. This 'ill never dae. Tak yin o' my pistols, for I'll never miss it. And see, gin ye tak my advice and gin ye're gaun to Barns, gang off the Peebles road at Leadburn, and haud doun by the Brochtoun and Newlands ways, for a' the way atween Leadburn and Peebles is hotchin' wi' sodgers and what-ye-may-ca'-thems. Guid e'en to ye, and a safe journey." The man rode off and almost instantly was lost to my sight; but his act gave me assurance that there was still some good left in the world, though in the most unlikely places.

And now I saw before me the black woods of Rosslyn and Hawthornden, and in the near distance the roofs of the clachan of Penicuik. There I knew danger would await me, so taking a random turning to the right, I struck towards the hills in the direction of Carlops. The place was rough and moory, and full of runlets of water, but Maisie was well used to such land, for it was no worse than the haughs of Manor, and level turf compared with the brow of the Deid Wife or the shoulder of Scrape. So in a little, when the lights of Penicuik were well on the left, I came to the Hawes Burn, which passes the inn of Leadburn, and tracking it downward, came to the bald white house which does duty for a hostel.

I dared not enter, though I was woefully thirsty, but kept straight on to the crossroads where the two paths to Tweeddale part asunder. One—the way by which I had gone when I set out on my travels—goes over the moor by the springs of the Eddleston Water, through the village of that name, and thence down the vale to Peebles. The other, longer and more circuitous, cuts straight over the rough moorlands to the little village of Newlands, then over much wild country to Kirkurd, and the high hills which hem in the hamlet of Broughton, whence it is but five miles to the house of Dawyck. It is a road which I have always hated as being dismal and wild beyond any of my knowledge, but now I was glad to be on it, for every step brought me nearer to my love.

The country, in the main, is desolate heather and bog, with here and there a white cot-house where dwells a shepherd. Of late I hear that many trees have been planted and the bogs are being drained, but at the time I speak of all was still in its virginal wilderness. The road, by a good chance, is dry and easy to find, else there had been difficulties awaiting me. The night was clear and sharp, and a bright moon made the path as plain as daylight. I found time to curse that moon whenever I neared human dwellings, and to bless it heartily when I was in the desert morasses again.

In a little I saw a hilltop which, by its broad, flat shape I knew for the Black Mount, which lies above the village of Dolphinton on the way to the west country. This is a landmark of great note in the countryside, and now I could guess my whereabouts. I made out that I must be scarce two miles from the jumble of houses lining the highway which is named Kirkurd, at which spot the road fords the deep, sullen stream of Tarth. Now this same Tarth a little way down flows into the Lyne, which enters Tweed almost opposite the house of Barns. At other times I had ridden the path down its side, for it is many miles the shorter way. But I knew well that Barns would be watched like the courtyard of the Parliament House, and I durst not for my life venture near it. I deemed it unprofitable to run the risk of capture for the sake of an hour or two saved. So after passing Kirkurd, I held straight on over the black moors which lie towards the watershed of the Broughton burn.

By good luck I had dismounted just after the bridge and buckled Maisie's girth tight and eased the saddle, for I suspected that now I was entering the more dangerous country. The issue showed that I had guessed rightly, for just at the sharp turn of the road over the Hell's Cleuch burn, I came near to my end. I was riding carelessly at a rapid pace through the thick wood which cloaks the turn, when suddenly, ere ever I knew, I was into the middle of a detachment of horse riding leisurely in the same direction.

I do not well know how I acted, save that my pistol went off in the mellay, and I saw a man clap his hand to his shoulder in a vast hurry and swear freely. Half a dozen hands were stretched to my bridle, half a dozen pistols covered me at once. Now I had no leave to use my hands, my pistol I had fired, so I was wholly at their mercy. What happened I can only guess, for I was in too great a flurry to have any clear remembrance of the thing. I was conscious of striking one man fiercely on the cheek with my empty pistol, and of kicking another on the shins with all my might. But my sudden appearance had startled the horses so thoroughly that all the soldiers' time was taken up in curbing them, so they had no leisure to take aim at me. A dozen shots cracked around me, all going high into the air, and in a second I was through them and on the high road beyond, some twenty paces in advance.

But by this time they were getting their horses under, and I felt that there was no time to be lost if I wished to see many more days on the earth. I patted Maisie's neck, which to a beast of her spirit was the best encouragement, and set myself to a race for life. I kicked off my great boots to ease her, and then, leaning forward, began the trial of speed. Behind me I heard shouting and the beat of horses getting into their stride. Before me was the long, thin highway, and black hills, and endless peat mosses. I had half a mind to leave the road and ride for the hills, where I made sure no man of them could ever follow me. But I reflected that this would shut for me the way to Dawyck, and I should have to lie hid in these regions for weeks, for when my path was once seen they would guard it more closely. My only chance was to outstrip them and so keep the country open before me.

So began the most terrible and desperate race that I was ever engaged in. I had tried my cousin Gilbert and beaten him on the side of Scrape; now his men were taking revenge for that episode in good earnest. At this time I was no more than out of pistol shot, and though I kept this interval, and all their balls fell short, it was an unpleasing thing to be riding with shots behind you, any one of which, for all you knew, might lodge in your spine. So I strained every nerve to increase the distance.

Maisie responded gallantly to my call. I felt her long, supple swing below me and the gathering of her limbs. I began to glory in the exhilaration of the thing, and my spirits rose at a bound. The keen, cool air blew about my face, the moonlight danced on the mare's neck, and the way in front was a long strip of light. Sometimes I could not tell whether or not I was dreaming. Sometimes I thought I was back in Holland asleep in the garden, and that all this shifting pageant of light and scenery, these cries and shots behind, and this long, measured fall of hooves were but the process of a dream. I experienced the most acute enjoyment, for all heavy cares for the future were driven away by the excitement of the chase. It was glorious, I thought, and I cared not a straw for the loss of place and fortune if the free life of the open air and the hills was to be mine. It was war to the hilt between my cousin and myself; both had flung away the scabbards; but I would master him yet and show him which was the better man.

But this braggadocio exhilaration soon passed, and in its place came some measure of forethought. I reflected that though I might distance my pursuers and win to Dawyck, I would surely be tracked and so bring misfortune on my mistress and myself. I had as yet no clear plans for the future. I had already all but burned my boats, for this night's work was like to get me into trouble on its own account. The wild notion of fleeing to the hills and trusting to God for the rest commended itself to me more and more. But one thing I must do—abide at Dawyck till such time as Nicol should be able to join me. I had the most perfect trust in him; I had proved him a hundred times, and I knew well that if mortal man could do aught to mend my fortunes, he could do it. So with this thought I matured a plan for the present. I must put forth all my speed and win clean away from my pursuers. Now at Broughton there was an inn, where abode an honest man, one Joshua Watson who had oft had dealings with me in the past. He was an old retainer of my house, and I knew that he would see his roof and gear in a blaze before his eyes ere he would see any harm come to a laird of Barns. To him I purposed to go and hide till the dragoons had passed. They had not recognized me, I knew, for they were not men of our countryside; and if left to themselves, would keep the highway to Moffat, and have never a thought of turning aside into Tweeddale.

I whispered something to Maisie, and the good mare set herself to the task. She was still unjaded, for I had used her to long wanderings, and she had not forgotten the lesson. I listened to her steady, rhythmical breath and the measured beat of her hooves, and I thanked Heaven that I had chanced on her. At first the pursuers were maybe an eighth of a mile behind. Soon the distance increased, little by little at first, then by more and more as my mare got into her long gallop and their coarse beasts began to tire. We passed the lonely cot of Lochurd, nestling under great green hills where the sheep bleat and the plovers cry alway. Then on by the lonely bog where men came once to dig marl and left a monstrous wide pit, filled with black water and with no bottom. I paused for a second to let Maisie drink from a burn which comes down from the Mount Hill. Soon we were at the turning where the road to Biggar and the west goes off from the highway. Here I stopped to listen for a moment. Far off and faint I heard the noise of my pursuers, and judged they were near a mile distant. Then off again; and now the road inclines downward, and as one rises over the crest of brae, which the shepherds call the Ruchill End, there bursts on the sight all the vast circle of hills, crowded and piled together, which marks the course of Tweed. Down the little glen of Broughton I rode, while the burn made music by the highway, and it was hard to think that death awaited a little behind. Soon the moors sank into fields, trees and cottages appeared, a great stone mill rose by the water, and I clattered into the village of Broughton.

The place was asleep, and, as I drew up at the inn, but one light was apparent. I hammered rudely at the door till the landlord came, sleepy and yawning, and bearing a candle in his hand. At the sight of me he started, for my danger was known all over Tweeddale. In a few words I told him of my pursuit and my request. He was a man of sparing speech, and, saying nothing, he led me to the barn and showed me a hole in a great bank of straw. Maisie he took to the stable. "Hae nae fear," he said. "Trust me, I'll settle the hash o' thae gentry."

Sure enough, I had not been three minutes in the place when I heard voices and the sound of horses, and creeping to the narrow, unglazed window, saw the dragoons draw up at the inn door. Much shouting brought down the landlord, who made a great show of weariness, and looked like one just aroused from sleep.

"Heard you or saw you any man pass on horseback about five minutes syne?" they asked.

"I dare say I did," said he. "At ony rate, I heard the sound o' a horse, and it's verra likely it was on the Moffat road. There's a hantle o' folk pass by here at a' 'oors."

"Ye're sure he didna come in here?" they said again. "We'll search the house to see."

"Weel," said the landlord, "ye can dae as ye like, but it seems a gey fule's errand. I tell ye it's lang past midnight, and we've a' been asleep here, and naebody could hae gotten in unless I had opened the door, for I hae a' the keys. But come and look, gentlemen, and I'll fetch ye some yill."

They drank the ale, and then seemed to think better of their purpose, for they remounted. "He'll be aff to the hills at the heid o' Tweed," they said. "He would never, gin he had ony sense, gang doun Tweeddale, where there's nae hiding for man or beast." So with many wanton oaths they set off again at a lazy gallop.

CHAPTER III

THE HOUSE OF DAWYCK

I knew well that I had little time to lose, and that what must be done must be done quickly. So, as soon as the tails of them were round the hillside, I came out from my hiding-place and mounted Maisie once more. I thanked the landlord, and with a cry that I would remember him if I ever got my affairs righted again, I turned sharply through the burn and down the path to Peebles. It was touch or miss with me, for it was unlikely that the highway between the west country and the vale of Peebles would be freed from the military.

Yet freed it was. It may have been that the folk of Tweedside were little caring about any religion, and most unlike the dour carles of the Westlands, or it may have been that the soldiers were not yet stirring. At any rate I passed unmolested. I struck straight for the ridge of Dreva, and rounding it, faced the long valley of Tweed, with Rachan woods and Drummelzier haughs and the level land of Stobo. Far down lay the forest of Dawyck black as ink on the steep hillside. Down by the Tweed I rode, picking my way very carefully among the marshes, and guarding the deep black moss holes which yawned in the meadows. Here daybreak came upon us, the first early gleam of light tingling in the east, and changing the lucent darkness of the moonlit night to a shadowy grey sunrise. Scrape raised his bald forehead above me, and down the glen I had a glimpse of the jagged peaks of the Shieldgreen Kips, showing sharp against the red dawn. In a little I was at the avenue of Dawyck and rode up the green sward, with the birds twittering in the coppice, eager to see my love.

The house was dead as a stone wall, and no signs of life came from within. But above me a lattice was opened to catch the morning air. I leapt to the ground and led Maisie round to the stables which I knew so well. The place was deserted; no serving-man was about; the stalls looked as if they had been empty for ages. A great fear took my heart. Marjory might be gone, taken I knew not whither. I fled to the door as though the fiend were behind me, and knocked clamorously for admittance. Far off in the house, as it were miles away, I heard footsteps and the opening of doors. They came nearer, and the great house door was opened cautiously as far as possible without undoing the chain; and from within a thin piping inquired my name and purpose.

I knew the voice for the oldest serving-man who dwelt in the house.

"Open, you fool, open," I cried. "Do you not know me? The Laird of Barns!"

The chain was unlocked by a tremulous hand.

"Maister John, Maister John," cried the old man, all but weeping. "Is't yoursel' at last? We've had sair, sair need o' ye. Eh, but she'll be blithe to see ye."

"Is your mistress well?" I cried with a great anxiety.

"Weel eneuch, the puir lass, but sair troubled in mind. But that'll a' be bye and dune wi', noo that ye're come back."

"Where is she? Quick, tell me," I asked in my impatience.

"In the oak room i' the lang passage," he said, as quick as he could muster breath.

I knew the place, and without more words I set off across the hall, running and labouring hard to keep my heart from bursting. Now at last I should see the dear lass whom I had left. There was the door, a little ajar, and the light of a sunbeam slanting athwart it.

I knocked feebly, for my excitement was great.

"Come," said that voice which I loved best in all the world.

I entered, and there, at the far end of the room, in the old chair in which her father had always sat, wearing the dark dress of velvet which became her best, and with a great book in her lap, was Marjory.

She sprang up at my entrance, and with a low cry of joy ran to meet me. I took a step and had her in my arms. My heart was beating in a mighty tumult of joy, and when once my love's head lay on my shoulder, I cared not a fig for all the ills in the world.

I cannot tell of that meeting; even now my heart grows warm at the thought; but if such moments be given to many men, there is little to complain of in life.

"O John," she cried, "I knew you would come. I guessed that every footstep was yours, coming to help us. For oh! there have been such terrible times since you went away. How terrible I cannot tell you," and her eyes filled with tears as she looked in mine.

So we sat down by the low window, holding each other's hands, thinking scarce anything save the joy of the other's presence. The primroses were starring the grass without, and the blossom coming thick and fast on the cherry trees. So glad a world it was that it seemed as if all were vanity save a dwelling like the Lotophagi in a paradise of idleness.

But I quickly roused myself. It was no time for making love when the enemy were even now at the gates.

"Marjory, lass," I said, "tell me all that has been done since I went away."

And she told me, and a pitiful tale it was—that which I had heard from Nicol, but more tragic and sad. I heard of her brother's ruin: how the brave, generous gentleman, with a head no better than a weathercock, had gone down the stages to besotted infamy. I heard of Gilbert's masterful knavery, of his wooing at Dawyck, and how he had despoiled the house of Barns. It seemed that he had spent days at Dawyck in the company of Michael Veitch, putting my poor Marjory to such a persecution that I could scarce bide still at the hearing of it. He would importune her night and day, now by gallantry and now by threats. Then he would seek to win her favour by acts of daring, such as he well knew how to do. But mostly he trusted to the influence of her brother, who was his aider and abetter in all things. I marvelled how a gentleman of family could ever sink so low as to be the servant of such cowardice. But so it was, and my heart was sore for all the toils which the poor girl had endured in that great, desolate house, with no certain hope for the future. She durst not write a letter, for she was spied on closely by her tormentors, and if she had bade me return, they well knew I

145

would come with the greatest speed, and so in knowing the time of my arrival, would lay hands on me without trouble. The letter which reached me was sealed under her brother's eyes and the postscript was added with the greatest pains and sent by Tam Todd, who sat at Barns in wrath and impotence. Truly things had gone wrong with a hearty goodwill since I had ridden away.

But the matter did not seem much better now that I had returned. I was an outlawed man, with no dwelling and scarce any friends, since the men of my own house were either hostile or powerless to aid. My estates were a prey to my enemies. I had naught to trust to save my own good fortune and a tolerably ready sword, and, to crown all, my love was in the direst danger. If she abode at Dawyck the bitter persecution must be renewed, and that the poor maid should suffer this was more than I could endure. I had no fear of her faithfulness, for I knew of old the steadfast heart and brave spirit, but I feared my cousin as I feared no other on earth. He cared not a fig for the scruples of ordinary men, and he was possessed of a most devilish cunning, before which I felt powerless as a babe. Yet I doubtless wronged him by suspicion, for, after all, he was a Burnet, and fought as a man of honour should. But he had a gang of marauding ruffians at his heels, and God alone knew what might happen.

At all events, I must wait till what time my servant Nicol should arrive from Leith. I had no fear of his failing, for he had the readiest wit that ever man had, and I verily believe the longest legs. He should be at Dawyck ere noonday, when he should advise me as to my course. Nor was there any immediate danger pressing, for so long as Gilbert abode at Leith he could not come to Dawyck, and unless our schemes grievously miscarried, he could not yet have been apprised of my escape. Moreover, the soldiers to whom I had given the slip the night before, could as yet have no inkling either of my identity or my present harbour. So for the meantime I was safe to meditate on the future.

Marjory, woman-like, was assured that now I had come back her sorrows were at an end. She would hear nothing of danger to be. "Now that you are here, John," she would say, "I am afraid of nothing. I do not care if Gilbert return and plague me a

146

thousandfold more; I shall well support it if I know that you are in the land. It is for you I fear, for what must you do save go to the hills and hide like the hillmen in caves and peat-bogs. It is surely a sad use for your learning, sir."

So the morning passed so quickly that I scarce knew it. We went together to a little turret-room facing the north and fronting the broad avenue which all must pass who come to the house; and here we waited for the coming of Nicol. I felt a fierce regret as I looked away over the woods and meadows to the little ridge of hills beyond which lay Barns, and saw the fair landscape all bathed in spring sunshine. It was so still and peaceful that I felt a great desire to dwell there with Marjory in quiet, and have done for ever with brawling and warfare. I had come home from the Low Countries with a longing for the plain country life of Tweeddale, such as I had been bred to. I was prepared in heart to get ready my fishing-rods and see to my guns, and begin again my long-loved sports. But harsh fate had decreed otherwise, and I was to fare forth like a partridge on the mountains, and taste the joys of the chase in a new manner. But at the thought my spirits rose again. I would love dearly to play a game of hide-and-go-seek with my cousin Gilbert, and so long as I had my sword and my wits about me, I did not fear. My one care was Marjory, and this, in truth, was a sore one. I cursed my cousin right heartily, and all his belongings, and vowed, deep down in my heart, to recompense him some day.

It is true that all this while it lay open to me to brazen it out before his Majesty's Council, and try to clear my name from guilt. But as the hours passed this method grew more distasteful to me. There I should be in a strange place among enemies and scenes of which I knew nothing. Innocent though I might be, it was more than likely that I should find myself worsted. More, it seemed the gallanter thing to contest the matter alone among the hills, a fight between soldiers, with no solemn knaves to interfere. So by this time I had all but resolved on the course which my servant had first advised.

About twelve of the clock we saw a long figure slinking up the avenue, keeping well in the shade of the trees, and looking warily

147

on all sides. I knew my man, and going down to the door, I set it open, and waited for his coming. When he saw me he changed his walk for a trot, and came up breathing hard, like a hound which has had a long run. I led him into the dining-hall and Marjory prepared for him food and drink. Never a word spoke he till he had satisfied his hunger. Then he pushed back his chair, and looking sadly at my lady, shook his head as though in dire confusion.

"A bonny bigging, Maister John," he said "but ye'll sune hae to leave it."

"That's a matter on which I have waited for your coming," said I, "but I would hear how you fared since I left you."

"I've nae guid news," he said sadly, "but such as they are ye maun e'en hear them."

And this was the tale he told.

CHAPTER IV

HOW MICHAEL VEITCH MET HIS END

"When you left," began Nicol, "I just waited till I heard your footsteps gang oot o' the yaird. Syne I gaed dounstairs to the landlord, whae is a decent, comfortable kind o' man wi' no muckle ill aboot him. I telled him that my maister was terrible unweel, and on no accoont maun be disturbit, but that he maun hae the room to himsel' for the nicht. The man was verra vexed to hear aboot ye. 'Sae young a chiel,' says he, 'it's awfu'.' So I got my will, and I kenned I wad be troubled by nae folk comin' and speirin' aboot the place. There was nae reason why I shouldna gang awa' and leave the lawin', but I had a kind o' irkin' to get anither glisk o' the sodgers, so I e'en gaed into the room aside them.

"They were noo mair uproarious than afore. Nane were drunk, for 'faith, the Captain wasna the man to let his men dae that, but a' were geyan wild and carin' little aboot their language. The Captain sits at the heid o' the table sippin' his toddy wi' that

148

dour stieve face o' his that naething could move, and that ye think
wad be ashamed to sae muckle as lauch. But Maister Veitch
wasna like him. He was singin' and roarin' wi' the loudest, and
takin' great wauchts frae the bowl, far mair than was guid for
him.

"By-and-by he gets up on his feet.

" 'A health to the Captain,' he says. 'Drink, lads, to the welfare
o' that most valiant soldier and gentleman, Captain Gilbert
Burnet. Ye a' ken the errand ye're come on, to lay hands on a
rebel an' take him to his proper place, and I drink to your guid
success in the matter.' And he lifts up his glass and spills some o'
it ower the table.

"At this there was a great uproar, and they a' rose wi' their
glasses and cried on the Captain. He sat a' the while wi' a sort o'
scornfu' smile on his face, as if he were half pleased, but thocht
little o' the folk that pleased him.

" 'I thank you,' he says at last. 'I thank you all, my men, for
your goodwill. We have done well together in the past, and we'll
do better in time to come. I will prove to the rebel folk o' this land
that Gilbert Burnet will make them obey.'

" 'Faith, Gilbert,' says Maister Veitch, 'hae ye no the grace to
speak o' your verra guid friend? I think ye're beholden to me for
a hantle o' your success.'

"The Captain looks at him wi' a glint o' guid humour. 'No
more, Michael,' says he, 'than the cook owes to the scullion. You
do my dirty work.'

" 'Dirty work, quotha,' cried Maister Veitch, who was hot and
flustered with wine. 'I wouldna tak that from any other than
yoursel', Gilbert, and maybe no from you.'

" 'Take it or not, just as you please,' said the Captain
scornfully. 'It's no concern o' mine.'

"This angered the other, and he spoke up fiercely:

" 'I am of as guid blood as yoursel', Gilbert Burnet. Is a
Tweeddale gentleman no as guid as a bit westland lairdie?'

" 'Faith, that is too much,' says the Captain. 'Michael, I'll
make you answer for this yet.' So he sat with lowered brows,
while Maister Veitch, to a' appearance, had forgotten the words

he had spoken.

"In a little the Captain dismisses the men to their sleeping quarters, and the pair were left alone, save for mysel', whae being in the dark shadows near the door escaped the sicht o' a'. The two gentlemen sat at the board eyeing each other with little love. By-and-by Gilbert speaks:

" 'Ye called me a bit westland lairdie no long syne, Maister Veitch, if ye'll be remembering.'

"The ither looks up. 'And what if I did?' says he. 'Is't no the fact?'

" 'That it's no the fact I have a damned good mind to let you see,' says the ither.

"Michael looks at him askance. 'This is a gey queer way to treat your friends. I've done a' in my power to aid you in a' your pliskies. I've turned clean against the Laird o' Barns, who never did me ony ill, a' for the sake o' you. And forbye that, I've done what I could to further your cause wi' my sister, who is none so well inclined to you. And this is a' the thanks I get for it, Gilbert?'

"I saw by the dour face o' the Captain that he was mortal thrawn.

" 'And a' the thanks ye are likely to get,' says he. 'Is't no enough that a man o' my birth and fame should be willing to mate wi' one o' your paltry house, a set o' thieves and reivers wi' no claim to honour save the exaltation o' the gallows rope? Gad, I think it's a mighty favour that I should be so keen to take the lass from among you.'

" 'By Heaven, that is too much to swallow!' said Maister Michael, as some sparks o' proper feeling rose in him at last; and he struggled to his feet.

"The Captain also rose and looked at him scornfu'-like.

" 'What would you do?' said he.

" 'This,' said the other, clean carried wi' anger; and he struck him a ringing lick on the face.

"Gilbert went back a step, and (for his honour I say it) kept his wrath doun.

" 'That's a pity,' says he; 'that was a bad action o' yours, Michael, as ye'll soon ken. I'll trouble ye to draw.'

150

"I hae felt vexed for mony folk in my life, but never for yin sae muckle as puir Maister Veitch. He reddened and stumbled and plucked his sword from its sheath. He was dazed wi' wine and drowsiness, but his enemy made nocht o' that.

"They crossed swirds and I watched them fall to. I was terrible feared, for I saw fine that the yin was as angry as a bull, the ither as helpless as a sheep. It was agin a' decency to let sic a thing gang on, so I ran forrit and cried on them to stop. 'D'ye no see the man's fair helpless?' I cried out; but they never seemed to hear me, but went at it as hard as ever.

"At first baith fought nane sae bad, for baith were braw swordsmen, and even in sic a plight Michael's skill didna desert him. Gilbert, too, was quieter than was to be expectit. But of a sudden a wild fury seized him. 'I'll teach ye to speak ill o' me and my house,' he cried in a voice like thunder, and cam on like a storm o' hail.

"Michael fell back and tried to defend himsel'. But the puir lad was sae dazed and foundered that frae the first he had nae chance. His blade wabbled at every guaird, and he never risked a cut. It was just like a laddie gettin' his paiks frae a maister and keepin' off the clouts wi' yae airm.

"And then he let his sword drop, whether wi' weariness or no I canna tell, and stood glowrin' afore him. The Captain never stopped. I dinna think he ettled it, for when he began I think he didna mean mair than to punish him for his words. But now he lunged clean and true. Nae sword kept it aff, nae coat o' mail wardit it, but deep into Michael's breast it sank. Wi' yae groan he fell back, and the breath gaed frae his body.

"I could hardly contain mysel' wi' rage. At first I was for rinnin' forrit and throttlin' the man, but I got a glimpse o' his face, and that keepit me. It was dark as a thunder-clud, and regret and unquenched anger lookit oot o' his een.

" 'This is a black business,' he says to himsel', 'a black, damnable business. God knows I never meant to kill the fool.' And he began to walk up and down wi' his heid on his breast.

"I felt that I had seen eneuch. My hert was sick wi' the peety o' the thing, and forbye it was time for me to be going if I was ever

151

to win to Tweedside. So I slips frae the house, which was still quiet, for naebody kenned o' the deed, and far away somewhere I heard the lilt o' a sodger's song. I sped doun the Harbour Walk and syne into Embro', as though the deil were ahint me. When I won to Auchendinny it was aboot three in the mornin', and I made a' the haste I could. I think I maun hae run a' the road frae there to Leidburn. Then I took ower the Cloch hills and doun by Harehope and the Meldons. I crossed Lyne abune the brig, and came doun Stobo burn, and here I am. I never met a soul for good or ill, so the land's quieter thereaways than folk make it oot. But doun by the Eddleston Water there's a geyan nest o' sodgers, so ye've nae time to lose, Laird, if ye wad win to the hills."

When I turned to Marjory at the close of this tale she was weeping silently; yet there was little bitterness in her tears. Her brother had, after all, made a better end than one could have guessed from his life. Indeed, I had small cause to feel kindness to him, for he had betrayed his trust, and had been the author of all the ills which had come upon my mistress. But for her sake I was sad.

"Marjory," I said, "I have many scores to settle with my cousin, for all his life he has done me ill, and the time will come when I shall pay them. I will add this to the others. Be assured, dear, that your brother shall not be unavenged."

And Marjory dried her tears, and from that hour spake never a word of Michael. But I knew well that deep in her heart remained an abiding sorrow which chastened the gaiety of her spirits.

CHAPTER V

I CLAIM A PROMISE, AND WE SEEK THE HILLS

And now I set myself resolutely to think out something that might be the saving of my life and my love. I was in a perilous case, for when Gilbert found that I had escaped him, he would come on forthwith to Dawyck, and, in all likelihood, be here ere nightfall. One thing was clear—that I could not bide myself nor leave Marjory to his tender mercies. The hills for me; and for her—ah, that was the rub in the matter!

At last I made out some semblance of a plan. On the edge of Douglasdale, in the shire of Lanark, dwelt William Veitch at the house of Smitwood, the uncle of the dead Sir John, an old man well fallen in the vale of years. He was unmolested by all, being a peaceable soldier who had served the king in his day, and now thought of nothing save making a good ending. He would gladly take the lass, I knew, and shelter her till such time as I should come and take her again. Nor would Gilbert follow her thither, for no word should come to his ear of her destined harbour, and he knew naught of the place nor the relationship. The plan came upon me with such convincing force that I took no other thought on the matter. Nicol should be left there both as a guard of the place—and who so vigilant?—and as some means of communication between me and my mistress. For my own part, when once I had seen my lass safely sheltered, I should take to the hills with a light heart.

I told the thing to Nicol and he gladly agreed. Then I sought out Marjory, who had gone to make some preparations for my flight, and found her talking gravely to the old man, the only remaining servant. I drew her to the little oak parlour.

"Marjory, lass," I said, "I am but new come home, and I little thought to have to take flight again so soon. Do you mind ere I went to the Low Countries I came here to bid you farewell, and you sang me a song?"

"I mind it well," said she.

"Have you a remembrance of the air, my dear? How did it go?" and I whistled a stave.

"Ay, even so. You have a good ear, John."

"I think, too, that I know a verse or so," said I. "There was one which ran like this:

> " 'And if he were a soldier gay,
>   And tarried from the town,
> And sought in wars, through death and scars,
>   To win for him renown,

153

I'd place his colours in my breast,
        And ride by moor and lea,
And win his side, there to abide,
        And bear him company.'

Was it not so?"

"Yes," she said, smiling; "how well you remember, John."

"And there was a refrain, too," I went on.

" 'For sooth a maid, all unafraid
        Should by her lover be,
With wile and art to cheer his heart,
        And bear him company.' "

Marjory blushed. "Why do you remind me of my old song?" she said. "It pains me, for I used to sing it ere the trouble came upon us, and when we were all as happy as the day was long."

"Nay," I said, "it is a song for the time of trouble. It was your promise to me, and I have come to claim its fulfilment. I am for the hills, Marjory, and I cannot leave you behind. Will you come and bear me company? I will take you to Smitwood, where even the devil and my cousin Gilbert could not follow you. There you will be safe till I come again when this evil time is past, for pass it must. And I will go to the hills with a blithe heart, if once I knew you were in good keeping."

"O John, to be sure I will follow you," she said, "even to the world's end. I will fare among rough hills and bogs if I may but be near you. But I will go to Smitwood, for most terribly I dread this place."

So it was all brought to a conclusion, and it but remained to make ready with all speed and seek the uplands. We trusted ourselves to Nicol's guidance, for he knew the way as he knew his own name, and had a wide acquaintance with the hillmen and their hiding-places. On him it lay to find shelter for us on the road and guide us by the most unfrequented paths. So we set about the preparing of provisions and setting the house in order. The old man, who was the sole servant remaining, was left in charge of the place against our uncertain return. For myself I should have taken but one horse, Marjory's roan mare, and tramped along on foot; but Nicol bade me take Maisie, for, said he, "I'll tak ye by little-kenned ways, where ye may ride as easy as walk; and forbye, if it cam to the bit, a horse is a usefu' cratur for rinnin' awa on. I could trot fine on my feet mysel', but though ye're a guid man at the sma'-swird, Laird, I doubt ye'd no be muckle at that." The words were wise, so I saddled Maisie and prepared to ride her to Smitwood, and there leave her.

It was, I think, about three hours after midday when we were ready to start on our journey. A strange cavalcade we formed— Marjory on the roan, dressed plainly as for the hills, and with a basket slung across the saddlebow, for all the world like a tinker's pannier; I myself on Maisie, well-mounted and armed, and Nicol on foot, lean and ill-clad as ever. It was not without a pang that we set out, for it is hard to leave the fair and settled dwellings of home for haphazard lodging among rough morasses. Marjory in especial could scarce refrain from tears, while I own that as I looked down the vale and saw the woods of Barns and the green hills of Manor, I could have found it in me to be despondent.

But once we left the valley and began to ascend the slopes, our spirits returned. It was an afternoon among a thousand, one such as only April weather and the Tweed valley can bring. The sky was cloudless and the wind sharp, and every hill and ridge in the great landscape stood out clear as steel. The grass was just greening beneath our feet, the saugh bushes were even now assuming the little white catkins, and the whole air was filled with a whistling and twittering of birds. We took our road straight through the pine wood which clothes the western slopes of Scrape. The ground was velvet-dry, and the deer fled swiftly as we neared their coverts. It was glorious to be abroad and feel the impulse of life stirring everywhere around. Yet I could not keep from the reflection that at this very time the day before I had been nearing the port of Leith in the *Seamaw*, expecting nothing save a pleasant home-coming, and thereafter a life of peace. Truly in one short day and night I had led a somewhat active life, and now was fleeing from the very place I had most longed to return to.

Soon we left the woods and came out on the heathery brow of Scrape, and crossing it, entered the deep glen where the burn of Scrape flows to join the Powsail. The heather had been burned, as is the custom here in the early spring, and great clouds of fine white dust rose beneath the hooves of our horses. A dry crackling of twigs and the strident creak of the larger roots as they grated on one another filled our ears. Then once more we ascended, high and ever higher, over rocks and treacherous green well-eyes and great spaces of red fern, till we gained the brow of the hill which they call Glenstivon Dod, and looked down into the little glen of Powsail.

We crossed the lovely burn of Powsail, which is the most beautiful of all Tweedside burns, since the water is sapphire and emerald and topaz, flashing in every ray like myriad jewels. Here we watered our horses, and once more took the hills. And now we were on the wild ridge of upland which heads the glens of Stanhope and Hopecarton and Polmood, the watershed 'twixt the vales of Tweed and Megget. Thence the sight is scarce to be matched to my knowledge in the south country of Scotland—an endless stretching of hills, shoulder rising o'er shoulder, while ever and again some giant lifts himself clean above his fellows, and all the while in the glen at our feet Tweed winding and murmuring.

I asked Nicol what was the purpose of our journey, for this was by no means the shortest way to Douglasdale and Smitwood. He answered that to go straight to our destination would be to run our heads into the lion's mouth. He purposed that we should go up Tweed to a hiding-place which he knew of on the Cor Water, and then make over by the upper waters of the Clyde and the Abington moors to the house of Smitwood. These were the more deserted and least accessible places, whereas the villages and lowlands around the skirts of the hills were watched like the High Street of Edinburgh.

In a little we passed the wild trough where the Stanhope Burn flows toward Tweed. It was now drawing toward the darkening, and the deep, black glen seemed dark as the nether pit. Had we

156

not had a guide to whom the place was familiar as his own doorstep, we should soon have been floundering over some craig. As it was, our case was not without its danger. It is not a heartening thing to go stumbling on hilltops in the dusk of an April evening, with black, horrific hill slopes sinking on all sides. Marjory grew frightened, as I knew by the tightened clutch at her horse's rein, and her ever seeking to draw nearer me, but like the brave lass that she was, she breathed never a word of it. Every now and then an owl would swoop close to our faces, or a curlew dart out of the night with its shrill scream, and vanish again into the dark. It was an uncanny place at that hour, and one little to be sought by those who love comfort and peace. But the very difficulty of the way gladdened us, for it gave us assurance that we would be unmolested by wayfaring dragoons. By-and-by stars came out and the moon rose, glorious and full as on the night before, when I had ridden from Leith. Then it served to light my course to Dawyck, now to guide me from it.

We were now descending a steep hillside, all rough with sklidders, and coming to the Water of Talla, which we forded at a shallow a little below the wild waterfall called Talla Linns. Even there we could hear the roar of the cataract, and an awesome thing it was in that lonely place. But we tarried not a minute, but urged our horses up a desperate ravine till once more we were on the crest of the hills. And now a different land was around us. Far to the right, where the Talla joins the Tweed, we could mark the few lights of the little village of Tweedsmuir. The higher hills had been left behind, and we were on a wide expanse of little ridges and moor which the people of Tweedside call "The Muirs," and which extends from the upper Clyde waters to the source of the Annan and the monstrous hills which line its course. I had been but once before in the place, in the winter time, when I was shooting the duck which come here in great plenty. To me, then, it had seemed the bleakest place in God's creation, but now, under the silver moonlight, it was a fantastic fairyland, and the long, gleaming line of Tweed like the fabled river which is the entrance to that happy domain.

We were now near our journey's end, and in the very heart of

157

the moors of Tweed. The night was bright with moonlight, and we went along speedily. Soon we came to a narrow upland valley, walled with precipitous green hills. Here Nicol halted.

"There'll be watchers aboot," he said, "and our coming 'll hae been tell't to the folk in the cave. We'd better gang warily." So we turned our horses up the glen, riding along the narrow strip of meadow land beside the burn. I had heard of the place before, and knew it for the Cor Water, a stream famous for trout, and at this time no less renowned among the hillmen as a hiding-place. For in the steep craigs and screes there were many caves and holes where one might lie hid for months.

Soon we came to a steep, green bank, and here we drew rein. Nicol whistled on his fingers, with a peculiar, piercing note like a whaup's cry. It was answered by another from the near neighbourhood. Again Nicol whistled with a different pitch, and this time a figure came out from the hillside, and spoke.

"Whae are ye," he said, "that come here, and what do ye seek? If ye come in the Lord's name, welcome and a night's lodging await ye. If no, fire and a sword."

"I'm Nicol Plenderleith," said my servant, "as weel ye ken, John Laidlaw. And these are twae gentlefolk, whose names are no convenient to be mentioned here, for hillsides hae ears. If ye come near, I'll whisper it in your lug."

The man approached and appeared well satisfied.

He bade us dismount and led the horses off, while we waited. Then he returned, and bidding us follow, led the way up a steep gully which scarred the hillside. In a little he stopped at an out-jutting rock, and crept round the corner of it. At the side next the hill was an opening large enough to allow a man of ordinary stature to pass, and here he entered and motioned us to follow.

CHAPTER VI

THE CAVE OF THE COR WATER

The place we found ourselves in was a narrow passage, very lofty and very dark, with countless jags of rough stone on all sides to affront the stranger. Some few paces led us into a wider place, lit by some opening on the hillside, for a gleam as of pale moonlight was all about it. There stood a sentinel, a tall, grave man, dressed in coarse homespun. Through this again we passed into another straitened place, which in a little opened into a chamber of some magnitude.

When I grew accustomed to the candle-light, I made out that it was a natural cave in the whinstone rocks, maybe thirty feet in height, square in shape, and not less than thirty feet long. The black sides were rough and crusted, and hung in many parts with articles of household gear and warlike arms. But the place was less notable than the people who were sitting there, and greeted us as we entered. In the midst was a table of rough-hewn wood, whereon lay the remnant of a meal. Lit pine staves cast an eerie glow over all things, and in the light I saw the faces of the company clear.

On a settle of stone covered with a sheep's fleece sat an old man, large of limb and tall, but bent and enfeebled with age. His long hair fell down almost to his shoulders; his features as the light fell upon them were strong, but his eyes were sightless and dull as stone. He had a great stick in his hand which he leaned on, and at our entrance he had risen and stared before him into vacancy, conscious of some new presence, but powerless to tell of it. Near him, along by the table-side, were two men of almost like age, square, well-knit fellows, with the tanned faces of hillmen. I guessed them to be shepherds or folk of that sort who had fled to this common refuge. Beyond these again stood a tall, slim man of a more polished exterior than the rest; his attitude had something of grace in it, and his face and bearing proclaimed

159

him of better birth. Forbye, there were one or two more, gaunt, sallow folk, such as I had learned to know as the extreme religionists. These were busy conversing together with bowed heads and earnest voices, and took no heed of our arrival. To add to all, there were two women, one with a little child, clearly the wives of the shepherds.

Our guide went forward to the man who stood by the wall and whispered something to him. In an instant he came to us, and, bowing to Marjory, bade us welcome. "We are glad to see you here, Master Burnet," said he. "I am rejoiced to see the gentlemen of the land coming forth for the Covenant. It is you and such as you that we need, and we are blithe to give you shelter here as long as you care to bide with us. It is a queer thing that two men of the same house should be engaged in this business on different sides."

Here one of the others spoke up.

"I trust, Master Burnet, ye have brought us good news from the Lawlands. We heard that ye had great converse with the godly there, and we will be glad to hear your account of how the guid cause prospers over the water."

Now I felt myself in a position of much discomfort. The cause of my outlawry had clearly got abroad, and here was I, credited with being a zealous religionist and a great man among the Scots exiles in Holland. Whereas, as I have already said, I recked little of these things, being not of a temper which finds delight in differences of creed or details of ecclesiastical government, but caring little in what way a man may worship his Maker. Indeed, to this day, while I can see the advantage of having fixed rites and a Church established, I see little use in making a pother about any deviation. So I now found myself in an unpleasing predicament. I must avow my utter ignorance of such matters and my worldly motives for thus seeking shelter, and in all likelihood win the disfavour of these folk, nay, even be not suffered to remain.

"I thank you for your welcome," said I, "but I must hasten to set matters right between us. I am not of your party, though it is my misfortune to have to seek safety among the hills. It is true I have been in the Low Countries, but it was for the purposes of study and seeing the world, and not for the sake of religion. If I must speak the truth, when I abode there I had little care of such things, for they were never in my way. Now that I am returned and find myself a fugitive, I am not a whit more concerned with them. My misfortunes arise from the guile of a kinsman, and not from my faith. So there you have my predicament."

I made the declaration crudely and roughly, for the necessity was urgent upon me of making it very plain at the outset. Another man would have been repelled or angered, but this man had the penetration to see through my mask of callousness that I was not ill-disposed to his cause.

"It is no matter," he said. "Though you were the most rabid malignant, we would yet give you shelter. And, indeed, though you may not be of our way of thinking in all matters, yet I doubt not you are with us on the essentials. Forbye, you are a gentleman of Tweeddale, and it would be queer if you werena a right-hearted, Master John Burnet."

Some one of the disputants grumbled, but the others seemed to share in this opinion, and bidding us sit down, they removed our travelling gear, and set food before us. Our appetites were sharp with the long hill journey, and we were not slow in getting to supper. Meanwhile, the long man to whom we had first spoken busied himself with serving us, for in that desert place every man was his own servant. Afterwards Marjory went to the women, and soon won their liking, for the heart would be hard indeed which was not moved by her graces.

When I had done I sat down on the settle with the rest, and the fire which burned in a corner of the cave was made up, and soon the place was less dismal but a thousandfold more fantastic. I could scarce keep from thinking that it was all a dream; that my landing, and midnight ride, and Nicol's news, and my perilous predicament were all figments of the brain. I was too tired to have any anxiety, for I would have you remember that I had ridden all the night and most of the day without a wink of sleep, besides having just come off a sea voyage. My eyelids drooped, and I was constantly sinking off into a doze. The whole place tended to drowsiness; the shadows and the light, the low hum of talk, the

161

heavy air, for the outlet for smoke was but narrow. But the man I have spoken of came and sat down beside me and would engage me in talk.

"I do not think you know me, Master Burnet," said he; "but I knew your father well, and our houses used to be well acquaint. I am one o' the Carnwath Lockharts, that ye may hae heard o'. My name is Francis Lockhart o' the Beltyne."

I knew him when he uttered the words, for I had often heard tell of him for a gallant gentleman who had seen service under Gustavus and in many Low Country wars. I complimented myself on his acquaintance, which kindness he proceeded to repay. So we fell to discussing many things—men I had known in Leyden, men I had known in Tweeddale, together with the more momentous question of the future of each of us. I gave him a full account of my recent fortunes, that he might have wherewith to contradict any rumours as to my reasons for taking to the hills. He in turn spoke to me of his life, and his sorrow at the fate of his land. The man spoke in such unfeigned grief, and likewise with such a gentleman-like note of fairness, that I felt myself drawn to him. It was while thus engaged that he spoke a word which brought upon him the condemnation of one of the others.

"Oh," said he, "I would that some way might be found to redd up thae weary times and set the king richt on his throne, for I canna but believe that in this matter loyalty and religion go hand in hand; and that were James Stewart but free from his wanchancy advisers there would be less talk of persecuting."

At this one of the others, a dark man from the West, spoke up sharply. "What do I hear, Maister Lockhart? It's no by ony goodwill to James Stewart that we can hope to set things richt in thae dark times. Rather let our mouths be filled with psalms and our hands with the sword-hilt, and let us teach the wanton and the scorner what manner o' men are bred by the Covenant and the Word."

The speech was hateful to me, and yet as I looked in the dark, rugged face of the man I could not keep from liking it. Here, at any rate, was a soul of iron.

Then the old man, him whom I have spoken of, beckoned to

me with his staff and bade me come and sit by him. He looked so king-like even in his affliction that I thought on the old blind king Œdipus in the Greek play.

"Ye kenna me, John Burnet, but weel ken I you. Often in the auld days your father and me had gey ploys hunting and fechting roond a' the muirs o' Tweed. He was a guid man was Gilbert, and I hear he had glimpses o' grace in the hinner end."

"Maybe," said I, being in perplexity, for from the grace that he spoke of my father had ever been far.

"Ay, and I was sair vexed I saw him so little. For he had to bide at hame for the last years, and I was aye busied wi' other work. Yeddie o' the Linns was never an idle man, and less than ever in thae days."

At the mention of his name a flood of recollection came upon me. I minded how I had heard of the son of Lord Fairley, a great soldier who had won high renown in the wars abroad: how he had returned a melancholy man, weighed down with the grave cares of religion, and gone to the wilds of Tweed to a hut just above the Linns of Talla, where he spent his days in prayer and meditation. The name of Yeddie o' the Linns, as he was called among the shepherds and folk of these parts, became an equivalent for high-hearted devotion. Then when the wars began tales of him grew over the countryside. In stature he was all but gigantic, famed over half the towns of France for feats of strength, and no evil living had impaired his might. So at the outbreak of the persecution he had been a terror to the soldiers who harried these parts. The tale ran of the four men whom he slew single-handed at the Linns, hemming them in a nook of rocks, and how often he had succoured fugitives and prisoners, coming like an old lion from the hills and returning no one knew whither. There was also the tale of his blinding by a chance splinter from a bullet shot, and how he had lived among the caves and hills, dangerous even in his affliction. Had I but known it, this cave was his finding, and half the retreats in Tweeddale and Clydesdale were known to him. But now he was an old man, who had long left his youth, and his strength had all but gone from him. He sat alone in his great darkness, speaking little to the

163

inmates or the chance comers, save when he knew them for gentlemen of birth; for though he might risk his life for the common people, he had no care to associate with them, being of the old Kirkpatricks of that ilk, as proud a house as is to be found in the land.

"You are not of us," he said suddenly. "I heard you say a moment agone that you had no share in the inheritance of Jacob, but still chose to dwell among the tents of sin."

"Nay," I said very gently, for he was very old and of noble presence, "do not speak thus. Surely it is no sin to live at peace in the good earth in honour and uprightness, and let all nice matters of doctrine go by, esteeming it of more importance to be a good man and true than a subtle disquisitioner—thinking, too, that all such things are of little moment and change from age to age, and that to concern one's self much with them is to follow vain trifles. For the root of the whole matter is a simple thing on which all men are agreed, but the appurtenances are many, and to me at least of such small significance that I care for them not at all. I do not mind how a man worship his Maker, if he have but real devoutness. I do not care how a Church is governed if the folk in it are in very truth God's people."

"You speak well, my son," said he, "and at one time I should have gone with you. But you are young and the blood is still rich in your veins and the world seems a fair place, with many brave things to be achieved. I am old and have seen the folly of all things, how love is only a delusion, and honour a catchword, and loyalty a mockery. And as the things of earth slip away from me, and the glory of my strength departs, I see more clearly the exceeding greatness of the things of God. So I love to bide in these dark moors where the pomp of the world comes not, among men of grave conversation, for I have leisure and a fitting place to meditate upon the things to come."

"It may be," said I, "that some day I also be of your way of thinking. At present the world, though the Devil is more loose in it than I love, seems to me so excellent that I would pluck the heart of it before I condemn it. But God grant that I may never lose sight of the beauty of His Kingdom."

"Amen to that," said the old man very reverently.

Truly, my thoughts on things were changing. Here was I in the very stronghold of the fanatics, and in the two chiefs, the old man and Master Lockhart, I found a reasonable mind and a lofty purpose. And thus I have ever found it, that the better sort of the Covenanters were the very cream of Scots gentlefolk, and that 'twas only in the *canaille* that the gloomy passion of fanatics was to be found.

Meantime Nicol, who cared for none of these things, was teaching the child how to play at the cat's garterns.

CHAPTER VII

HOW TWO OF HIS MAJESTY'S SERVANTS MET WITH THEIR DESERTS

The next morn broke fair and cloudless, and ere the sun was up I was awake, for little time must be lost if we sought to win to Smitwood ere the pursuit began. The folk of the cave were early risers, for the need for retiring early to rest made them so; and we broke our fast with a meal of cakes and broiled fish almost before daylight. Then I went out to enjoy the fresh air, for it was safe enough to be abroad at that hour. Nothing vexed the still air on the green hillside save the flapping peewits and the faint morning winds.

Marjory meantime ran out into the sunshine with all the gaiety in the world. She was just like a child let loose from school, for she was ever of a light heart and care sat easily upon her. Now, although we were in the direst peril, she was taking delight in spring, as if we were once again children in Dawyck, catching trout in the deep pools of the wood. She left me to go out from the little glen, which was the entrance to the cave, into the wider dale of the Cor Water which ran shallow between lone green braes. I heard her singing as she went down among the juniper bushes and flinty rocks, and then it died away behind a little shoulder of hill.

So I was left to my own reflections on the plight in which I found myself. For the first time a sort of wounded pride began to vex me. Formerly I had thought of nothing save how to save my own head and keep my love from my enemy, and cared not, if in the effecting of it, I had to crouch with the fox and be chased by the basest scum of the land. I cared not if I were put out of house and home and outlawed for years, for the adventurous spirit was strong within me. But now all my pride of race rose in rebellion at the thought that I was become a person without importance, a houseless wanderer, the sport of my enemies. It made me bitter as gall to think of it, and by whose aid my misfortune had been effected. A sort of hopeless remorse came over me. Should I ever win back the place I had lost? Would the Burnets ever again be great gentlemen of Tweeddale, a power in the countryside, having men at their beck and call? Or would the family be gone for ever, would I fall in the wilds, or live only to find my lands gone with my power, and would Marjory never enter Barns as its mistress? I could get no joy out of the morning for the thought, and as I wandered on the hillside I had little care of what became of me.

Now at this time there happened what roused me and set me once more at peace with myself. And though it came near to being a dismal tragedy, it was the draught which nerved me for all my later perils. And this was the manner of it.

Marjory, as she told me herself afterwards, had gone down to the little meadows by the burnside, where she watched the clear brown water and the fish darting in the eddies. She was thus engaged, when she was aware of two horsemen who rode over the top of the glen and down the long hill on the other side. They were almost opposite before she perceived them, and there was no time for flight. Like a brave lass she uttered no scream, but stood still that they might not see her. But it was of no avail. Their roving eyes could not miss in that narrow glen so fair a sight, and straightway one called out to the other that there was a girl at the burnside.

Now had the twain been out on an ordinary foray it would have gone hard indeed with us. For they would have turned aside to search out the matter, and in all likelihood the hiding-place would have been discovered. But they had been on some night errand and were returning in hot haste to their quarters at Abington, where their captain had none too gentle a temper. So they contented themselves with shouting sundry coarse railleries, and one in the plenitude of his great-heartedness fired his carbine at her. Without stopping further they rode on.

The bullet just grazed her arm above the wrist, cutting away a strip of dress. She cried out at the pain, but though frightened almost to death, she was brave enough to bide where she was, for if she had run straight to the cave it would have shown them the hiding-place. As soon as they passed out of view she came painfully up the slope, and I, who had heard the shot and rushed straightway to the place whence it came, met her clasping her wounded wrist and with a pitiful white face.

"O Marjory, what ails you?" I cried.

"Nothing, John," she answered; "some soldiers passed me and one fired. It has done me no harm. But let us get to shelter lest they turn back."

At her words I felt my heart rise in a sudden great heat of anger. I had never felt such passion before. It seemed to whelm and gulf my whole being.

"Let me carry you, dear," I said quietly, and lifting her I bore her easily up the ravine to the cave.

When I got her within our shelter there was a very great to-do. The women ran up in grief to see the hurt, and the men at the news of the military wore graver faces. Master Lockhart, who was something of a surgeon, looked at the wound.

"Oh," he says, "this is nothing—a scratch, and no more. It will be well as ever tomorrow. But the poor maid has had a fright which has made her weak. I have some choice French cordial which I aye carry with me for the fear of such accidents. Some of that will soon restore her."

So he fetched from some unknown corner the bottle which he spake of, and when her lips had been moistened, Marjory revived and declared her weakness gone. Now my most pressing anxiety was removed, which up till this time had been harassing me sore.

For if my lady were to be hurt in this unfriendly place, what hope of safety would there be for either? When I saw that the wound was but trifling, the anger which had been growing in my heart side by side with my care, wholly overmastered me. To think that the lady who was the dearest to me in the world should be thus maltreated by scurrilous knaves of dragoons stirred me to fury. I well knew that I could get no peace with the thought, and my inclination and good judgment alike made me take the course I followed.

I called to Nicol, where he sat supping his morning porridge by the fire, and he came to my side very readily.

"Get the two horses," said I quietly, that none of the others might hear of my madness, "one for me and one for yourself." Now the beasts were stabled in the back part of the cave, which was roomy and high, though somewhat damp. The entrance thereto lay by a like rift in the hillside some hundred yards farther up the glen. When I had thus bidden my servant I sauntered out into the open air and waited his coming with some impatience.

I asked him, when he appeared, if he had the pistols, for he had a great trick of going unarmed and trusting to his fleet legs and mother wit rather than the good gifts of God to men, steel and gunpowder.

"Ay, Laird, I hae them. Are ye gaun to shoot muirfowl?"

"Yes," said I, "I am thinking of shooting a muirfowl for my breakfast."

Nicol laughed quietly to himself. He knew well the errand I was on, or he would not have consented so readily.

I knew that the two dragoons had ridden straight down the Cor Water glen, making for the upper vale of Tweed and thence to the Clyde hills. But this same glen of Cor is a strangely winding one, and if a man leave it and ride straight over the moorland he may save a matter of two miles, and arrive at the Tweed sooner than one who has started before him. The ground is rough, but, to one used to the hills, not so as to keep him from riding it with ease. Also at the foot of the burn there is a narrow nick through which it thrusts itself in a little cascade to join the larger stream; and through this place the road passes, for all the hills on either side are steep and stony, and offer no foothold for a horse. Remembering all these things, a plan grew up in my mind which I hastened to execute.

With Nicol following, I rode aslant the low hills to the right and came to the benty tableland which we had travelled the day before. The sun was now well up in the sky, and the air was so fresh and sweet that it was pure pleasure to breathe it.

After maybe a quarter-hour's stiff riding we descended, and keeping well behind a low spur which hid us from the valley, turned at the end into the glen mouth, at the confluence of the two waters. Then we rode more freely till we reached the narrows which I have spoken of, and there we halted. All was quiet, nor was there any sound of man or horse.

"Do you bide there," said I to my servant, "while I will wait here. Now I will tell you what I purpose to do. The two miscreants who shot Mistress Marjory are riding together on their way to their quarters. One will have no shot in his carbine; what arms the other has I cannot tell; but at any rate we two with pistols can hold them in check. Do you cover the one on the right when they appear, and above all things see that you do not fire."

So we waited there, sitting motionless in our saddles, on that fair morning when all around us the air was full of crying snipe and twittering hill linnets. The stream made a cheerful sound, and the little green ferns in the rocks nodded beneath the spray of the water. I found my mind misgiving me again and again for the headstrong prank in which I was entered, as unworthy of one who knew something of better things. But I had little time for self-communings, for we had scarce been there two minutes before we heard the grating of hooves on the hill gravel, and our two gentlemen came round the corner not twenty yards ahead.

At the sight of us they reined up and stared stock still before them. Then I saw the hands of both reach to their belts, and I rejoiced at the movement, for I knew that the arms of neither were loaded.

"Gentlemen," said I, "it will be at your peril that you move. We have here two loaded pistols. We are not soldiers of his Majesty, so we have some skill in shooting. Let me assure you on

169

my word that your case is a desperate one."

At my words the one still looked with a haughty, swaggering stare, but the jaw of the other dropped and he seemed like a man in excess of terror.

"Today," I went on, "you shot at a lady not half an hour agone. It is for this that I have come to have speech with you. Let us understand one another, my friends. I am an outlawed man and one not easy to deal with. I am the Laird of Barns—ah, I see you know the name—and let this persuade you to offer no resistance."

One of the twain still stood helpless. The other's hand twitched as if he would draw his sword or reach to his powder flask, but the steely glitter of our barrels and my angry face deterred him.

"What do you want with us?" he said, in a tone of mingled sulkiness and bravado. "Let me tell you, I am one of his Majesty's dragoons, and you'll pay well for any ill you do to me. I care not a fig for you, for all your gentrice. If you would but lay down your pop-guns and stand before me man to man, I would give you all the satisfaction you want."

The fellow was a boor but he spoke like a man, and I liked him for his words. But I replied grimly—

"I will have none of your bragging. Go and try that in your own sty, you who shoot at women. I will give you as long as I may count a hundred, and if before that you have not stripped off every rag you have on and come forward to me here, by God I will shoot you down like the dogs you are."

And with this I began solemnly to count aloud.

At first they were still rebellious, but fear of the death which glinted to them from the barrels of the pistols won the mastery. Slowly and with vast reluctance they began to disrobe themselves of belt and equipments, of coat and jackboots, till they stood before me in the mild spring air as stark as the day they were born. Their faces were heavy with malice and shame.

"Now," said I to Nicol, "dismount and lay on to these fellows with the flat of my sword. Give me your pistol, and if either makes resistance he will know how a bullet tastes. Lay on, and do not spare them."

So Nicol, to whom the matter was a great jest, got down and laid on lustily. They shouted most piteously for mercy, but none they got till the stout arm of my servant was weary.

"And now, gentlemen, you may remount your horses. Nay, without your clothes; you will ride more freely as you are. And give my best respects to your honourable friends, and tell them I wish a speedy meeting."

But as I looked in the face of one, him who had been so terror-stricken at the outset, I saw that which I thought I recognized.

"You, fellow," I cried, "where have I seen you before?"

And as I looked again, I remembered a night the year before on the Alphen road, when I had stood over this very man and questioned him on his name and doings. So he had come to Scotland as one of the foreign troops.

"I know you, Jan Hamman," said I. "The great doctor Johannes Burnetus of Lugdunum has not forgotten you. You were scarcely in an honest trade before, but you are in a vast deal less honest now. I vowed if ever I met you again to make you smart for your sins, and I think I have kept my word, though I had the discourtesy to forget your face at first sight. Good morning, Jan. I hope to see you again ere long. Good morning, gentlemen both."

So the luckless pair rode off homeward, and what reception they met with from their captain and their comrades who shall say?

Meanwhile, when they were gone for some little time, Nicol and I rode back by a roundabout path. When I began to reflect, I saw the full rashness of my action. I had burned my boats behind me with a vengeance. There was no choice of courses before me now. The chase would be ten times hotter against me than before, and besides, I had given them some clue to my whereabouts. You may well ask if the danger to my love were not equally great, for that by this action they would know at least the airt by which she had fled. I would answer that these men were of Gilbert's own company, and one at least of them, when he heard my name, must have had a shrewd guess as to who the lady was. My cousin's love affairs were no secret. If the man had revealed the tale in its entirety, his own action must necessarily have been exposed, and God help him who had insulted one whom Gilbert cared for. He would have flayed the skin from him at the very mention.

To my sober reason today the action seems foolhardy in the extreme, and more like a boyish frolic than the work of a man. But all I knew at the time, as I rode back, was that my pride was for the moment soothed, and my heart mightily comforted.

CHAPTER VIII

OF OUR WANDERINGS AMONG
THE MOORS OF CLYDE

If there had been haste before in our journey there was the more now, when in a few hours the countryside would be alive with our foes. I hurriedly considered in my mind the course of events. In three hours' riding the soldiers, all stark as they were, would come to Abington, and in three more the road to Douglasdale would be blocked by a dozen companies. It was no light thing thus to have set the whole hell's byke in Clydesdale buzzing about my ears.

We were not long in reaching the cave. Here, to my joy, I found Marjory all recovered from her fright, and the wound hurting her no more than a pin's scratch. When I spoke of immediate progress she listened gladly, and was for setting out forthwith. I did not tell her of the soldiers' discomfiture, for I knew that she would fall to chiding me for my foolhardiness, and besides she would have more dismal fears for my future if she knew that I had thus incensed the military against me.

It was with much regret that I bade farewell to Master Lockhart and the old man; nor would they let me go without a promise that if I found myself hard pressed at any time in the days to come I would take refuge with them. I was moved by the sight of the elder, who, laying his hand on my lady's head, stroked her fair golden hair gently and said, "Puir lass, puir lass, ye're no for the muirs. I foresee ill days coming for ye when ye'll hae nae guid sword to protect ye. But lippen weel to the Lord, my bairn, and He'll no forsake ye." So amid the speaking of farewells and well-wishes we rode out into the green moors.

How shall I tell of that morning ride? I have seen very many days in April now, for I am a man ageing to middle life, but never have I seen one like that. The sky was one sheet of the faintest blue, with delicate white clouds blown lightly athwart it. The air was so light that it scarce stirred the grass, so cool that it made our foreheads as crisp and free as on a frosty winter's day, so mild that a man might have fancied himself still in the Lowlands. The place was very quiet save for a few sounds and these the most delectable on earth—the cries of sheep and the tender bleating of young lambs, the rise and fall of the stream, the croon of rock pigeons, and the sterner notes of curlew and plover. And the grass was short and lawn-like, stretching in wavy ridges to the stream, seamed with little rush-fringed rills and patched with fields of heath. Only when we gained the edge had we any view of country, and even then it was but circumscribed. Steep fronting hills, all scarred with ravines; beyond, shoulders and peaks rising ever into the distance, and below us the little glen which holds the head-waters of Tweed.

We crossed the river without slacking rein, for the water scarce reached above our horses' pasterns. And now we struck up a burn called the Badlieu, at the foot of which was a herd's shieling. The spirit of the spring seemed to have clean possessed Marjory, and I had never seen her so gay. All her past sorrows and present difficulties seemed forgotten, and a mad gaiety held her captive. She, who was for usual so demure now cast her gravity to the winds, and seemed bent on taking all the joys of the fair morning. She laughed, she sang snatches of old songs, and she leaped her horse lightly over the moss-trenches. She stooped to pluck some early white wind-flowers, and set some in her hair and some at her saddle-bow.

"Nay, John," she cried, "if you and I must take to the hills let us do it with some gallantry. It is glorious to be abroad. I would give twelve months of sleepy peace at Dawyck for one hour of this life. I think this must be the Garden of Perpetual Youth in the fairy tale."

The same mad carelessness took hold on me also. Of a sudden my outlook on the world changed round to the opposite, and the black forebodings which had been ever present to distress me, seemed to vanish like dew before the sun. Soon I was riding as gaily as she; while Nicol, as he ran with great strides and unfaltering breath, he too became light-hearted, though to tell the truth care was not a commodity often found with him.

Soon we had climbed the low range which separates the Clyde glen from the Tweed and turned down the narrow ravine of the burn which I think they call Fopperbeck, and which flows into the Evan Water. Now it would have been both easier and quieter to have ridden down the broad, low glen of the Medlock Water, which flows into Clyde by the village of Crawford. But this would have brought us perilously near the soldiers at Abington, and if once the pursuit had begun every mile of distance would be worth to us much gold. Yet though the danger was so real I could not think of it as any matter for sorrow, but awaited what fate God might send with a serene composure, begotten partly of my habitual rashness and partly of the intoxication of the morn.

We kept over the rocky ravine through which the little river Evan flows to Annan, and came to the wide moorlands which stretch about the upper streams of Clyde. Here we had a great prospect of landscape, and far as eye could see no living being but ourselves moved in these desolate wastes. Far down, just at the mouth of the glen where the vale widens somewhat, rose curling smoke from the hamlet of Elvanfoot, a place soon to be much resorted to and briskly busy, since, forbye lying on the highway 'twixt Edinburgh and Dumfries, it is there that the bypath goes off leading to the famous lead mines, at the two places of Leadhills and Wanlockhead. But now it was but a miserable roadside clachan of some few low huts, with fodder for neither man nor beast.

As we rode we looked well around us, for we were in an exceeding dangerous part of our journey. To the right lay

Abington and the lower Clyde valley, where my sweet cousin and his men held goodly fellowship. Even now they would be buckling saddle-straps, and in two hours would be in the places through which we were now passing. To the left was the long pass into Nithsdale, where half a score of gentlemen did their best to instil loyalty into the Whigs of the hills. I hated the land to that airt, for I had ever loathed the south and west countries, where there is naught but sour milk and long prayers without a tincture of gentrice or letters. I was a man of Tweeddale who had travelled and studied and mingled among men. I had no grudge against sheltering with the Tweedside rebels, who were indeed of my own folk; but I had no stomach for Nithsdale and Clydesdale rant and ill fare. Had not necessity driven me there I vow I should never have ventured of myself; and as I rode I swore that once I were free of my errand I would seek my refuge in my own countryside.

And now we were climbing the long range which flanks the Portrail Water, which is the larger of the twin feeders of Clyde. Now we turned more to the north, and skirting the wild hills which frown around the pass of Enterkin, sought the upper streams of the Duneaton Water. I cannot call to mind all the burns we crossed or the hills we climbed, though they have all been told to me many a time and again. One little burn I remember called the Snar, which flowed very quietly and pleasantly in a deep, heathery glen. Here we halted and suffered our horses to graze, while we partook of some of the food which the folk of the Cor Water had sent with us. Now the way which we had come had brought us within seven miles of the dragoons' quarters at Abington, for it was necessary to pass near them to get to Douglasdale and Smitwood. But they had no clue to our whereabouts, and when they set forth against us must needs ride first to the Tweed valley.

Here in this narrow glen we were in no danger save from some chance wandering soldier. But this danger was the less to be feared, since if Gilbert had any large portion of his men out on one errand he would be sure to set the rest to their duties as garrison. For my cousin had no love for lax discipline, but had all the family pride of ordering and being obeyed to the letter. So we kindled a little fire by the streamside, and in the ashes roasted some eggs of a muirfowl which Nicol had picked up on the journey; and which, with the cheese and the cakes we had brought, made a better meal than I might hope for for many days to come. We sat around the fire in the dry heather 'neath the genial sun, thanking God that we were still alive in the green world and with few cares save the frustrating of our foes. Marjory was somewhat less cheerful than in the morning, partly from the fatigue of riding, which in these waste places is no light thing, and partly because anxiety for my safety and sorrow at our near parting were beginning to oppress her. For herself, I verily believe, she had no care, for she was brave as a lion in the presence of what most women tremble at. But the loneliness of a great house and the never-appeased desire for knowledge of my safety were things which came nearer so rapidly that I did not wonder she lost her gaiety.

"Oh, what will you do alone in these places?" she said. "If you had but one with you, I should be comforted. Will you not let Nicol accompany you?"

Now when my lady looked at me with melting eyes and twined her hands in her eagerness, it was hard to have to deny her. But I was resolved that my servant should abide at Smitwood to guard her and bring me tidings if aught evil threatened.

"Nay, dear," I said, "that may not be. I cannot have you left with an old man who is helpless with age and a crew of hireling servants. I should have no heart to live in the moors if I had not some hope of your safety. Believe me, dear, I can very well defend myself. My skill of hillcraft is as good as any dragoon's, and I have heard folk say that I am no ill hand with a sword. And I know the countryside like the palm of my own hand, and friends are not few among these green glens. Trust me, no ill will come near me, and our meeting will be all the merrier for our parting."

I spoke heartily, but in truth I was far from feeling such ease of mind. For my old cursed pride was coming back, and I was beginning to chafe against the beggarly trade of skulking among the moors when I had a fine heritage for my own, and above all when I was a scholar and had thought of peaceful days. I found it hard to reconcile my dream of a philosophic life wherein all things should be ordered according to the dictates of reason, with the rough-and-ready times which awaited me, when my sword must keep my head, and my first thought must be of meat and lodging, and cunning and boldness would be qualities more valuable than subtle speculation and lofty imagining.

In a little we were rested and rode on our way. Across the great moors of Crawfordjohn we passed, which is a place so lonely that the men in these parts have a proverb, "Out of the world and into Crawfordjohn." We still kept the uplands till we came to the springs of a burn called the Glespin, which flows into the Douglas Water. Our easier path had lain down by the side of this stream past the little town of Douglas. But in the town was a garrison of soldiers—small, to be sure, and feeble, but still there—who were used to harry the moors around Cairntable and Muirkirk. So we kept the ridges till below us we saw the river winding close to the hill and the tower of Smitwood looking out of its grove of trees. By this time darkness was at hand, and the last miles of our journey were among darkening shadows. We had little fear of capture now, for we were on the lands of the castle, and Veitch of Smitwood was famed for a cavalier and a most loyal gentleman. So in quiet and meditation we crossed the stream at the ford, and silently rode up the long avenue to the dwelling.

CHAPTER IX

I PART FROM MARJORY

"I've travelled far and seen many things, but, Gad, I never saw a stranger than this. My niece is driven out of house and home by an overbold lover, and you, Master Burnet, come here and bid me take over the keeping of this firebrand, which, it seems, is so obnoxious to his Majesty's lieges."

So spake the old laird of Smitwood, smiling. He was a man of full eighty years of age, but still erect with a kind of soldierly bearing. He was thin and tall, and primly dressed in the fashion of an elder day. The frosty winter of age had come upon him, but in his ruddy cheek and clean-cut face one could see the signs of a hale and vigorous decline. He had greeted us most hospitably, and seemed hugely glad to see Marjory again, whom he had not set eyes on for many a day. We had fallen to supper with keen appetite, for the air of the moors stirs up the sharpest hunger; and now that we had finished we sat around the hall fire enjoying our few remaining hours of company together. For myself I relished the good fare and the warmth, for Heaven knew when either would be mine again. The high oak-roofed chamber, hung with portraits of Veitches many, was ruddy with firelight. Especially the picture in front of the chimney by Vandyke, of that Michael Veitch who died at Philiphaugh, was extraordinarily clear and lifelike. Master Veitch looked often toward it; then he took snuff with a great air of deliberation, and spoke in his high, kindly old voice.

"My brother seems well tonight, Marjory. I have not seen him look so cheerful for years." (He had acquired during his solitary life the habit of talking to the picture as if it were some living thing.) "I can never forgive the Fleming for making Michael hold his blade in so awkward a fashion. Faith, he would have been little the swordsman he was, if he had ever handled sword like that. I can well remember when I was with him at Etzburg, how he engaged in a corner two Hollanders and a Swiss guard, and beat them back till I came up with him and took one off his hands."

"I have heard of that exploit," said I. "You must know that I have just come from the Low Countries, where the names of both of you are still often on men's lips."

The old man seemed well pleased.

"Ah," he said, "so you have come from abroad. In what place did you bide, may I inquire?"

"In the town of Leyden," said I, "for my aim was no more than to acquire learning at the college there. But I forgathered with many excellent Scots gentlemen from whom I heard the talk of the camp and the state."

"Say you so? Then what do you here? Did you return on the single errand of protecting my fair niece? But stay! I am an old man who cares not much for the chatter of the country, but I have heard—or am I wrong?—that you were not of the true party, but leaned to the Whigs?"

"Nay," I cried, "I beseech you not to believe it. God knows I am a king's man out and out, and would see all whigamores in perdition before I would join with them. But fate has brought me into a strange mixture of misfortunes. I land at Leith, expecting nothing save a peaceful home-coming, and lo! I find my cousin waiting with a warrant for my arrest. I am accused of something I am wholly innocent of, but I cannot prove it; nay, there is evidence against me, and my enemies in the Council are all-powerful. Moreover, if I suffer myself to be taken, Marjory is at the mercy of my foes. I take the only course; give the dragoons the slip, and ride straight to Tweeddale, escort her to a house where she will be safe and unknown; and when this is done take to the hills myself with a light heart. They are too ill-set against me for my setting any hope in going to Edinburgh and pleading my case. Was there any other way?"

"None," said Master Veitch, "but it is a hard case for yourself. Not the hiding among the moors; that is a noble trade for any young man of spirit. But the consorting with the vile fanatics of these deserts must go sore against your heart."

Now I, who had just come from the folk of the Cor Water, had no such dread of the hillmen, but I forbore to say it. For Master Veitch had been brought up in one school, those men in another. Both were blind to the other's excellencies; both in their own ways were leal-hearted men. It is a strange providence that has so ordered it that the best men in the world must ever remain apart through misunderstanding.

"But to come to my errand," said I. "I have brought you your niece for protection. You are a king's man, a soldier, and well known in the countryside. It is more than unlikely that any troops will come nigh you. Nor is it possible that the maid can be traced hither. I ask that you suffer her to abide in the house, while I take myself off that there be the less danger. And oh, I beseech you, do not refuse me. She is your own flesh and blood. You cannot deny her shelter."

The old man's face darkened. "You take me for a strange kinsman, Master Burnet," he said, "if you think I would refuse my best aid to a kinswoman in distress. Do you think that you are the sole protector of my house?"

I bowed before his deserved rebuke.

"But, for certain, Marjory may abide here as long as she will," he added cheerfully. "We will do our best to entertain her, though I am too old to remember well the likings of girls. And if any one comes seeking her on errand of no good, by God, he will learn that William Veitch has not lost the use of his arm."

"May I ask," said I, "that my servant be allowed to stay? He knows the hills as scarce any other living man, he is faithful, and clever as you would hardly believe were I to tell you. With him in the house I should have no fear for its safety."

"So be it," said the old man; "I will not deny that my servants are not so numerous nor so active that another would not be something of an improvement. Has he any skill in cooking?" This he asked in a shamefaced tone, for old as he was he had not lost his relish for good fare.

"I will ask him," said I, and I called Nicol from the servants' quarters.

"Your master gives me a good account of you," said the cracked voice of the laird of Smitwood, "and I would fain hope it true. I wished to interrogate you about—ah, your powers— ah, of cooking pleasing dishes," and he waved his hand deprecatingly.

"Oh, your honour, I am ready for a'thing," said Nicol. "Sheep's heid, singit to a thocht, cockyleeky and a' kind o' soup, mutton in half a dozen different ways, no to speak o' sic trifles as confections. I can cook ye the flesh o' the red deer and the troots frae the burn, forbye haggis and brose, partan pies and rizzard haddies, crappit-heids and scate-rumples, nowt's feet, kebbucks, scadlips, and skink. Then I can wark wi' custocks and carlings, rifarts and syboes, farles, fadges, and bannocks, drammock, brochan, and powsowdie."

"That will do, you may go," said the old man, rubbing his hands with glee. "By my word, a genuine Scots gastronome, skilled in the ancient dishes of the land. I anticipate a pleasing time while he bides here."

It was long ere the worthy gentleman could get over his delight in the project of my servant's presence. Even after he had gone he sat and chuckled to himself, for he was known among his friends to have a fine taste for dainties. Meantime, the light was dying out of doors, and more logs were laid on the fire, till it crackled and leaped like a live thing. I have ever loved the light of a wood fire, for there is no more heartsome thing on earth than its cheerful crackle when one comes in from shooting on the hills in the darkening of a winter's day. Now I revelled in the comfort of it, since on the morrow I would have no other cheer than a flaming sunset.

So we sat around the hearth and talked of many things till the evening was late. The old man fell to the memories of former folk, and told us tales of our forbears as would have made them turn in their graves could they have heard them. Of my house he had scarce a good word to speak, averring that they were all 'scape-the-gallows every one, but gallant fellows in their way. "There was never a Burnet," he cried, "who would scruple to stick a man who doubted his word, or who would not ride a hundred miles to aid a friend. There were no lads like the Burnets in all the countryside for dicing and feasting and riding break-neck on the devil's errand. But, Gad, if they were stubborn as bulls when they were down themselves, they were as tender as women to folk in trouble."

"There's one of their name like to be in trouble for many days to come," said I.

"Meaning yourself? Well, it will do you no ill. There's naught better for a young man than to find out how little the world cares whether he be dead or alive. And, above all, you that pretend to be a scholar, it will ding some of the finespun fancies out of your head. But for the Lord's sake, laddie, dinna get a bullet in your skull or you'll have me with all my years taking the field to pay

181

back them that did it." He spoke this so kindly that I was moved to forget the first half of his words through the excellence of the second. In truth I much needed the rough lessons of hardship and penury, for at that time I was puffed up in a self-conceit and a certain pride of letters as foolish as it was baseless.

"I must be off in the morning before the dawning, for I have to be on the hills ere the soldiers get abroad. I must beg of you not to disturb yourself, Master Veitch, for my sake, but just to bid them make ready for me some provisions; and I will slip off ere the household be awake. It is better to say farewell now than to have many sad leave-takings at the moment of departure. I have no fear of my journey, for my legs are as good as any man's, and I can make my hands keep my head. Also, my mind is easy since I know that Marjory is safe."

"Then I will even bid you goodbye, John," said he, "for I am an old man and keep early hours. If you will follow me I will take you to your chamber. Alison will take you to the old room, Marjory, where you have not been since you were a little lass scarce up to my knee." And with obvious intent he walked out.

"God keep you, John," my dear lass whispered on my shoulder. "I will never cease to think of you. And oh, be not long in coming back."

And this was the last I saw of my lady for many days.

CHAPTER X

OF THE MAN WITH THE ONE EYE AND THE ENCOUNTER IN THE GREEN CLEUCH

I promise you I slept little that night, and it was with a heavy heart that I rose betimes and dressed in the chill of the morning. There was no one awake, and I left the house unobserved, whistling softly to keep up my spirits.

Just without, some one came behind me and cried my name. I turned sharply round, and there was my servant Nicol, slinking after me for all the world like a collie dog which its master has left at home.

"What do you want with me?" I cried.

"Naething," he groaned sadly. "I just wantit to see ye afore ye gaed. I am awfu' feared, sir, for you gaun awa' yoursel'. If it werena for Mistress Marjory, it wad be a deal mair than your word wad keep me frae your side. But I cam to see if there was nae way o' gettin' word o' ye. My leddy will soon turn dowie, gin she gets nae sough o' your whereabouts. Ye'd better tell me where I can get some kind o' a letter."

"Well minded!" I cried. "You know the cairn on the back side of Caerdon just above the rising of Kilbucho Burn. This day three weeks I will leave a letter for your mistress beneath the stones, which you must fetch and give her. And if I am safe and well every three weeks it will be the same. Good day to you, Nicol, and see you look well to the charge I have committed to you."

"Guid day to you, sir," he said, and I protest that the honest fellow had tears in his eyes; and when I had gone on maybe half a mile and looked back, he was still standing like a stone in the same spot.

At first I was somewhat depressed in my mind. It is a hard thing thus to part from one's mistress when the air is thick with perils to both. So as I tramped through the meadows and leaped the brooks, it was with a sad heart, and my whole mind was taken up in conjuring back the pleasant hours I had spent in my lady's company, the old frolics in the wood of Dawyck, the beginnings of our lovemaking, even the ride hither from the Cor Water. Yesterday, I reflected, she was with me here; now I am alone and like to be so for long. Then I fell to cursing myself for a fool, and went on my way with a better heart.

But it was not till I had crossed the wide stream of the Douglas Water and begun to ascend the hills, that I wholly recovered my composure. Before, I had been straggling in low meadows which do not suit my temper, since I am above all things hill-bred and a lover of dark mountains. So now on the crisp spring grass of the slopes my spirits rose. Was not I young and strong and skilled in the accomplishments of a man? The world was before me—that wide, undiscovered world which had always attracted the more heroic spirits. What hardship was there to live a free life among the hills, under the sunshine and the wind, the clouds and the blue sky?

But my delight could never be unmixed though I tried. After all, was I free? I felt of a sudden that I was not one half equipped for a gipsy life. I was tied down to custom and place with too many ties. I came of a line of landed gentlemen. The taint of possession, of mastery and lordship over men and land, was strong in me. I could not bring me to think of myself as a kinless and kithless vagabond, having no sure place of abode. Then my love of letters, my learning, my philosophy, bound me down with indissoluble bands. To have acquired a taste for such things was to have unfitted myself for ever for the life of careless vagabondage. Above all there was my love; and ever, as I went on, my thoughts came home from their aerial flights and settled more and more in a little room in a house in a very little portion of God's universe. And more and more I felt myself a slave to beloved tyrants, and yet would not have been free if I could.

It was always thus with me when alone: I must fall to moralizing and self-communing. Still perhaps the master feeling in my mind was one of curiosity and light-heartedness. So I whistled as I went, all the old tunes of my boyhood which I was wont to whistle when I went out to the hills with my rod and gun, and stepped briskly over the short heather, and snapped my fingers in the face of the world.

Now I dared not go back to Tweeddale by the way by which I had come, for the Clyde valley above Abington would be a hunting-ground of dragoons for many days. There was nothing for it but to make for the lower waters, ford the river above Coulter, and then come to Tweeddale in the lower parts, and thence make my way to the Water of Cor. Even this course was not without its dangers; for the lower glen of Tweed was around Dawyck and Barns, and this was the very part of all the land the most perilous to me at the moment. To add to this, I was well at home among the wilder hills; but it was little I knew of Clydesdale below Abington, till you come to the town of Lanark. This may at first seem a trifling misfortune, but in my present case it was a very great one. For unless a man knows every house and the character of its inmates he is like to be in an ill way if close watched and threatened. However, I dreaded this the less, and looked for my troubles mainly after I had once entered my own lands in Tweeddale.

At the time when the sun rose I was on a long hill called Craigcraw, which hangs at the edge of the narrow crack in the hills through which goes the bridle road from Lanark to Moffat. I thought it scarce worth my while to be wandering aimlessly among mosses and craigs when something very like a road lay beneath me; so I made haste to get down and ease my limbs with the level way. It was but a narrow strip of grass, running across the darker heath, and coiling in front like a green ribbon through nick or scaur or along the broad brae-face.

Soon I came to the small, roofless shieling of Redshaw, where aforetime lived a villain of rare notoriety, with whose name, "Redshaw Jock," Jean Morran embittered my childhood. I thought of all these old pleasing days, as I passed the bare rickle of stones in the crook of the burn. Here I turned from the path, for I had no desire to go to Abington, and struck up a narrow howe in the hills, which from the direction I guessed must lead to the lower Clyde. It was as lonesome a place as ever I have seen. The spring sunshine only made the utter desolation the more apparent and oppressive. Afar on the hillside, by a clump of rowan trees, I saw the herd's house of Wildshaw, well named in its remote solitude. But soon I had come to the head of the burn and mounted the flat tableland, and in a little came to the decline on the other side, and entered the glen of the Roberton Burn.

Here it was about the time of noon, and I halted to eat my midday meal. I know not whether it was the long walk and the rough scrambling, or the clean, fresh spring air, or the bright sunshine, or the clear tinkle of the burn at my feet, or the sense of freedom and adventurous romance, but I have rarely eaten a meal with such serene satisfaction. All this extraordinary day I had been alternating between excessive gaiety and sad regrets. Now the former element had the mastery, and I was as hilarious as a young horse when he is first led out to pasture.

185

And after a little as I sat there my mirth grew into a sober joy. I remembered all the poets who had sung of the delight of the open air and the unshackled life. I laughed at my former feeling of shame in the matter. Was there any ignominy in being driven from the baseness of settled habitation to live like a prince under God's sky? And yet, as I exulted in the thought, I knew all too well that in a little my feelings would have changed and I would be in the depths of despondency.

In less than an hour I had turned a corner of hill, and there before me lay the noble strath of Clyde. I am Tweedside born and will own no allegiance save to my own fair river, but I will grant that next to it there is none fairer than the upper Clyde. Were it not that in its lower course it flows through that weariful west country among the dull whigamores and Glasgow traders, it would be near as dear to me as my own well-loved Tweed. There it lay, glittering in light, and yellow with that strange yellow glow that comes on April waters. The little scrubs of wood were scarce seen, the few houses were not in the picture; nothing caught the eye save the giant mouldings of the hills, the severe barren vale, and the sinuous path of the stream.

I crossed it without any mishap, wading easily through at one of the shallows. There was no one in sight, no smoke from any dwellings; all was as still as if it were a valley of the dead. Only from the upper air the larks were singing, and the melancholy peewits cried ever over the lower moorlands. From this place my course was clear; I went up the prattling Wandel Burn, from where it entered the river and soon I was once more lost in the windings of the dark hills. There is a narrow bridle-path which follows the burn, leading from Broughton in Tweeddale to Abington, so the way was easier walking.

And now I come to the relation of one of the strangest adventures of this time, which as often as I think upon it fills me with delight. For it was a ray of amusement in the perils and hardships of my wanderings.

A mile or more up this stream, just before the path begins to leave the waterside and strike towards the highlands, there is a little green cleuch, very fair and mossy, where the hills on either

186

side come close and the glen narrows down to half a hundred yards. When I came to this place I halted for maybe a minute to drink at a pool in the rocks, for I was weary with my long wanderings.

A noise in front made me lift my head suddenly and stare before me. And there, riding down the path to meet me, was a man. His horse seemed to have come far, for it hung its head as if from weariness and stumbled often. He himself seemed to be looking all around him and humming some blithe tune. He was not yet aware of my presence, for he rode negligently, like one who fancies himself alone. As he came nearer I marked him more clearly. He was a man of much my own height, with a shaven chin and a moustache on his upper lip. He carried no weapons save one long basket-handled sword at his belt. His face appeared to be a network of scars; but the most noteworthy thing was that he had but one eye, which glowed bright from beneath bushy brows. Here, said I to myself, is a man of many battles.

In a moment he caught my eye, and halted abruptly not six paces away. He looked at me quietly for some seconds, while his horse, which was a spavined, broken-winded animal at best, began to crop the grass. But if his mount was poor, his dress was of the richest and costliest, and much gold seemed to glisten from his person.

"Good day, sir," said he very courteously. "A fellow-traveller, I perceive." By this time I had lost all doubt, for I saw that the man was no dragoon, but of gentle birth by his bearing. So I answered him readily.

"I little expected to meet any man in this deserted spot, least of all a mounted traveller. How did you come over these hills, which if I mind right are of the roughest?"

"Ah," he said, "my horse and I have done queer things before this," and he fell to humming a fragment of a French song, while his eye wandered eagerly to my side.

Suddenly he asked abruptly: "Sir, do you know aught of swordplay?"

I answered in the same fashion that I was skilled in the rudiments.

He sprang from his horse in a trice and was coming towards me.

"Thank God," he cried earnestly, "thank God. Here have I been thirsting for days to feel a blade in my hands, and devil a gentleman have I met. I thank you a thousand times, sir, for your kindness. I beseech you to draw."

"But," I stammered, "I have no quarrel with you."

He looked very grieved. "True, if you put it in that way. But that is naught between gentlemen, who love ever to be testing each other's prowess. You will not deny me?"

"Nay," I said, "I will not," for I began to see his meaning, and I stripped to my shirt and, taking up my sword, confronted him.

So there in that quiet cleuch we set to with might and main, with vast rivalry but with no malice. We were far too skilled to butcher one another like common rufflers. Blow was given and met, point was taken and parried, all with much loving kindness. But I had not been two minutes at the work when I found I was in the hands of a master. The great conceit of my play which I have always had ebbed away little by little. The man before me was fencing easily with no display, but every cut came near to breaking my guard, and every thrust to overcoming my defence. His incomprehensible right eye twinkled merrily, and discomposed my mind, and gave me no chance of reading his intentions. It is needless to say more. The contest lasted scarce eight minutes. Then I made a head-cut which he guarded skilfully, and when on the return my blade hung more loose in my hand he smote so surely and well that, being struck near the hilt, it flew from my hand and fell in the burn.

He flung down his weapon and shook me warmly by the hand.

"Ah, now I feel better," said he. "I need something of this sort every little while to put me in a good humour with the world. And, sir, let me compliment you on your appearance. Most admirable, most creditable! But oh, am I not a master in the craft?"

So with friendly adieux we parted. We had never asked each other's name and knew naught of each other's condition, but that single good-natured contest had made us friends; and if ever

I see that one-eyed man again in life I shall embrace him like a brother. For myself, at that moment I felt on terms of good comradeship with all, and pursued my way in a settled cheerfulness.

CHAPTER XI

HOW A MILLER STROVE WITH
HIS OWN MILL WHEEL

I lay that night on the bare moors, with no company save the birds, and no covering save a dry bush of heather. The stars twinkled a myriad miles away, and the night airs blew soft, and I woke in the morning as fresh as if I had lain beneath the finest coverlet on the best of linen. Near me was a great pool in the burn, and there I bathed, splashing to my heart's content in the cold water. Then I ate my breakfast, which was no better than the remnants of the food I had brought away with me the day before from Smitwood; but I gulped it down heartily and hoped for something better. There will be so much complaining, I fear, in my tale ere it is done, that I think it well to put down all my praise of the place and the hours which passed pleasingly.

By this time I was on a little plateau, near the great black hill of Coomb Dod, a place whence three streams flow—the Camps Water and the Coulter Water to the Clyde, and the burn of Kingledoors to Tweed. Now here, had I been wise, I should at once have gone down the last-named to the upper waters of Tweed near the village of Tweedsmuir, whence I might have come without danger to the wilder hills and the Cor Water hiding-place. But as I stayed there desire came violently upon me to go down to the fair green haughlands about the Holmes Water, which is a stream which rises not far off the Kingledoors burn, but which flows more to the north and enters Tweed in the strath of Drummelzier not above a few miles from Barns itself and almost at the door of Dawyck. Here I knew was the greater danger, because it lay on the straight line between Abington and

189

Peebles, a way my cousin Gilbert travelled often in those days. But I was not disposed at that moment to think of gradations of danger; and indeed, after my encounter on the previous afternoon, I was in a haphazard, roystering mood, and would have asked for nothing better than a chance of making holes in my cousin or his company,

Now in Holmes Water glen there dwelled many who would receive me gladly and give me shelter and food if I sought it. There were the Tweedies of Quarter and Glencotho, kin to myself on the mother's side, not to speak of a score of herds with whom I had dealings. But my uppermost reason was to see once more that lovely vale, the fairest, unless it be the Manor, in all the world. It is scarce six miles long, wide at the bottom and set with trees and rich with meadows and cornland, but narrowing above to a long, green cleft between steep hills. And through it flows the clearest water on earth, wherein dwell the best trout—or did dwell, for, as I write, I have not angled in it for many days. I know not how I can tell of the Holmes Water. It tumbles clear and tremulous into dark brown pools. In the shallows it is like sunlight, in the falls lie virgin snow. And over all the place hangs a feeling of pastoral quiet and old romance, such as I never knew elsewhere.

Midday found me in the nick of the hill above Glencotho debating on my after course. I had it in my mind to go boldly in and demand aid from my kinsman. But I reflected that matters were not over-pleasant between us at the time. My father had mortally offended him on some occasion (it would be hard to name the Tweedside gentleman whom my father had not mortally angered), and I could scarce remember having heard that the quarrel had been made up. I knew that in any case if I entered they would receive me well for the honour of the name, but I am proud, and like little to go to a place where I am not heartily welcome. So I resolved to go to Francie Smails, the herd's, and from him get direction and provender.

The hut was built in a little turn of the water beneath a high bank. I knocked at the door, not knowing whether some soldier might not come to it, for the dragoons were quartered everywhere. But no one came save Francie himself, a great godly man who lived alone, and cared not for priest or woman. He cried aloud when he saw me.

"Come in by," he says, "come in quick; this is nae safe place the noo."

And he pulled me in to the hearth, where his midday meal was standing. With great goodwill he bade me share it, and afterward, since he had heard already of my case and had no need for enlightenment thereon, he gave me his good counsel.

"Ye maunna bide a meenute here," he said. "I'll pit up some cauld braxy and bread for ye, for it's a' I have at this time o' year. Ye maun get oot o' the glen and aff to the hills wi' a' your pith, for some o' Maister Gilbert's men passed this morn on their way to Barns, and they'll be coming back afore nicht. So ye maun be aff, and I counsel ye to tak the taps o' the Wormel and syne cross the water abune the Crook, and gang ower by Talla and Fruid to the Cor. Keep awa' frae the Clyde hills for ony sake, for they're lookit like my ain hill i' the lambin' time; and though it's maybe safer there for ye the noo, in a wee it'll be het eneuch. But what are ye gaun to dae? Ye'll be makkin' a try to win ower the sea, for ye canna skip aboot on thae hills like a paitrick for ever."

"I do not know," said I; "I have little liking for another sea journey, unless all else is hopeless. I will bide in the hills as long as I can, and I cannot think that the need will be long. For I have an inkling, and others besides me, that queer things will soon happen."

"Guid send they dae," said he, and I bade him goodbye. I watched him striding off to the hill, and marvelled at the life he led. Living from one year's end to another on the barest fare, toiling hard on the barren steeps for a little wage, and withal searching his heart on his long rounds by the canon of the book of God. A strange life and a hard, yet no man knows what peace may come out of loneliness.

Now had I taken his advice I should have been saved one of the most vexatious and hazardous episodes of my life. But I was ever self-willed, and so, my mind being set on going down the Holmes vale, I thought nothing of going near the Wormel, but set off down the bridle way, as if I were a king's privy councillor and not a branded exile.

I kept by the stream till patches of fields began to appear and the roofs of the little clachan. Then I struck higher up on the hillside and kept well in the shade of a little cloud of birk trees which lay along the edge of the slope. It was a glorious sunny day, such as I scarce ever saw surpassed, though I have seen many weathers under many skies. The air was as still and cool as the first breath of morning, though now it was mid-afternoon. All the nearer hills stood out clear-lined and silent; a bird sang in the nigh thicket; sheep bleated from the meadow; and around the place hung the low rustle of the life of the woods.

Soon I came to a spot above the bend of the water near the house called Holmes Mill. There dwelt my very good friend the miller, a man blessed with as choice a taste in dogs as ever I have seen, and a great Whig to boot—both of which tricks he learned from a westland grandfather. Lockhart was his name, and his folk came from the Lee near the town of Lanark to this green Tweedside vale. From the steading came the sound of life. There was a great rush of water out of the dam. Clearly the miller was preparing for his afternoon's labours. The wish took me strongly to go down and see him, to feel the wholesome smell of grinding corn, and above all to taste his cakes, which I had loved of old. So without thinking more of it, and in utter contempt for the shepherd's warning, I scrambled down, forded the water, and made my way to the house.

Clearly something was going on at the mill, and whatever it was there was a great to-do. Sounds of voices came clear to me from the mill-door, and the rush of water sang in my ears. The miller has summoned his family to help him, thought I: probably it is the lifting of the bags to the mill-loft.

But as I came nearer I perceived that it was not a mere chatter of friendly tongues, but some serious matter. There was a jangling note, a sound as of a quarrel and an appeal. I judged it wise therefore to keep well in the shadow of the wall and to go through the byre and up to the loft by an old way which I remembered—a place where one could see all that passed without being seen of any.

And there sure enough was a sight to stagger me. Some four soldiers with unstrung muskets stood in the court, while their horses were tethered to a post. Two held the unhappy miller in their stout grip, and at the back his wife and children were standing in sore grief. I looked keenly at the troopers, and as I looked I remembered all too late the shepherd's words. They were part of my cousin's company, and one I recognized as my old friend Jan Hamman of the Alphen road and the Cor Water.

The foremost of the soldiers was speaking.

"Whig though ye be," said he, "ye shall hae a chance of life. Ye look a man o' muscle. I'll tell ye what I'll dae. Turn on the sluice and set the mill-wheel gaun, and then haud on to it; and if ye can keep it back, your life ye shall hae, as sure as my name's Tam Gordon. But gin ye let it gang, there'll be four bullets in ye afore ye're an hour aulder, and a speedy meeting wi' your Maker. Do ye wish to mak the trial?"

Now the task was hopeless from the commencement, for big though a man be, and the miller was as broad and high a man as one may see in Tweeddale, he had no chance against a millrace. But whether he thought the thing possible or whether he wanted to gain a few minutes' respite from death, the man accepted and took off his coat to the task. He opened the sluice and went forward to the wheel.

Soon the water broke over with a rush and the miller gripped a spoke like grim death. For a moment the thing was easy, for it takes some minutes for the water to gather body and force. But in a little it became harder, and the sinews on his bare arms began to swell with the strain. But still he held on valiantly and the wheel moved never an inch. Soon the sweat began to run over his face, and the spray from the resisted water bespattered him plentifully. Then the strain became terrible. His face grew livid as the blood surged to his head, his eyeballs stood out, and his arms seemed like to be torn from their sockets. The soldiers, with the spirit of cruel children, had forgot their weapons, and crowded round the wheel to see the sport.

I saw clearly that he could not hold out much longer, and that unless I wanted to see a friend butchered before my eyes I had better be up and doing. We were two resolute men: I armed and with considerable skill of the sword, he unarmed, but with the strength of a bull. The most dangerous things about our opponents were their weapons. Could I but get between them and their muskets we could make a fight for it yet.

Suddenly as I looked the man failed. With a sob of weariness he loosed his hold. The great wheel caught the stream and moved slowly round, and he almost fell along with it. His tormentors laughed cruelly, and were about to seize him and turn back, when I leaped from the loft window like some bolt from a clear sky.

My head was in a whirl and I had no thought of a plan. I only knew that I must make the venture at any cost, or else be branded in my soul as a coward till my dying day.

I fell and scrambled to my feet.

"Lockhart," I cried, "here man, here. Run."

He had the sense to see my meaning. Exhausted though he was, he broke from his astonished captors, and in a moment was beside me and the weapons.

As I looked on them I saw at a glance where our salvation lay.

"Take these two," I said, pointing to the muskets. "I will take the others."

I cleared my throat and addressed the soldiers. "Now, gentlemen," said I, "once more the fortune of war has delivered you into my hands. We, as you perceive, command the weapons. I beg your permission to tell you that I am by no means a poor shot with the musket, and likewise that I do not stick at trifles, as doubtless my gallant friend Master Hamman will tell you."

The men were struck dumb with surprise to find themselves thus taken at a disadvantage. They whispered for a little among themselves. Doubtless the terrors of my prowess had been so magnified by the victims in the last escapade to cover their shame that I was regarded as a veritable Hector.

"Are you the Laird of Barns?" said the leader at last, very politely. I bowed.

"Then give us leave to tell you that we are nane sae fond o' the Captain, your cousin," said he, thinking to soothe me.

"So much the worse for my cousin," said I.

"Therefore we are disposed to let you gang free."

"I am obliged," said I, "but my cousin is my cousin, and I tolerate no rebellion toward one so near of blood. I am therefore justified, gentlemen, in using your own arms against you, since I have always believed that traitors were shot."

At this they looked very glum. At last one of them spoke up.

"If ye'll tak the pick o' ony yin o' us and stand up to him wi' the sma'-sword, we'll agree to bide by the result."

"I thank you," I said, "but I am not in the mood for sword exercise. However, I will be merciful, though that is a quality you have shown little of. You shall have your horses to ride home on, but your arms you shall leave with me as a pledge of your good conduct. Strip, gentlemen."

And strip they did, belt and buckler, pistol and sword. Then I bade them go, not without sundry compliments as one by one they passed by me. There were but four of them, and we had all the arms, so the contest was scarcely equal. Indeed, my heart smote me more than once that I had not accepted the fellow's offer to fight. The leader spoke up boldly to my face.

"Ye've gotten the better o' us the noo, but it'll no be long afore ye're gettin' your kail through the reek, Master John Burnet."

At which I laughed, and said 'twas a truth I could not deny.

CHAPTER XII

I WITNESS A VALIANT ENDING

They had scarce been five minutes gone when the full folly of my action dawned upon me. To be sure I had saved the miller from death, but I had now put my own neck in the noose. I had given them a clue to my whereabouts: more, I had brought the hunt down on lower Tweeddale, which before had been left all but unmolested. It was war to the knife. I could look for no quarter, and my only chance lay in outstripping my pursuers. The dragoons dared not return immediately, for four unarmed soldiers would scarcely face two resolute men, fully armed and strongly posted. They could only ride to Abington, and bring the whole hornet's nest down on my head.

Another reflection had been given to me by the sight of these men. In all likelihood Gilbert had now returned and resumed the chief command of the troop, for otherwise there would have been no meaning in the journey to Dawyck and lower Tweeddale which these fellows had taken. And now that my dear cousin had come back I might look for action. There was now no more any question of foolish and sluggish soldiery to elude, but a man of experience and, as I well knew, of unmatched subtlety.

The miller was for thanking me on his knees for my timely succour, but I cut him short. "There is no time," said I, "for long thanks. You must take to the hills, and if you follow my advice you will hold over to the westlands where your friends are, and so keep the pursuit from Tweeddale, which little deserves it. As for myself, I will go up the Wormel, and hide among the scrogs of birk till evening. For the hills are too bare and the light too clear to travel by day. To be kenspeckle in these times is a doubtful advantage."

So without more ado I took myself off, crossed the fields with great caution, and going up a little glen in the side of the big hill, found a very secure hiding-place in the lee of a craig among a tangle of hazel bushes. I had taken some food with me from the mill to provision me during my night journey, and now I used a little of it for my afternoon meal. In this place I lay all the pleasant hours after midday till I saw the shadows lengthen and the sun flaming to its setting over the back of Caerdon. Then the cool spring darkness came down on the earth, and I rose and shook myself and set out on my way.

I shall ever remember that long night walk over hill and dale to the Cor Water for many reasons. First, from the exceeding beauty of the night, which was sharp and yet not cold, with a sky glittering with stars, and thin rails of mist on the uplands. Second, from the exceeding roughness of the way, which at this season of the year makes the hills hard for walking on. The frost and snow loosen the rocks, and there are wide stretches of loose shingle, which is an accursed thing to pass over. Third, and above all, for the utter fatigue into which I fell just past the crossing of Talla. The way was over the Wormel and the Logan Burn hills as far as Kingledoors. There I forded Tweed and struck over the low ridge to Talla Water. Thence the way was straight, and much the same as that which I had come with Marjory. But now I had no such dear escort, and I give my word that my limbs ached and my head swam oftentimes ere I reached my journey's end.

It was early dawning when I crossed the last ridge and entered the Cor Water valley. There was no sign of life in that quiet green glen, a thing that seemed eerie when one thought that somewhere in the hill in front men were dwelling. I found that short as had been my absence I had almost forgotten the entrance to the cave, and it was not without difficulty that I made out the narrow aperture in the slate-grey rock and entered.

In the first chamber all was dark, which struck me with astonishment, since at five o'clock on a good spring day folk should be stirring. But all was still, and it was not till I had come into the second chamber, which, as I have told, was the largest in the place, that there were any signs of life. This was illumined in the first instance by a narrow crevice in the rock which opened into a small ravine. The faint struggling light was yet sufficient to see with, and by its aid I made out the old man who had spoken with me on that first night of my journey.

He was sitting alone, staring before him as is the way with the blind, but at the sound of my steps he rose slowly to his feet. One could see that the natural acuteness of his hearing was little impaired by years. I paused at the threshold and he stood listening; then he sank back in his seat as if convinced it was no enemy.

"Come in, John Burnet," he said, "I ken you well. How have you fared since you left us? I trust you have placed the maid in safe keeping."

I had heard before of that marvellous quickness of perception which they possess who have lost some other faculty; but I have never yet had illustration of it. So I was somewhat surprised, as I told him that all as yet was well, and that my lady was in good hands.

"It is well," said he; "and, Master Burnet, I fear you have come back to a desolate lodging. As ye see, all are gone and only I am left. Yestreen word came that that had happened which we had long expected. There was once a man among us whom we cast out for evil living. He has proved the traitor and there is no more safety here. They scattered last night, the puir feckless folk, to do for themselves among the moors and mosses, and I am left here to wait for the coming of the enemy."

"Do you hold your life so cheap," I cried, "that you would cast it away thus? I dare not suffer you to bide here. I would be a coward indeed if I did not take care of you."

A gleam of something like pleasure passed over his worn face. But he spoke gravely. "No, you are too young and proud and hot in blood. You think that a strong arm and a stout heart can do all. But I have a work to do in which none can hinder me. My life is dear to me, and I would use it for the best. But you, too, are in danger here; the soldiers may come at any moment. If you go far to the back you'll find a narrow way up which you can crawl. It'll bring ye out on the back side of the hill. Keep it well in mind, lad, when the time comes. But now, sit ye down, and give us your crack. There's a heap o' things I want to speir at ye. And first, how is auld Veitch at Smitwood? I once kenned him well, when he was a young, 'prising lad; but now I hear he's sair fallen in years and gien ower to the pleasures of eating and drinking."

I told him all of the Laird of Smitwood that I could remember.

"It would be bonny on the muirs o' Clyde in this weather. I havena been out o' doors for mony a day, but I would like fine to feel the hill wind and the sun on my cheek. I was aye used wi' the open air," and his voice had a note of sorrow.

To me it seemed a strange thing that in the presence of the most deadly danger this man should be so easy and undisturbed. I confess that I myself had many misgivings and something approaching fear. There was no possibility of escape now, for though one made his way out of the cave when the soldiers came, there was little hiding on the bare hillside. This, of course, was what the old man meant when he bade me stay and refused to go out of doors. It was more than I could do to leave him, but yet I ever feared the very thought of dying like a rat in a hole. My forebodings of my death had always been of an open, windy place, with a drawn sword and more than one man stark before me. It was with downcast eyes that I waited for the inevitable end, striving to commend my soul to God and repent of my past follies.

Suddenly some noise came to the quick ear of the old man, and he stood up quivering.

"John," he cried, "John, my lad, gang to the place I told ye. Ye'll find the hole where I said it was, and once there ye needna fear."

'Twas true I was afraid, but I had given no signs of fear, and he had little cause to speak of it. "Nay," I said haughtily, "I will not move from your side. It were a dastardly thing to leave you, and the two of us together may account for some of the fiends. Besides, there is as much chance of life here as out on the braeside, where a man can be seen for miles."

He gripped me fiercely by the arm so that I almost cried out for pain, and his voice came shrill and strange. "Gang where I tell ye, ye puir fool. Is this a time for sinfu' pride o' honour or mettle? Ye know not what evil is coming upon these men. Gang quick lest ye share it also."

Something in his voice, in his eye, overcame me, and I turned to obey him.

As I went he laid his hand on my head. "The blessing o' man availeth little, but I pray God that He be ever near you and your house, and that ye may soon hae a happy deliverance from all your afflictions. God bless and keep ye ever, and bring ye at the end to His ain place."

With a heart beating wildly between excitement and sorrow I found the narrow crevice, and crept upward till I came to the turning which led to the air. Here I might have safely hid for long, and I was just on the point of going back to the old man and forcing him to come with me to the same place of refuge, when I heard the sound of men.

From my vantage-ground I could see the whole cave clearly

and well. I could hear the noise of soldiers fumbling about the entrance, and the voice of the informer telling the way. I could hear the feet stumbling along the passage, the clink of weapons, and the muttered words of annoyance; and then, as I peered warily forth, I saw the band file into the cave where sat the old man alone. It was as I expected: they were some twenty men of my cousin's company, strangers to me for the most; but what most occupied my thoughts was that Gilbert was not with them.

"By God, they're off," said the foremost, "and nothing left but this auld dotterel. This is a puir haul. Look you here, you fellow," turning to the guide, "you are a liar and a scoundrel, and if your thick hide doesna taste the flat o' my sword ere you're five hours aulder, my name's no Peter Moriston. You," this to the old man, "what's your name, brother well-beloved in the Lord?"

At their first coming he had risen to his feet and taken his stand in the middle of the cave, by the two great stone shafts which kept up the roof, for all the world like the pillars in some mighty temple. There he stood looking over their heads at something beyond, with a strange, almost pitying smile, which grew by degrees into a frown of anger.

"Ye've come here to taunt me," said he, "but the Lord has prepared for you a speedy visitation. Puir fools, ye shall go down quick to the bottomless pit like Korah, Dathan, and Abiram, and none shall be left to tell the tale of you. Ye have led braw lives. Ye have robbed the widow and the fatherless, ye have slain by your numbers men ye darena have come near singly, ye have been the devil's own braw servants, and, lads, ye'll very soon get your wages. Ye have made thae bonny lands o' Tweedside fit to spew ye forth for your wickedness. And ye think that there is nae jealous God in heaven watching ower you and your doings and biding His time to repay. But, lads, ye're wrang for yince. The men ye thocht to take are by this time far from ye, and there is only one left, an auld feckless man, that will no bring muckle credit to ye. But God has ordained that ye shall never leave here, but mix your banes to a' time wi' the hillside stanes. God hae pity on your souls, ye that had nae pity on others in your lives."

And even as I watched, the end came, sudden and awful.

Stretching out his great arms, he caught the two stone shafts and with one mighty effort pushed them asunder. I held my breath with horror. With a roar like a world falling the roof came down, and the great hillside sank among a ruin of rock. I was blinded by dust even in my secure seat, and driven half-mad with terror and grief. I know not how I got to the air, but by God's good providence the passage where I lay was distinct from the cave, and a rift in the solid rock. As it was, I had to fight with falling splinters and choking dust all the way. At last—and it seemed ages—I felt free air and a glimmer of light, and with one fresh effort crawled out beneath a tuft of bracken.

And this is why at this day there is no cave at the Cor Water, nothing but the bare side of a hill strewn with stones.

When I gained breath to raise myself and look around, the sight was strange indeed. The vast cloud of dust was beginning to settle and the whole desolation lay clear. I know not how to tell of it. It was like some battlefield of giants of old time. Great rocks lay scattered amid the beds of earth and shingle, and high up toward the brow of the hill one single bald scarp showed where the fall had begun.

A hundred yards away, by his horse's side, gazing with wild eyes at the scene, stood a dragoon, doubtless the one whom the ill-fated company had set for guard. I hastened toward him as fast as my weak knees would carry me, and I saw without surprise that he was the Dutchman, Jan Hamman, whom I had already met thrice before. He scarce was aware of my presence, but stood weeping with weakness and terror, and whimpering like a child. I took him by the shoulder and shook him, until at last I had brought him back to his senses, and he knew me.

"Where are they gone?" and he pointed feebly with his finger to the downfall.

"To their own place," I said shortly. "But tell me one word. Where is your captain, Gilbert Burnet, that he is not with you today?"

The man looked at me curiously.

"He is gone on another errand, down Tweed toward Peebles."

Then I knew he was seeking for Marjory high and low and

would never rest till he found her.

"I will let you go," said I to the man, "that you may carry the tidings to the rest. Begone with you quick. I am in no mood to look on such as you this day."

The man turned and was riding off, when he stopped for one word. "You think," he said, "that I am your enemy and your cousin's friend, and that I serve under the captain for his own sweet sake. I will tell you my tale. Three years ago this Captain Gilbert Burnet was in Leyden, and there also was I, a happy, reputable man, prosperous and contented, with the prettiest sweetheart in all the town. Then came this man. I need not tell what he did. In a year he had won over the silly girl to his own desires, and I was a broken man for evermore. I am a servant in his company who worked my fall. Remember then that the nearer I am to Gilbert Burnet the worse it will fare with him." And he rode off, still pale and shivering with terror.

I mused for some time with myself. Truly, thought I, Gilbert has his own troubles, and it will go hard with him if his own men turn against him. And I set it down in my mind that I would do my best to warn him of the schemes of the foreigner. For though it was my cousin's own ill-doing that had brought him to this, and my heart burned against him for his villainy, it was yet right that a kinsman should protect one of the house against the plots of a foreign soldier.

CHAPTER XIII

I RUN A NARROW ESCAPE FOR MY LIFE

This was in April, and now the summer began to grow over the land. The days grew longer and the air more mild, the flowers came out on the hills, little mountain pansies and eyebright and whortleberry, and the first early bells of the heath; the birds reared their young and the air was all filled with the cries of them; and in the streams the trout grew full fleshed and strong.

And all through these days I lay close hid in the wilds, now in one place, now in another, never wandering far from Tweeddale. My first hiding was in a narrow glen at the head of the Polmood Burn in a place called Glenhourn. It was dark and lonesome, but at first the pursuit was hot after me and I had no choice in the matter. I lived ill on the fish of the burn and the eggs of wildfowl, with what meal I got from a shepherd's house at the burnfoot. These were days of great contemplation, of long hours spent on my back in the little glen of heather, looking up to the summer sky and watching the great clouds fleeting athwart it. No sound came to disturb me, I had few cares to vex me; it was like that highest state of being which Plotinus spoke of, when one is cumbered not with the toils of living. Here I had much grave communing with myself on the course of my life, now thinking upon it with approval, now much concerned at its futility. I had three very warring moods of mind. One was that of the scholar, who would flee from the roughness of life. This came upon me when I thought of the degradation of living thus in hiding, of sorting with unlettered men, of having no thoughts above keeping body and soul together. The second was that of my father's son, whose pride abhorred to flee before any man and hide in waste places from low-born soldiers and suffer others to devour his patrimony. But the third was the best, and that which I ever sought to keep with me. It was that of the gentleman and cavalier who had a wide, good-humoured outlook upon the world, who cared not for houses and lands, but sought above all things to guard his honour and love. When this was on me I laughed loud at all my misfortunes, and felt brave to meet whatever might come with a light heart.

In this place I abode till near the middle of the month of June. Twice I had gone to the cairn on Caerdon and left a letter, which I wrote with vast difficulty on fragments of paper which I had brought with me, and received in turn Marjory's news. She was well and in cheerful spirits, though always longing for my return. The days passed easily in Smitwood, and as none came there she was the better hidden. I wrote my answers to these letters with great delight of mind, albeit much hardship. The ink in the inkhorn which I had always carried with me soon became dry, and my pen, which I shaped from a curlew's feather, was never of the best. Then after the writing came the long journey, crouching in thickets, creeping timorously across the open spaces, running for dear life down the hill slopes, until I came at length to the cairn on Caerdon and hid the letter 'neath the grey stones.

But about mid June I bethought me that I had stayed long enough in that lonely place and resolved to move my camp. For one thing I wished to get nearer Barns, that I might be within reach of my house for such provisions as I required. Also there were signs that the place was no longer safe. Several times of late I had heard the voice of soldiers on the moors above my hiding, and at any moment a chance dragoon might stray down the ravine. So late one evening about midsummer I bade adieu to the dark Glenhourn, and took off across the wild hills to the lower vale of Tweed.

The place I chose was just at the back of Scrape between that mountain and a height called the Pykestone hill. It was a stretch of moss hags and rough heather, dry as tinder at this time, but, as I well knew, in late autumn and winter a treacherous flow. Thither I had been wont to go to the duck shooting in the months of November and February, when great flocks of mallard and teal settled among the pools. Then one has to look well to his feet, for if he press on eager and unthinking, he is like to find himself up to the armpits. But if he know the way of the thing, and walk only on the tufted rushes and strips of black peat, he may have the finest sport that I know of. Here then I came, for the place was high and lonesome, and with a few paces I could come to the top of the Little Scrape and see the whole vale of Tweed from Drummelzier to Neidpath. I had the less fear of capture, for the place was almost impassable for horses; also it was too near the house of Barns to be directly suspected, and the country below it was still loyal and with no taint of whiggery.

Here then I settled myself, and made a comfortable abode in a dry burn channel, overarched with long heather. The weather was unusually warm and dry, the streams were worn to a narrow thread of silver trickling among grey stones, and the hot sun blazed from morn to night in a cloudless sky. The life, on the whole, was pleasing. There was cold water from a mossy well hard by when I was thirsty. As for food, I made at once an expedition to the nearest cottage on my lands, where dwelt one Robin Sandilands, who straightway supplied all my needs and gave me much useful information to boot. Afterwards he came every second day to a certain part of the hill with food, which he left there for me to take at my convenience. Hence the fare was something better than I had had in my previous hiding-place. Also it was a cheerful life. Up there on the great flat hilltop, with nothing around me but the sky and the measureless air, with no noises in my ear but the whistle of hill birds, with no view save great shoulders of mountain, the mind was raised to something higher and freer than of old. Earthly troubles and little squabbles and jealousies seemed of less account. The more than Catonian gravity of these solemn uplands put to flight all pettiness and small ambition. It has been an immemorial practice in our borderland that those of ruined fortunes, broken men, should take to the hills for concealment, if need be, and in any case for satisfaction. Verily twelve months of that pure air would make a gentleman of a knave, and a hero of the most sordid trader.

However, ere June had merged in July, I found myself in want of some companion to cheer my solitude. I would have given much for some like-minded fellow-wayfarer, but since that might not be had I was fain to content myself with a copy of Plotinus, which I had got with all the difficulty in the world from the house of Barns. It happened on a warm afternoon, when, as I lay meditating as was my wont in the heather, a great desire came upon me for some book to read in. Nothing would do but that I must straightway set out for Barns at the imminent peril of my own worthless life. It was broad daylight; men were working in the fields at the hay; travellers were passing on the highway; and for all I knew soldiers were in the house. But with a mad recklessness I ventured on the quest, and, entering the house boldly, made my way to the library and was choosing books. Then I was startled by the noise of approaching steps, and seizing hastily the first volume I could lay hands on, set off for the hills at the top of my speed. The visit had renewed old recollections, and I spent a bitter evening reflecting upon my altered position.

But toward the end of August, when the nights grew longer and the sunsets stormy, a change came over the weather. The Lammas floods first broke the spell of the drought, and for three clear days the rain fell in torrents, while I lay in my hole, cold and shivering. On the fourth I made an incursion down to my own lands to the cottage of my ally. There I heard evil news. The soldiers had come oftener than of late and the hunt had been renewed. The reward on my head had been doubled, and with much sorrow I had the news that the miller of Holmes Mill had been taken and carried to Edinburgh. In these dim grey days my courage fell, and it took all the consolations of philosophy, all my breeding and manly upbringing to sustain my heart. Also it became more difficult to go at the three weeks' end to the cairn on Caerdon with the letter for Marjory.

It was, as far as I remember, for I did not keep good count, on the second day of September, that I set out for Caerdon on my wonted errand. I had had word from Robin Sandilands that the countryside was perilous; but better, I thought, that I should run into danger than that my lady should have any care on my account. So I clapped the written letter in my pocket and set out over the hills in a fine storm of wind.

I went down the little burn of Scrape, which flows into Powsail about a mile above the village of Drummelzier. Had I dared I would have crossed the lowlands just above the village, and forded Tweed at Merlin's Grave, and so won to Caerdon by Rachan and Broughton. But now it behoved me to be cautious, so I kept straight over the hills; and, striking the source of a stream called Hopecarton, followed it to where it joined the river in the Mossfennan haughs. All the time the wind whistled in my teeth and the sharpest of showers bit into my skin. I was soon soaked to the bone, for which I cared very little, but pushed steadfastly on through the rapidly rising waters of Tweed, and scrambled up the back of the Wormel. Here it was stiff work, and my legs ached mightily ere I reached the top and flung myself on the damp heather to spy out the Holmes valley.

All seemed quiet. The stream, now changed from its clearness to a muddy brown, was rolling on its way through the fields of stubble. The few houses smoked in peace. The narrow road was empty of travellers. Without hesitation I ran down the slopes, caring not to look circumspectly to the left and right.

I had not run far till something before me brought me to a halt and sent me flat among the grass. Just below the house of Quarter, coming from the cover of the trees, were half a score of soldiers.

My first thought was to turn back and give up the project. My second, to go forward and find a way to cross the valley. Happily the foliage was still there, the heath was still long, the grass was dense: a man might succeed in crossing under cover.

With a beating heart I crawled through the heather to the rushes beside a little stream. This I followed, slowly, painfully, down to the valley, looking sharply at every bare spot, and running for dear life when under cover of bank or brae. By-and-by I struck the road, and raised myself for a look. All was quiet. There was no sign of any man about, nothing but the beating of the rain and the ceaseless wind. It was possible that they had gone down the vale, and were by this time out of sight. Or may be they had gone up the water on their way to the moors of Clyde. Or still again they might have gone back to the house of Quarter, which they doubtless loved better than the rainy out-of-doors. In any case they were not there, and nothing hindered me from making a bold sally across the open.

I rose and ran through the cornfield, cleaving my way amid the thick stubble. The heavy moisture clung to my soaked clothes and the sweat ran over my face and neck, but I held straight on till I gained the drystone dyke at the other side and scrambled across it. Here I fell into the stream and was soaked again, but the place was not deep and I was soon through. Now I was direct beneath the house, but somewhat under the cover of the trees; and still there was no sign of man or beast. I began to think that after all my eyes had deceived me, and taken nowt for dragoons. Such a trick was not impossible; I had found it happen before at the winter's shooting. With this pleasing hope I straightened my

207

back and ran more boldly up the planting's side till I gained the moorlands above. Here I paused for a second to enjoy my success and look back upon the house.

Suddenly something cracked in the thicket, and a voice behind me cried, "Stop. Gang another step and I fire." So the cup of safety was dashed from my lips at the very moment of tasting it.

I did not obey, but dashed forward to the high moors with all my speed. It was conceivable that the men were unmounted and their horses stabled, in which case I might get something of a lead. If not, I should very soon know by the clear convincing proof of a shot in my body.

My guess was right, and it was some little time ere I heard the cries of pursuers behind me. I had made straight for the top of the ridge where the ground was rough for horses, and I knew that they could not follow me with any speed. I was aye a swift runner, having been made long and thin in the shanks and somewhat deep-chested. I had often raced on the lawn at Barns with my cousin for some trifling prize. Now I ran with him again, but for the prize of my own life.

I cannot tell of that race, and to this day the thought of it makes my breath go faster. I only know that I leaped and stumbled and ploughed my way over the hillside, sobbing with weariness and with my heart almost bursting my ribs. I never once looked behind, but I could measure the distance by the sound of their cries. The great, calm face of Caerdon was always before me, mocking my hurry and feebleness. If I could but gain the ridge of it, I might find safety in one of the deep gullies. Now I had hope, now I had lost it and given myself up for as good as dead. But still I kept on, being unwilling that any one should see me yield, and resolving that if I needs must die I would stave it off as long as might be.

In the end, after hours—or was it minutes?—I reached the crest and crawled down the other side. They were still some distance behind and labouring heavily. Near me was a little ravine in which a slender trickle of floodwater fell in a long cascade. I plunged down it, and coming to a shelter of over-lapping rock crawled far in below, and thanked God for my present safety.

Then I remembered my errand and my letter. I clapped my hand to my pocket to draw it forth. The place was empty—the letter was gone. With a sickening horror I reflected that I had dropped it as I ran, and that my enemies must have found it.

CHAPTER XIV

I FALL IN WITH STRANGE FRIENDS

I lay there, still with fright and anxiety, while the wind roared around my hiding-place, and the noise of the horses' feet came to my ears. My first thought was to rush out and meet them, engage the company and get the letter back by force. But a moment's reflection convinced me that this was equal to rushing on my death. There was nothing for it but to bide where I was, and pray that I might not be discovered.

The noise grew louder, and the harsh voices of the men echoed in the little glen. I lay sweating with fear and I know not what foreboding, as I heard the clatter of hooves among the slates and the heavy tread of those who had dismounted and were searching every tuft of heather. I know not to this day how I escaped. It may be that their eyes were blinded with mist and rain; it may be that my hiding-place was securer than I thought, for God knows I had no time to choose it; it may be that their search was but perfunctory, since they had got the letter; it may be that they thought in their hearts that I had escaped over the back of Caerdon and searched only to satisfy their leader. At any rate, in a little all was still, save for the sound of distant voices, and with vast caution and great stiffness of body I drew myself from the hole.

I have rarely felt more utterly helpless and downcast. I had saved my skin, but only by a hairbreadth, and in the saving of it I had put the match to my fortunes. For that luckless letter gave the man into whose hands it might fall a clue to Marjory's whereabouts. It is true that the thing was slight, but still it was there, and 'twas but a matter of time till it was unravelled. All was up with me. Now that I was thus isolated on Caerdon and the far western ridges of the Tweedside hills I could have little hope of getting free, for to return to safety I must cross either Holmes Water, which was guarded like a street, or the lower Tweed, which, apart from the fact that it was in roaring flood, could no more be passed by me than the gates of Edinburgh. But I give my word it was not this that vexed me; nay, I looked forward to danger, even to capture, with something akin to hope. But the gnawing anxiety gripped me by the throat that once more my poor lass would be exposed to the amenities of my cousin, and her easy, quiet life at Smitwood shattered for ever. An unreasoning fit of rage took me, and I dashed my foot on the heather in my hopeless vexation. I cursed every soldier, and damned Gilbert to the blackest torments which my heart could conjure.

But rage, at the best, is vain and I soon ceased. It was indeed high time that I should be bestirring myself. I could not stay where I was, for in addition to being without food or decent shelter, I was there on the very confines of the most dangerous country. Not two miles to the north from the place where I lay the hills ceased, and the low-lying central moorlands succeeded, which, as being a great haunt of the more virulent Whigs, were watched by many bands of dragoons. If my life were to be saved I must get back once more to the wild heights of the upper Tweed.

I climbed the gully and, keeping lower down the hill, made for the mountain, named Coulter Fell, which is adjacent to Caerdon. I know not why I went this way, save through a fantastic idea of getting to the very head of the Holmes Water and crossing there. Every step I took led me into more perilous ground, for it took me farther to the westward. It was my sole chance, and in the teeth of the wind I wrestled on over the long heather and grey sklidders, slipping and stumbling with weariness and dispirit. Indeed I know not if anything could have sustained me save the motto of my house, which came always to my mind. *Virescit vulnere virtus!* The old proud saw cheered my heart wondrously. I shall not shame my kin, said I to myself; it shall never be said that misfortune did aught to one of my name save raise his valour.

When I reached the head of the ridge I thought that the way was clear before me and that I had outdistanced my pursuers. I stood up boldly on the summit and looked down on the Holmes Water head. The next minute I had flung myself flat again and was hastening to retrace my steps.

For this was what I saw. All up the stream at irregular intervals dragoons were beating the heather in their quest for me. Clearly they thought that I had made for the low ground. Clearly, also, there was no hope of escape in that quarter.

With a heavy heart I held along the bald face of the great Coulter Fell. I know no more heartless mountain on earth than that great black scarp, which on that day flung its head far up into the mist. The storm, if anything, had increased in fury. Every now and then there came a burst of sharp hail, and I was fain to shelter for a moment by lying on the earth. Very circumspectly I went, for I knew not when through the wall of mist a gleam of buff coats or steel might meet me. In such a fashion, half creeping, half running, I made my way down the hills which flank the Coulter Water, and came at length to the range of low heights which look down upon Biggar and the lowlands of Clyde.

I struggled to the top and looked over into the misty haughs. The day was thick, yet not so thick that I could not see from this little elevation the plain features of the land below. I saw the tall trees of Coulter House and the grey walls and smoking chimney. Beyond was the road, thick in mud, and with scarce a traveller. All seemed quiet, and as I looked a wild plan came into my head. Why should I not go through the very den of the lion? What hindered me from going down by the marsh of Biggar and the woods of Rachan, and thence to my hiding-place? It was the high roads that were unwatched in these days, and the byways which had each their sentinel.

But as I looked again the plan passed from my mind. For there below, just issuing from the gateway of Coulter House, I saw a man on horseback, and another, and still another. I needed no more. A glance was sufficient to tell me their character and purport. Gilbert verily had used his brains to better advantage than I had ever dreamed of. He had fairly outwitted me, and the three airts of north and south and west were closed against me.

There still remained the east, and thither I turned. I was shut in on a triangle of hill and moorland, some three miles in length and two in breadth. At the east was the spur of hill at the foot of the Holmes Water and above the house of Rachan. If I went thither I might succeed in crossing the breadth of the alley and win to the higher hills. It was but a chance, and in my present weakness I would as soon have laid me down on the wet earth and gone to sleep. But I forced myself to go on, and once more I battled with the snell weather.

I do not very well remember how I crossed the Kilbucho glen, and stumbled through the maze of little streams and sheep drains which cover all the place. I had no more stomach for the work than an old dog has for coursing. To myself I could give no reason for my conduct save a sort of obstinacy which would not let me give in. At a place called Blendewing I lay down on my face and drank pints of water from the burn—a foolish action, which in my present condition was like to prove dangerous. In the pine wood at the back of the shieling I laid me down for a little to rest, and when once more I forced myself to go on, I was as stiff as a ship's figurehead. In this state I climbed the little hills which line the burn, and came to the limit of the range above the place called Whiteslade.

It was now about two o'clock in the afternoon, and the storm, so far from abating, grew every moment in fierceness. I began to go hot and cold all over alternately, and the mist-covered hills were all blurred to my sight like a boy's slate. Now, by Heaven, thought I, things are coming at last to a crisis. I shall either die in a bog-hole, or fall into my cousin's hands before this day is over. A strange perverted joy took possession of me. I had nothing now to lose, my fortunes were so low that they could sink no farther; I had no cause to dread either soldier or weather. And then my poor silly head began to whirl, and I lost all power of anticipation.

To this day I do not know how I crossed the foot of the Holmes valley—for this was what I did. The place was watched most

212

jealously, for Holmes Mill was there, and the junction of the roads to the upper Tweed and the moors of Clyde. But the thing was achieved, and my next clear remembrance is one of crawling painfully among the low birk trees and cliffs on the far side of the Wormel. My knees and hands were bleeding, and I had a pain in my head so terrible that I forgot all other troubles in this supreme one.

It was now drawing towards evening. The grey rain clouds had become darker and the shadows crept over the sodden hills. All the world was desert to me, where there was no shelter. Dawyck and Barns were in the hands of the enemy. The cave of the Cor Water was no more. I had scarce strength to reach my old hiding-place in the hags above Scrape, and if I did get there I had not the power to make it habitable. A gravelled and sanded couch with a heathery roof is pleasant enough in the dry weather, but in winter it is no better than a bog-hole.

Nevertheless I slid down the hill as best I could and set myself to crossing the valley. It was half filled with water pools which the flood had left, and at the far side I saw the red-raging stream of Tweed. I remember wondering without interest whether I should ever win over or drown there. It was a matter of little moment to me. The fates had no further power to vex me.

But ere I reached the hill foot I saw something which gave me pause, reckless though I had come to be. On the one hand there was a glimpse of men coming up the valley—mounted men, riding orderly as in a troop. On the other I saw scattered soldiers dispersing over the haughland. The thought was borne in upon me that I was cut off at last from all hope of escape. I received the tidings with no fear, scarcely with surprise. My sickness had so much got the better of me that though the heavens had opened I would not have turned my head to them. But I still staggered on, blindly, nervelessly, wondering in my heart how long I would keep on my feet.

But now in the little hollow I saw something before me, a glimpse of light, and faces lit by the glow. I felt instinctively the near presence of men. Stumbling towards it I went, groping my way as if I were blindfold. Then some great darkness came over my brain and I sank on the ground.

CHAPTER XV

THE BAILLIES OF NO MAN'S LAND

The next period in my life lies still in my mind like a dream. I have a remembrance of awaking and an impression of light, and strange faces, and then all was dark again. Of those days my memory is a blank; there is nothing but a medley of sickness and weariness, light and blackness, and the wild phantoms of a sick man's visions.

When I first awoke to clear consciousness, it was towards evening in a wild glen just below the Devil's Beef Tub at the head of the Annan. I had no knowledge where I was. All that I saw was a crowd of men and women around me, a fire burning and a great pot hissing thereon. All that I heard was a babel of every noise, from the discordant cries of men to the yelping of a pack of curs. I was lying on a very soft couch made of skins and cloaks in the shade of a little roughly made tent. Beyond I could see the bare hillsides rising shoulder on shoulder, and the sting of air on my cheek told me that it was freezing hard. But I was not cold, for the roaring fire made the place warm as a baker's oven.

I lay still and wondered, casting my mind over all the events of the past that I could remember. I was still giddy in the head, and the effort made me close my eyes with weariness. Try as I would I could think of nothing beyond my parting from Marjory at Smitwood. All the events of my wanderings for the moment had gone from my mind.

By-and-by I grew a little stronger, and bit by bit the thing returned to me. I remembered with great vividness the weary incidents of my flight, even up to its end and my final sinking. But still the matter was no clearer. I had been rescued, it was plain, but by whom, when, where, why? I lay and puzzled over the thing with a curious mixture of indifference and interest.

Suddenly a face looked in upon me, and a loud strident voice cried out in a tongue which I scarce fully understood. The purport of its words was that the sick man was awake and looking about him. In a minute the babel was stilled, and I heard a woman's voice giving orders. Then some one came to me with a basin of soup.

"Drink, lad," said she; "ye've had a geyan close escape, but a' is richt wi' ye noo. Tak this and see how ye feel."

The woman was tall and squarely built like a man; indeed, I cannot think that she was under six feet. Her face struck me with astonishment, for I had seen no woman for many a day since Marjory's fair face, and the harsh commanding features of my nurse seemed doubly strange. For dress she wore a black hat tied down over her ears with a kerchief, and knotted in gipsy fashion beneath her chin. Her gown was of some dark blue camlet cloth, and so short that it scarce reached her knees, though whether this fashion was meant for expedition in movement or merely for display of gaudy stockings, I know not. Certainly her stockings were monstrously fine, being of dark blue flowered with scarlet thread, and her shoon were adorned with great buckles of silver. Her outer petticoat was folded so as to make two large pockets on either side, and in the bosom of her dress I saw a clasp-knife.

I drank the soup, which was made of some wild herbs known only to the gipsy folk, and lay back on my couch.

"Now, sleep a wee, lad," said the woman, "and I'll warrant ye'll be as blithe the morn as ever."

I slept for some hours, and when I awoke sure enough I felt mightily strengthened. It was now eventide and the camp-fire had been made larger to cook the evening meal. As I looked forth I could see men squatting around it, broiling each his own piece of meat in the ashes, while several cauldrons sputtered and hissed on the chains. It was a wild, bustling sight, and as I lay and watched I was not sorry that I had fallen into such hands. For I ever loved to see new things and strange ways, and now I was like to have my fill.

They brought me supper, a wild duck roasted and coarse home-made bread, and a bottle of very tolerable wine, got I know not whence unless from the cellars of some churlish laird. I ate heartily, for I had fasted long in my sickness, and now that I was recovered I had much to make up.

Then the woman returned and asked me how I did. I told her, "Well," and thanked her for her care, asking her how I had been rescued and where I was. And this was the tale she told me.

She was of the clan of the Baillies, the great gipsies of Tweeddale and Clydesdale, offshoots of the house of Lamington, and proud as the devil or John Faa himself. They had been encamped in the little haugh at the foot of the Wormel on the night of my chase. They had heard a cry, and a man with a face like death had staggered in among them and fainted at their feet. Captain William Baillie, their leader, of whom more anon, had often been well-entreated at Barns in my father's time, and had heard of my misfortunes. He made a guess as to who I was and ordered that I should be well looked after. Meantime the two companies of soldiers passed by, suspecting nothing, and not troubling to look for the object of their search, who all the while was lying senseless beneath a gipsy tent. When all was safe they looked to my condition, and found that I was in a raging fever with cold and fatigue. Now the gipsies, especially those of our own countryside, are great adepts in medicine, and they speedily had all remedies applied to me. For three weeks I lay ill, delirious most of the time, and they bore me with them in a litter in all their wanderings. I have heard of many strange pieces of generosity, but of none more strange than this—to carry with much difficulty a helpless stranger over some of the roughest land in Scotland, and all for no other motive than sheer kindliness to a house which had befriended them of old. With them I travelled over the wild uplands of Eskdale and Ettrick, and with them I now returned to the confines of Tweeddale.

"The Captain's awa' the noo," added she, "but he'll be back the morn, and blithe he'll be to see ye so weel."

And she left me and I slept again till daybreak.

When I awoke again it was morning, just such a day as the last, frosty and clear and bright. I saw by the bustle that the camp was making preparations for starting, and I was so well recovered that I felt fit to join them. I no longer needed to be borne like a child in a litter, but could mount horse and ride with the best of them.

I had risen and gone out to the encampment and was watching the activity of man and beast, when one advanced from the throng toward me. He was a very tall, handsome man, dark in face as a Spaniard, with fine curling moustaches. He wore a broad blue bonnet on his head, his coat was of good green cloth and his small-clothes of black. At his side he carried a sword and in his belt a brace of pistols, and save for a certain foreign air in his appearance he seemed as fine a gentleman as one could see in the land. He advanced to me and made me a very courtly bow, which I returned as well as my still aching back permitted me.

"I am glad you are recovered, Master John Burnet," said he, speaking excellent English, though with the broad accent which is customary to our Scots lowlands. "Permit me to make myself known to you. I have the honour to be Captain William Baillie at your service, captain of the Ragged Regiment and the Egyptian Guards." All this he said with an air as if he were his Majesty's first general.

At the mention of his name I called to mind all I had heard of this extraordinary man, the chief of all the south-country gipsies, and a character as famous in those days and in those parts as Claverhouse or my lord the King. He claimed to be a bastard of the house of Lamington, and through his mother he traced descent, also by the wrong side of the blanket, to the Gay Gordons themselves. Something of his assumed gentrice showed in his air and manner, which was haughty and lofty as any lord's in the land. But in his face, among wild passions and unbridled desires, I read such shrewd kindliness that I found it in my heart to like him. Indeed, while the tales of his crimes are hawked at every fair, the tales of his many deeds of kindness are remembered in lonely places by folk who have cause to bless the name of Baillie. This same captain had indeed the manners of a prince, for when he bought anything he was wont to give his purse in payment, and indignantly refuse to receive change of any kind. It is only fair to add that the money was not got by honest means, but by the plunder of the rich and churlish. Yet though his ways were roguish his acts were often most Christian-like and courteous, and there were worse men in higher places than this William Baillie. More, he was reputed the best swordsman in all Scotland, though, as being barred from the society of men of birth and education, his marvellous talent was seldom seen. He was of the most indomitable courage and self-possession, and even in the court, when on his trial, he spoke fearlessly to his judges. I do not seek to defend him; but to me and mine he did a good deed and I would seek to be grateful. When long afterwards he was killed in a brawl in the alehouse of Newarthill, I heard the tidings with sorrow, for he died bravely, though in an ignoble quarrel.

He now informed me with great civility of the incidents of my escape and sickness. When I thanked him he waved me off with a great air.

"Tut, tut," said he, "that is a small matter between gentlefolk. I have often had kindness from your father, and it is only seemly that I should do my best for the son. Besides, it is not my nature to see a man so sore pressed by the soldiery and not seek to deliver him. It is a predicament I have often been in myself."

A horse was brought for me, a little wiry animal, well suited for hills and sure-footed as a goat. When I felt myself in the saddle once again, even though it were but a gipsy hallion, I was glad; for to one who has scrambled on his own feet for so many days, a horse is something like an earnest of better times. Captain Baillie bade me come with him to another place, where he showed me a heap of gipsy garments. "It is necessary," said he, "if you would ride with us that you change your appearance. One of your figure riding among us would be too kenspeckle to escape folk's notice. You must let me stain your face, too, with the juice which we make for our bairns' cheeks. It will wash off when you want it, but till that time it will be as fast as sunburn." So taking a crow's feather and dipping it in a little phial, he with much skill passed it over my whole face and hands. Then he held a mirror for me to look, and lo and behold, I was as brown as a gipsy or a Barbary Moor. I laughed loud and long at my appearance, and when I was bidden put on a long green coat, the neighbour of the captain's, and a pair of stout untanned riding-boots, I swear my appearance was as truculent as the roughest tinker's.

218

Thus accoutred we set out, the men riding in front in pairs and threes, the women behind with donkeys and baggage shelties. It was a queer picture, for the clothing of all was bright-coloured, and formed a strange contrast with the clear, chilly skies and the dim moor. There was no fear of detection, for apart from the company that I was with, my disguise was so complete that not even the most vigilant dragoon could spy me out. Our road was that which I had already travelled often to my own great weariness—down Tweed by Rachan and the Mossfennan haughs. I had no guess at our destination; so when at Broughton we turned to the westward and headed through the moss towards the town of Biggar, I was not surprised. Nay, I was glad, for it brought me nearer to the west country and Smitwood, whither I desired to go with the utmost speed. For with my returning health my sorrows and cares came back to me more fiercely than ever. It could not be that my cousin should find out Marjory's dwelling-place at once, for in the letter there was no clear information: only indefinite hints, which in time would bring him there. The hope of my life was to reach the house before him and rescue my love, though I had no fixed plan in my mind and would have been at a sore loss for aid. Nevertheless, I was quieter in spirit, and more hopeful. For, after all, thought I, though Gilbert get my lass, he yet has me to deal with, and I will follow him to the world's end ere I let him be.

CHAPTER XVI

HOW THREE MEN HELD A TOWN IN TERROR

It was towards evening, a dark autumn evening, that we came near the little town of Biggar. The place lies on a sandy bank raised from the wide moss which extends for miles by the edge of the sluggish stream. It is a bleak, desolate spot, where whaups and snipe whistle in the back streets, and a lane, which begins from the causeway, may end in a pool of dark moss-water. But the street is marvellous broad, and there, at the tail of the autumn, is held one of the greatest fairs in the lowlands of Scotland, whither hawkers and tinkers come in hordes, not to speak of serving-men and serving-lasses who seek hire. For three days the thing goes on, and for racket and babble it is unmatched in the countryside.

We halted before the entrance to the town on a square of dry land in the midst of the waterway. The weather had begun to draw to storm, and from the east great masses of rolling cloud came up, tinged red and yellow with the dying sun. I know not how many the gipsies were, but, with women and children, they were not less in number than ninety or a hundred. They had with them a great quantity of gear of all kinds, and their animals were infinite. Forbye their horses and asses, they had dogs and fowls, and many tamed birds which travelled in their company.

One sight I yet remember as most curious. A great long man, who rode on a little donkey, had throughout the march kept an ugly raven before him, which he treated with much kindness; and on dismounting lifted off with assiduous care. And yet the bird had no beauty or accomplishment to merit his goodwill. It is a trait of these strange people that they must ever have something on which to expend their affection; and while the women have their children, the men have their pets. The most grim and quarrelsome tinker will tend some beast or bird and share with it his last meal.

When the camp was made, the fire lit, and the evening meal prepared, the men got out their violins and bagpipes, and set themselves to enliven the night with music. There in the clear space in front of the fire they danced to the tunes with great glee and skill. I sat beside the captain and watched the picture, and in truth it was a pleasing one. The men, as I have said, were for the most part lithe and tall, and they danced with grace. The gipsy women, after the age of twenty, grow too harsh-featured for beauty, and too manly in stature for elegance. But before that age they are uniformly pretty. The free, open-air life and the healthy fare makes them strong in body and extraordinarily graceful in movement. Their well-formed features, their keen, laughing black eyes, their rich complexions, and, above all, their masses of coal-black hair become them choicely well. So there in the ruddy firelight they danced to the quavering music, and peace for once in a while lay among them.

Meanwhile I sat apart with William Baillie, and talked of many things. He filled for me a pipe of tobacco, and I essayed a practice which I had often heard of before but never made trial of. I found it very soothing, and we sat there in the bield of the tent and discoursed of our several wanderings. I heard from him wild tales of doings in the hills from the Pentlands to the Cumberland fells, for his habits took him far and wide in the country. He told all with the greatest indifference, affecting the air of an ancient Stoic, to whom all things, good and evil alike, were the same. Every now and then he would break in with a piece of moralizing, which he delivered with complete gravity, but which seemed to me matter for laughter, coming, as it did, after some racy narrative of how he vanquished Moss Marshall at the shieling of Kippertree, or cheated the alewife at Newbigging out of her score.

On the morrow all went off to the fair save myself, and I was left with the children and the dogs. The captain had judged it better that I should stay, since there would be folk there from around Barns and Dawyck, who might penetrate my disguise and spread the tidings. Besides, I knew naught of the tinker trade, and should have been sorely out of place. So I stayed at home and pondered over many things, notably my present predicament. I thought of all my old hopes and plans—to be a scholar and a gentleman of spirit, to look well to my lands and have a great name in the countryside, to study and make books, maybe even to engage in Parliament and State business. And what did I now? Travelling in disguise among tinkers, a branded man, with my love and my lands in danger, nay all but lost. It was this accursed thought that made the bitterest part of my wanderings.

I was in such a mood when a servant came from a farmhouse near to get one of the gipsies to come and mend the kitchen pot. As I was the only one left, there was nothing for it but to go. The adventure cheered me, for its whimsicality made me laugh, and laughter is the best antidote to despair. But I fared very badly, for,

221

when I tried my 'prentice hand at the pot, I was so manifestly incapable that the goodwife drove me from the place, calling me an idle sorner, and a lazy vagabond, and many other well-deserved names. I returned to the camp with my ears still ringing from her cuff, but in a more wholesome temper of mind.

The greater part of the others returned at the darkening, most with well-filled pockets, though I fear it was not all come by honestly; and a special feast was prepared. That gipsy meal was of the strangest yet most excellent quality. There was a savoury soup made of all kinds of stewed game and poultry, and after that the flesh of pigs and game roasted and broiled. There was no seasoning to the food save a kind of very bitter vinegar; for these people care little for salt or any condiment. Moreover, they had the strange practice of grating some hard substance into their wine, which gave it a flavour as if it had been burned in the mulling.

The meal was over and I was thinking of lying down for the night, when William Baillie came back. I noted that in the firelight his face was black with anger. I heard him speak to several of his men, and his tone was the tone of one who was mastering some passion. By-and-by he came to where I sat and lay down beside me.

"Do you wish to pleasure me?" he said shortly.

"Why, yes," I answered; "you have saved my life and I would do all in my power to oblige you, though I fear that just now my power is little."

"It's a' I want," said he, leaving his more correct speech for the broad Scots of the countryside. "Listen, and I'll tell ye what happened the day at the fair. We tinker-folk went aboot our business, daein' ill to nane, and behavin' like dacent peaceable, quiet-mainnered men and women. The place was in a gey steer, for a heap o' Wast-country trash was there frae the backs o' Straven and Douglasdale, and since a' the godly and reputable folk thereaways hae ta'en to the hills, nane but the rabble are left. So as we were gaun on canny and sellin' our bits o' things and daein' our bits o' jobs, the drucken folk were dancin' and cairryin' on at the other end. By-and-by doun the fair comes a

222

drucken gairdener, one John Cree. I ken him weel, a fosy, black-hertit scoondrel as ever I saw. My wife, whom ye ken, for it was her that lookit after ye when ye were sick, was standin' at the side when the man sees her. He comes up to her wi' his leerin', blackgairdly face, and misca's her for a tinkler and a' that was bad, as if the warst in our tribe wasna better than him.

"Mary, she stands back, and bids him get out or she wad learn him mainners.

"But he wadna tak a tellin'. 'Oh, ho, my bawbee joe,' says he, 'ye're braw and high the day. Whae are you to despise an honest man? A wheen tinkler doxies!' And he took up a stane and struck her on the face.

"At this a' our folk were for pittin' an end to him there and then. But I keepit them back and bade them let the drucken fule be. Syne he gaed awa', but the folks o' the fair took him up, and we've got nocht but ill words and ill tongue a' day. But, by God, they'll pay for it the morn." And the captain looked long and fiercely into the embers.

"I hae a plan," said he, after a little, "and, Master Burnet, I want ye to help me. The folk o' the fair are just a wheen scum and riddlings. There are three o' us here, proper men, you and myself and my son Matthew. If ye will agree to it we three will mount horse the morn and clear oot that fair, and frichten the folk o' Biggar for the next twal'month."

"What would you do?" said I.

"I hae three suits," he said, "o' guid crimson cloth, which I got frae my grandfather and have never worn. I have three braw horses, which cam oot o' England three year syne. If the three o' us mount and ride through the fair there will be sic a scattering as was never heard tell o' afore i' the auld toun. And, by God, if that gairdener-body doesna gang wud wi' fricht, my name's no William Baillie."

Now, I do not know what madness prompted me to join in this freak. For certain it was a most unbecoming thing for a man of birth to be perched on horseback in the company of two reckless tinkers to break the king's peace and terrify his Majesty's lieges of Biggar. But a dare-devil spirit—the recoil from the morning's

223

despondency—now held me. Besides, the romance of the thing took me captive; it was as well that a man should play all the parts he could in the world; and to my foolish mind it seemed a fine thing that one who was a man of birth and learning should not scruple to cast in his lot with the rough gipsies.

So I agreed readily enough, and soon after went to sleep with weariness, and knew nothing till the stormy dawn woke the camp.

Then the three of us dressed in the crimson suits, and monstrously fine we looked. The day was dull, cloudy, and with a threat of snow; and the massing of clouds which we had marked on the day before was now a thousandfold greater. We trotted out over the green borders of the bog to the town, where the riot and hilarity were audible. The sight of the three to any chance spectator must have been fearsome beyond the common. William Baillie, not to speak of his great height and strange dress, had long black hair which hung far below his shoulders, and his scarlet hat and plume made him look like the devil in person. Matthew, his son, was something smaller, but broad and sinewy, and he sat his horse with an admirable grace. As for myself, my face was tanned with sun and air and the gipsy dye, my hair hung loosely on my shoulders in the fashion I have always worn it, and I could sit a horse with the best of them.

When we came near the head of the street we halted and consulted. The captain bade us obey him in all and follow wherever he went, and above all let no word come from our mouth. Then we turned up our sleeves above the elbows, drew our swords and rode into the town.

At the first sight of the three strange men who rode abreast a great cry of amazement arose, and the miscellaneous rabble was hushed. Then, in a voice of thunder, the captain cried out that they had despised the gipsies the day before, and that now was the time of revenge. Suiting the action to the word he held his naked sword before him, and we followed at a canter.

I have never seen so complete a rout in my life. Stalls, booths, tables were overturned, and the crowd flew wildly in all directions. The others of the tribe, who had come to see the show, looked on from the back, and to the terrified people seemed like fresh assailants. I have never heard such a hubbub as rose from the fleeing men and screaming women. Farmers, country-folk, ploughmen mingled with fat burgesses and the craftsmen of the town in one wild rush for safety. And yet we touched no one, but kept on our way to the foot of the street, with our drawn swords held stark upright in our hands. Then we turned and came back; and lo! the great fair was empty, and wild, fearful faces looked at us from window and lane.

Then, on our second ride, appeared at the church gate the minister of the parish, a valiant man, who bade us halt.

"Stop," said he, "you men of blood, and cease from disturbing the town, or I will have you all clapt in the stocks for a week."

Then the captain spoke up and told him of the wrong and insult of the day before.

At this the worthy man looked grave. "Go back to your place," he said, "and it shall be seen to. I am wae that the folk of this town, who have the benefit of my ministrations, set no better example to puir heathen Egyptians. But give up the quarrel at my bidding. 'Vengeance is mine, and I will repay,' saith the Lord."

"But haply, sir," said I, "as Augustine saith, we may be the Lord's executors." And with this we turned and rode off, leaving the man staring in open-mouthed wonder.

CHAPTER XVII

OF THE FIGHT IN THE MOSS OF BIGGAR

When we came to the camping-place it was almost deserted. The people had all gone to the fair, and nothing was to be seen save the baggage and the children. The morning had grown wilder and a thin snow was falling, the earnest of a storm. The mist was drawing closer and creeping over the boglands. I minded an old saying of Tam Todd's, "Rouk's snaw's wraith," and I looked for a wild storm with gladness, for it would keep the dragoon gentry at home and prohibit their ill-doing.

225

But just in front at the border of the fog and at the extremity of the dry land, the captain saw something which made him draw up his horse sharply and stare. Then he turned to Matthew, and I saw that his face was flushed. "Ride a' your pith, man," he said, "ride like the wind to the toun, and bid our folk hurry back. Nae words and be off." And the obedient son galloped away to do his bidding.

He gripped me by the arm and pulled me to the side. "Ye've guid een," he said. "D'ye see that ower by the laigh trees?" I looked and looked again and saw nothing.

"Maybe no," he said, "ye haena gipsy een; but in half an' oor we'll a' ken what it means. It's the Ruthvens wi' the Yerl o' Hell. I ken by their red-stripit breeks and their lang scythe-sticks. Ye maun ken that for lang we've had a bluid feud wi' that clan, for the Baillies are aye gentrice and hae nae trokins wi' sic blagyird tinklers. We've focht them yince and twice and aye gotten the better, and noo I hear that little Will Ruthven, that's him that they ca' the Yerl o' Hell for his deevilry, has sworn to fecht us till there's no a Baillie left to keep up the name. And noo they've come. 'Faith there'll be guid bluid spilt afore thae wratches learn their lesson."

The news struck me with astonishment and a little dismay. I had often longed to see a battle, and now I was to be gratified. But what a battle! A fight between two bloodthirsty gipsy clans, both as wild as peat reek, and armed with no more becoming weapons than bludgeons, cutlasses, and scythe-blades. More, the event would place me in a hard position. I could not fight. It would be absurd that I should be mixed up in their mellays. But the man at my side expected me to aid him. I owed my life to him and with these folk gratitude is reckoned one of the first of the virtues. To refuse William Baillie my help would be to offer him the deepest unkindness. Yet I dismissed the thought at once as preposterous. I could no more join the fight than I could engage in a pothouse or stable brawl. There was nothing for it but to keep back and watch the thing as a silent spectator.

In a little I began to see the band. It would number, as I guessed, some hundred and ten, with women and children. The captain, as he looked, grew fierce with excitement. His dark eyes blazed, and his brow and cheeks were crimson. Ever and anon he looked anxiously in the direction of the town, waiting for the help which was to come. As the foe came nearer he began to point me out the leaders. "There's Muckle Will," he cried, "him wi' the lang bare shanks, like the trams o' a cairt. He's the strongest and langest man frae the Forth to Berwick. My God, but it'll be a braw fellow that can stand afore him. And there's Kennedy himsel', that sonsy licht-coloured man. They say he's the best wi' the sma'-sword in a' Nithsdale, but 'faith, he's me to reckon wi' the day. And there's that bluidy deil, Jean Ruthven, whae wad fecht ony man in braid Scotland for a pund o' 'oo'. She's as guid as a man, and they say has been the death o' mair folk than the Yerl himsel'. But here come our ain men. Come on, Rob and Wat, and you, Mathy, gang wide to the right wi' some. It's a great day this. Nae wee cock fecht, but a muckle lang deidly battle." And the man's face was filled with fierce joy.

Meanwhile both the forces had taken up their position opposing one another, and such a babel of tinkler yells arose that I was deafened. Each side had their war-cry, and, in addition, the women and children screamed the most horrible curses and insults against the enemy. Yet the battle was not arrayed in haphazard fashion, but rather with some show of military skill. The stronger and bigger men of the clan with the captain himself were in the middle. On the right and left were their sons, with a more mixed force, and behind all the women were drawn up like harpies, looking wellnigh as fierce and formidable as the men.

"You'll come to the front wi' me, Maister Burnet," said the captain. "Ye're a guid man o' your hands, and we'll need a' we can get i' the middle."

"No," said I, "I cannot."

"Why?" he asked, looking at me darkly.

"Tut, this is mere foolery. You would not have me meddling in such a fray?"

"You think we're no worthy for you to fecht wi'," he said quietly, "we, that are as guid as the best gentlemen i' the land, and have saved your life for ye, Master John Burnet. Weel, let it be.

227

I didna think ye wad hae dune it." Then the tinker blood came out. "Maybe you're feared," said he, with an ugly smile.

I turned away and made no answer; indeed, I could trust myself to make none. I was bitterly angry and unhappy. All my misfortunes had drawn to a point in that moment. I had lost everything. A fatal mischance seemed to pursue me. Now I had mortally offended the man who had saved my life, and my outlook was drear enough.

I had been looking the other way for a second, and when I turned again the fray had begun. The Earl, with a cutlass, had engaged the captain, and the wings, if one may call them by so fine a word, had met and mingled in confusion. But still it was not a general mellay, but rather a duel between the two principal combatants. The little man with the short sword showed wondrous agility, and leaped and twisted like a tumbler at a fair. As for the Baillie, he had naught to do but keep him at a distance, for he was both better armed and better skilled. As he fought he let his eye wander to the others and directed them with his voice. "Come up, Mathy lad," he would cry. "Stand weel into them, and dinna fear the lasses." Then as he saw one of his own side creeping behind the Earl to strike a back blow, he roared with anger and bade him keep off. "Let the man be," he cried. "Is't no eneuch to hae to fecht wi' blagyirds that ye maun be blagyirds yoursel'?"

But in a little the crowd closed round them and they had less room for play. Then began a grim and deadly fight. The townspeople, at the word of the tinkers fighting, had left the fair and come out in a crowd to witness it. It was a sight such as scarce a man may see twice in his lifetime. The mist rolled low and thick, and in the dim light the wild, dark faces and whirling weapons seemed almost monstrous. Now that death had begun there was little shouting; nothing was heard save the rattle of the cutlasses, and a sort of sighing as blows were given and received. The bolder of the women and boys had taken their place, and at the back the little children and young girls looked on with the strangest composure. I grew wild with excitement, and could scarce keep from yelling my encouragements or my warnings;

but these had no thought of uttering a word. Had there been a cloud of smoke or smell of powder it would have seemed decent, but this quietness and clearness jarred on me terribly. Moreover, the weapons they fought with were rude, but powerful to inflict deep wounds, being all clubs and short swords and scythe-blades fixed on poles. Soon I saw ghastly cuts on the faces of the foremost and blood splashes on brow and cheek. Had there been horses it would not have seemed so cruel, for there would have been the rush and trample, the hot excitement of the charge and the recoil. But in the quiet, fierce conflict on foot there seemed nothing but murder and horror.

At first the battle was fought in a little space, and both sides stood compact. But soon it widened, and the wings straggled out almost to the edge of the bog water. The timid onlookers fled as from the plague, and I, in my station in the back, was in doubts whether I should bide still or no. But in front of me were the girls and children, and I thought if I could do naught else I might see to them. For the horns of the Ruthven's company (which was the larger) threatened to enclose the Baillies, and cut off their retreat. Meantime the mist had come down still closer, and had given that decent covering which one desires in a bloody fray. I could scarce see the front ranks of our opponents, and all I could make out of my friends was the captain's bright sword glinting as he raised it to the cut.

But that soon happened which I had feared. For the Ruthvens, enclosing our wings, had all but surrounded us, since the captain had put the weaker there and left all the more valiant for the centre. Almost before I knew I saw one and another great gipsy rush around and make towards the girls who had not joined the battle. In that moment I saw the bravest actions which it has ever been my lot to see. For these slim, dark-haired maids drew knives and stood before their assailants, as stout-hearted as any soldiers of the King's guard. The children raised a great cry and huddled close to one another. One evil-looking fellow flung a knife and pierced a girl's arm. . . . It was too much for me. All my good resolutions went to the wind, and I forgot my pride in my anger. With a choking cry I drew my sword and rushed for him.

229

After that I know not well what happened. I was borne back by numbers, then I forced my way forward, then back I fell again. At first I fought calmly, and more from a perverted feeling of duty than any lust of battle. But soon a tinker knife scratched my cheek, and a tinker bludgeon rattled sorely against my head. Then I grew very hot and angry. I saw all around me a crowd of fierce faces and gleaming knives, and I remember naught save that I hurled myself onward, sword in hand, hewing and slashing like a devil incarnate. I had never drawn blade in overmastering passion before, and could scarce have thought myself capable of such madness as then possessed me. The moss-trooping blood, which I had heired from generations of robber lords, stood me in good stead. A reckless joy of fight took me. I must have seemed more frantic than the gipsies themselves.

At last, I know not how, I found my way to the very front rank. I had been down often, and blood was flowing freely from little flesh wounds, but as yet I was unscathed. There I saw William Baillie laying about him manfully, though sore wounded in the shoulder. When he saw me he gave me a cry of welcome. "Come on," he cried, "I kenned ye wad think better o't. We've muckle need o' a guid man the noo." And he spoke the truth, for anything more fierce and awesome than the enemy I have never seen. The Earl of Hell was mangled almost to death, especially in the legs and thighs. The flesh was clean cut from the bone of one of his legs, and hung down over the ankles, till a man grew sick at the sight. But he was whole compared with his daughter, Jean Ruthven, who was the chief's wife. Above and below her bare breasts she was cut to the bone, and so deep were the gashes that the movement of her lungs, as she breathed, showed between the ribs. The look of the thing made me ill with horror. I felt giddy, and almost swooned; and yet, though white as death, she fought as undauntedly as ever. I shunned the sight, and strove to engage her husband alone, the great fair-haired man, who, with no weapon but a broken cutlass, had cleared all around him. I thrust at him once and again, and could get no nearer for the swing of his mighty arms. Then the press behind, caused I suppose by the Ruthvens at the back, drove me forward, and there was nothing

230

for it but to grapple with him. Our weapons were forced from our hands in the throng, and, with desperate energy, we clutched one another. I leaped and gripped him by the neck, and the next instant we were both down, and a great, suffocating wave of men pressed over us. I felt my breath stop, and yet I kept my grip and drew him closer. All was blackness around, and even as I clutched I felt a sharp thrill of agony through my frame, which seemed to tear the life from my heart, and I was lost to all.

CHAPTER XVIII

SMITWOOD

That I am alive to this day and fit to write this tale I owe to William Baillie. He saw me fall and the press close over me, and, though hard beset himself, he made one effort for my salvation. "Mathy," he cried, "and Tam and Andra, look after your man and get him up," and then once more he was at death-grips. They obeyed his bidding as well as they might, and made a little ring in the centre around me, defending me with their weapons. Then they untwined us and lifted me, senseless as I was, to the light and air. As for Kennedy, he was heavy and florid, and his life had gone from him at the first overthrow.

I do not know well how I was got from the fray. I think I would have been killed, had not the Ruthvens, whose best men were wounded, given way a little after. Their trick of surrounding the enemy, by spreading wide their wings, was not wise and met with sorry success. For it left their middle so weak, that when Kennedy and the valiant Earl had been mastered, there remained no resistance. So when my friends made haste to push with me to the back they found their path none so hard. And after all that there was nothing but confusion and rout, the one side fleeing with their wounded, the other making no effort to pursue, but remaining to rest and heal their hurts.

As I have said, I was unconscious for some time, and when I revived I was given a sleeping draught of the gipsies' own making. It put me into a profound slumber, so that I slept for the rest of the day and night and well on to the next morning. When I awoke I was in a rough cart drawn by two little horses, in the centre of the troop who were hurrying westward. I felt my body with care and found that I was whole and well. A noise still hummed in my head and my eyes were not very clear, as indeed was natural after the fray of the day before. But I had no sore hurt, only little flesh scratches, which twinged at the time, but would soon be healed.

But if this was my case it was not that of the rest of the band. The battle had been like all such gipsy fights—very terrible and bloody, but with no great roll of dead. Indeed, on our side we had not lost a man, and of the enemy Kennedy alone had died, who, being a big man and a full-blooded, had been suffocated in his fall by the throng above him. It was just by little that I had escaped the same fate, for we two at the time had been in death-grips, and had I not been thin and hardy of frame, I should have perished there and then. But the wounds were so terrible on both sides that it scarce seemed possible that many could ever recover. Yet I heard, in after days, that not one died as a result of that day's encounter. Even the Earl of Hell and his daughter Jean recovered of their wounds, and wandered through the country for many years. But the sight of the folk around me on the march was very terrible. One man limped along with a great gash in his thigh in which I could have placed my open hand. Another had three fingers shorn off, and carried his maimed and bandaged hand piteously. Still a third lay in the cart with a breast wound which gaped at every breath, and seemed certain ere long to bring death. Yet of such strength and hardihood was this extraordinary people that they made light of such wounds, and swore they would be healed in three weeks' time. Perhaps this tenacity of life is due in some part to their excellent doctoring, for it is certain that these folk have great skill in medicaments, and with herb concoctions, and I know not what else, will often perform wondrous cures. I have my own case as an instance—where first I was restored from a high fever by their skill, and, second, from a fit of suffocation far more deadly.

232

The storms of the day before had passed and a light frost set in which made the air clear and sharp and the countryside plain even to the distances. We were passing under the great mass of Tintock—a high, hump-backed hill which rises sheer from the level land and stands like a mighty sentinel at the gate of the upper Clyde valley. We travelled slow, for the wounded were not fit to bear much speed, and many of the folk walked to suffer the horses to be yoked to the carts After a little I espied the captain walking at the side, with his shoulder and cheeks bandaged, but as erect and bold as ever. Seeing that I was awake, he came over beside me and asked very kindly after my health. His tenderness toward me was as great as if I had been his son or nearest blood-kin. When I told him that I was well and would get down and walk beside him, he said that that would be a most unbecoming thing and would never do, but that he would have a horse brought me from the back. So a horse was brought, an excellent black, with white on its fetlocks, and I mounted; and despite some little stiffness, found it much to my liking.

He told of the end of the battle and all the details of its course. He was in the highest spirits, for though his folk were sore wounded, they had yet beaten their foes and sent them off in a worse plight than themselves. Above all he was full of a childish vanity in his own prowess. "Saw you that muckle hullion, Kennedy, Master Burnet? I gied him some gey licks, but I never could win near eneuch to him for his muckle airm. You grippit him weel, and he'll no bother us mair. His ain folk'll keep quiet eneuch aboot the affair, I'll warrant, so we may look to hear naething mair aboot it. I'm thinkin', tae, that the Yerl'll no seek to come back my gate again. I tried to mak him fecht like a gentleman, but faith, he wadna dae't. He just keepit cuttin' at my shanks till I was fair wild, and I telled some o' our ain folk to tak the legs frae the body wi' a scythe-stick. I haena seen a fecht like it since that at the Romanno Brig fifteen years syne, atween the Faas and the Shawes, when they were gaun frae Haddington to Harestane. Our folk wad hae been in't if they hadna come't up ower late and juist seen the end o't."

"And will you have no further trouble about the matter?" I

asked. "If justice gets word of it will you not suffer?"

"Na, na," he said, with conviction, "nae fear. Thae things dinna come to the lugs o' the law. We didna dae ony harm except to oorsels, and there's nane o' us killed save Kennedy whae dee'd a naitural death, so there can be nae word aboot that. Forbye, how's the law to grip us?" And he turned on me a face full of roguish mirth which looked oddly between the bandages. "If they heard we were at Biggar Moss yae day and cam after us, afore the morn we wad be in the Douglas Muirs or the Ettrick Hills. We're kittle cattle to fash wi'. We gang slow for ordinar, but when aucht presses we can flee like a flock o' stirlins."

"Then where are you going?" I asked.

"Where, but to Lanerick," he said. "There's a fair comes on there Monday three days, and the muir is grand beddin'. I didna ask your will on the maitter, for I kenned a' places the noo were muckle the same to ye, provided they were safe and no ower far away frae the wast country."

"That's true enough," I said, thinking sadly of Marjory and my miserable plight. I had not told Baillie anything of my story, for I did not care to commit it to such ears. But I was glad that we travelled in this airt, for I had still in my heart a wild hope that by some fortunate chance I should be in time to save my love.

About midday we came to Lanark Moor, where the baggage and shelties, as well as most of the women and children, were left behind to find an encampment. As for us, we pushed on to the town to see what was doing and hear some news of the country-side. I had no fear of detection, for in my new guise I passed for the veriest gipsy in the land. I was still clothed in my suit of crimson, but the fight had made it torn in many places, and all smirched with mire and bog-water. Also, my face was not only stained with the captain's dye, but the storms and dust of the encounter had deepened its colour to the likeness of an Ethiop. I had not a rag left of gentility, save maybe the sword which still swung at my side. In this fashion I rode by Baillie's elbow in a mood neither glad nor sad, but sunk in a sort of dogged carelessness. The entrance to the town was down a steep path from the moor, for the place is built above the gorge of Clyde, yet something lower than the surrounding moorlands. Far on all sides I had a view of the wide landscape, from the rugged high hills of Tweeddale and the upper Clyde to the lowlands in the west which stretch to Glasgow and the sea.

But when we came to the town there was a great to-do, men running about briskly and talking to one another, old women and young gossiping at house and close doors, and the upper windows filled with heads. There was a curious, anxious hum throughout the air, as if some great news had come or was coming ere long. I forgot for a moment my position and leaned from the saddle to ask the cause of a man who stood talking to a woman at the causeway side. He looked at me rudely. "What for d'ye want to ken, ye blackfaced tinkler? D'ye think it'll matter muckle to you what king there is when ye're hangit?" But the woman was more gracious and deigned to give me some sort of answer. "There's word o' news," she said. "We kenna yet what it is, and some think ae thing and some anither, but a' are agreed that it'll make a gey stramash i' the land. A man cam ridin' here an hour syne and has been closeted wi' the provost ever since. Honest man, his heid'll be fair turned if there's onything wrang, for he's better at sellin' tatties than reddin' the disorders o' the state." And then the man by her side bade her hold her peace, and I rode on without hearing more.

By-and-by we came to the market-place where stands the ancient cross of Lanerick, whereat all proclamations are made for the Westlands. Straight down from it one looks on the steep braes of Kirkfieldbank and the bridge which the Romans built over the river; and even there the murmur of the great falls in Clyde comes to a man's ear. The place was thronged with people standing in excited groups, and the expression on each face was one of expectancy. Folk had come in from the country round as on errands of inquiry, and the coats of a few of the soldiery were to be discerned among the rest. But I had no fear of them, for they were of the lowlands regiment, and had no knowledge of me. The sight of us, and of myself in especial, for Baillie had changed his garb, caused some little stir in the crowd and many inquisitive looks.

235

The captain came up to me. "There's dooms little to be dune here," he cried; "the place is in sic a fever, I canna think what's gaun to happen. We may as weel gang back to the muirs and wait till things quiet doun."

"I know not either," said I, and yet all the time I knew I was lying, for I had some faint guess at the approach of great tidings, and my heart was beating wildly.

Suddenly the crowd parted at the farther end and a man on a wearied grey horse rode up toward the cross. He held a bundle of papers in his hand, and his face was red with hurry and excitement. "News," he cried hoarsely, "great news, the greatest and the best that the land has heard for many a day." And as the people surged round in a mighty press he waved them back and dismounted from his horse. Then slowly and painfully he ascended the steps of the cross and leaned for a second against the shaft to regain his breath. Then he stood forward and cried out in a loud voice that all in the market-place might hear. "I have ridden post-haste from Edinbro' with the word, for it came only this morn. James Stewart has fled from the throne, and William of Orange has landed in the South and is on his way to London. The bloody house has fallen and the troubling of Israel is at an end."

At that word there went through the people a sound which I shall never forget as long as I live—the sigh of gratitude for a great deliverance. It was like a passing of a wind through a forest, and more terrible to hear than all the alarums of war. And then there followed a mighty shout, so loud and long that the roofs trembled, and men tossed bonnets in air and cried aloud and wept and ran hither and thither like madmen. At last the black cloud of the persecution had lifted from their land, and they were free to go and tell their kinsmen in hiding that all danger was gone for ever.

As for myself, what shall I say? My first feeling was one of utter joy. Once more I was free to go whither I liked, and call my lands my own. Now I could overmaster my cousin and set out to the saving of my lass. Indeed I, who am a king's man through and through, and who sorrowed in after days for this very event, am ashamed to say that my only feeling at the moment was one of irrepressible gladness. No one, who has not for many months been under the shadow of death, can tell the blessedness of the release. But even as I joyed, I thought of Marjory, and the thought recalled me to my duty.

"Have you a fast horse?" I said to the captain.

He looked at me in amazement, for the tidings were nothing to him, and in my face he must have read something of my tale.

"You mean—" he said.

"Yes, yes," said I; "it means that I am now safe, and free to save another. I must be off hotfoot. Will you lend me a horse?"

"Take mine," said he, "it's at your service, and take my guidwill wi' ye." And he dismounted and held out his hand.

I mounted and took his in one parting grip. "God bless you, William Baillie, for an honest man," and I was off without another word.

It must have been a strange thing for the people of Lanerick to see me on that day, as they ran hither and thither to tell the good tidings. For, in all my savage finery, I dashed up the narrow street, scattering folk to the right and left like ducks from a pond, and paying no heed to a hundred angry threats which rang out behind me. In a little I had gained the moor, and set my face for Douglasdale and my lady. Smitwood was but ten miles away and the path to it easy. In a short hour I should be there, and then— ah, then, it could not be otherwise, it must be, that Marjory should be there to greet me, and be the first to hear my brave news.

I passed over the road I had come, and had no time to reflect on the difference in my condition from two hours agone, when abject and miserable I had plodded along it. Now all my head was in a whirl, and my heart in a storm of throbbing. The horse's motion was too slow to keep pace with my thoughts and my desires; and I found me posting on ahead of myself, eager to be at my goal. In such wild fashion I rode over the low haughlands of Clyde, and forded the river at a deep place where it flowed still and treacherous among reeds, never heeding, but swimming my horse across, though I had enough to do to land on the other side.

Then on through the benty moorlands of Douglas-side and past the great wood of the Douglas Castle. My whole nature was centred in one great desire of meeting, and yet even in my longing I had a deadly suspicion that all might not be well—that I had come too late.

Then I saw the trees and the old house of Smitwood lying solemn among its meadows. I quickened my horse to fresh exertion. Like a whirlwind he went up the avenue, making the soft turf fly beneath his heels. Then with a start I drew him up at the door and cried loudly for admittance.

Master Veitch came out with a startled face and looked upon me with surprise.

"Is Marjory within?" I cried. "Marjory! Quick, tell me!"

"Marjory," he replied, and fell back with a white face. "Do you seek Marjory? She left here two days agone to go to you, when you sent for her. Your servant Nicol went after her."

"O my God," I cried, "I am too late"; and I leaned against my horse in despair.

BOOK IV

THE WESTLANDS

CHAPTER I

I HEAR NO GOOD IN THE INN
AT THE FORDS O' CLYDE

FOR a second I was so filled with despair at Master Veitch's news that my mind was the veriest blank and I could get no thought save that bitterest of all—that my lady was gone. But with an effort I braced myself to action.

"And what of my servant Nicol?" I asked, and waited breathlessly for the answer.

"Oh, he was away on the hills seeking ye, Master Burnet. When he got no word Marjory was in sic a terror that nothing would suffice her but that he maun off to Tweeddale and seek every heather buss for word of ye. He hadna been gone twae days when half a dozen men, or maybe more, came wi' horse and a' and a letter frae you yoursel', seekin' the lass. They said that a' was peaceably settled now, and that you had sent them to fetch her to meet you at Lanerick. I hadna a thocht but that it was a' richt, and neither had the lass, for she was blithe to gang. Next day, that was yestreen, here comes your servant Nicol wi' a face as red as a sodger's coat, and when he finds Marjory gone he sits down wi' his heid atween his hands and spak never a word to any man. Then aboot the darkening he gets up and eats a dinner as though he hadna seen meat for a twal'month. Then off he gangs, and tells na a soul where he was gaun." The old man had lost all his fine bearing and correct speech, and stood by the door shivering with age and anxiety.

A whirlwind of thoughts passed through my mind. Now that the old order was at an end, Gilbert's power had gone with it, and he was likely to find it go hard with him soon. There was but one refuge for him—in his own lands in the west, where, in his great house of Eaglesham or his town dwelling in Glasgow, he might find harbourage; for the very fact that they were in the stronghold of the Whigs made them the more secure. Thither he must have gone if he had any remnant of wit, and thither he had taken

241

my lady. And with the thought my whole nature was steeled into one fierce resolve to follow him and call him to bitter account. My first fit of rage had left me, and a more deadly feeling had taken its place. This earth was too narrow a place for my cousin and me to live in, and somewhere in these Westlands I would meet him and settle accounts once and for all. It was not anger I felt, I give you my word. Nay, it was a sense of some impelling fate behind driving me forward to meet this man, who had crossed me so often. The torments of baffled love and frustrated ambition were all sunk in this one irresistible impulse.

I clambered on my horse once more, and a strange sight I must have seemed to the gaping servants and their astonished master.

"I am off on the quest," I cried, "but I will give you one word of news ere I go. The king has fled the land, and Dutch William goes to the throne." And I turned and galloped down the avenue, leaving a throng of pale faces staring after my horse's tail.

Once on the road I lashed my animal into a mad gallop. Some devil seemed to have possessed me. I had oft thought fondly in the past that my nature was not such as the wild cavaliers whom I had seen, but more that of the calm and reasonable philosopher. Now I laughed bitterly at these vain imaginings. For when a man's heart is stirred to its bottom with love or hatred all surface graces are stripped from it and the old primeval passions sway him, which swayed his father before him. But in my heart I felt a new coolness and self-possession. A desperate calm held me. In a little all things would be settled, for this was the final strife, from which one or other of the combatants would never return.

The dull November eve came on me ere I reached the Clyde. 'Twas no vantage to ford the stream, so I rode down the left bank among the damp haughs and great sedgy pools. In a little I had come to the awful gorge where the water foams over many linns and the roar of the place is like the guns of an army. Here I left the stream side and struck into the country, whence I returned again nearly opposite the town of Lanark, at the broad, shallow place in the river which folk call the Fords o' Clyde.

Here there is a clachan of houses jumbled together in a crinkle of the hill, where the way from the Ayrshire moors to the capital comes down to the bank. Here there was an inn, an indifferent place, but quiet and little frequented; and since there was naught to be got by going farther I resolved to pass the night in the house. So I rode down the uneven way to where I saw the light brightest, and found the hostel by a swinging lamp over the door. Giving my horse to a stableman, with many strict injunctions as to his treatment, I entered the low doorway and found my way to the inn parlour.

From the place came a great racket of mirth, and as I opened the door a glass struck against the top and was shivered to pieces. Inside, around the long table, sat a round dozen of dragoons making merry after their boisterous fashion. One would have guessed little indeed from their faces that their occupation was gone, for they birled at the wine as if the times were twenty years back and King Charles (whom God rest) just come anew to his throne.

I had never seen the soldiers before, but I made a guess that they were disbanded men of my cousin's company, both from their air of exceeding braggadocio which clung to all who had any relation to Gilbert Burnet, and also since there were no soldiers in this special part of the Clyde dale save his. I was in no temper for such a racket, and had there been another room in the house I should have sought it; but the inn was small and little frequented, and the accommodation narrow at the best. However, I must needs make the most of it, so shutting the door behind I sought a retired corner seat. I was still worn with my exertions of yesterday and weary with long riding, so I was blithe to get my limbs at rest.

But it was clear that three-fourths of the company were in the last state of drunkenness, and since men in liquor can never let well alone, they must needs begin to meddle with me.

"Gidden," said one, "what kind o' gentleman hae we here? I havena seen sic a fellow sin' yon steeple-jaick at Brochtoun Fair. D'ye think he wad be willin' to gie us a bit entertainment?"

Now you must remember that I still wore my suit of torn and dirty crimson, and with my stained face and long hair I must have cut a rare figure.

But had the thing gone no further than words I should never have stirred a finger in the matter, for when a man's energies are all bent upon some great quarrel he has little stomach for lesser bickerings. But now one arose in a drunken frolic, staggered over to where I sat, and plucked me rudely by the arm. "Come ower," he said "my man, and let'sh see ye dance the 'Nancy kilt her Coats.' Ye see here twelve honest sodgers whae will gie ye a penny a piece for the ploy."

"Keep your hands off," I said brusquely, "and hold your tongue. 'Twill be you that will do the dancing soon at the end of a tow on the castle hill, when King William plays the fiddle. You'll be brisker lads then."

"What," said he in a second, with drunken gravity. "Do I hear ye shpeak treason against his Majesty King James? Dod, I'll learn ye better." And he tugged at his sword, but being unable in his present state to draw it with comfort, he struck me a hard thwack over the shoulder, scabbard and all.

In a moment I was ablaze with passion. I flung myself on the fellow, and with one buffet sent him rolling below the table. Then I was ashamed for myself, for a drunken man is no more fit for an honest blow than a babe or a woman.

But there was no time for shame or aught save action. Three men—the only three who were able to understand the turn of affairs—rose to their feet in a trice, and with drawn swords came towards me. The others sat stupidly staring, save two who had fallen asleep and rolled from their seats.

I picked up my chair, which was broad and heavy and of excellent stout oak, and held it before me like a shield. I received the first man's awkward lunge full on it, and, thrusting it forward, struck him fair above the elbow, while his blade fell with a clatter on the floor. Meantime the others were attacking me to the best of their power, and though they were singly feeble, yet in their very folly they were more dangerous than a mettlesome opponent, who will keep always in front and observe the rules of the game. Indeed, it might have gone hard with me had not the door been flung violently open and the landlord entered, wringing his hands and beseeching, and close at his heels another man, very tall and thin and dark. At the sight of this second my heart gave a great bound and I cried aloud in delight. For it was my servant Nicol.

In less time than it takes to write it we had disarmed the drunken ruffians and reduced them to order. And, indeed, the task was not a hard one, for they were a vast deal more eager to sleep than to fight, and soon sank to their fitting places on the floor. Forbye they may have had some gleam of sense, and seen how perilous was their conduct in the present regiment of affairs. Then Nicol, who was an old acquaintance of the host's, led me to another room in the back of the house, where we were left in peace; and sitting by the fire told one another some fragment of our tales.

And first for his own, for I would speak not a word till he had told me all there was to tell. He had had much ado to get to Caerdon, for the hills were thick with the military, and at that wild season of the year there is little cover. When he found no letter he set off for the hiding-place above Scrape, where he knew I had been, and found it deserted. Thence he had shaped his way again to Smitwood with infinite labour and told Marjory the fruit of his errand. At this her grief had been so excessive that nothing would content her but that he must be off again and learn by hook or crook some word of my whereabouts. So began his wanderings among the hills, often attended with danger and always with hardship, but no trace of me could he find. At last, somewhere about the Moffat Water, he had forgathered with a single tinker whom he had once befriended in the days when he had yet power to help. From this man he had learned that the Baillies had with them one whom he did not know for certain, but shrewdly guessed as the Laird of Barns. With all speed he had set off on this new quest and followed me in my journey right to the moss of Biggar. Here all signs of the band came to an end, for most of the folk of the place knew naught of the airt of the gipsy flight, and such as knew were loath to tell, being little in a mood to incur the Baillies' wrath. So naught was left for him but to return to the place whence he had started. Here he was met with the bitter news that I have already set down. He was thrown into a state of utter despondency, and sat for long in confusion of mind. Then he fell to reasoning. There was no place whither Gilbert could take a woman save his own house of Eaglesham, for Dawyck and Barns were too near the hills and myself. You must remember that at this time my servant had no inkling of the momentous event which had set our positions upside down. Now, if they took her to the west they would do so with all speed; they had but one day's start; he might yet overtake them, and try if his wits could find no way out of the difficulty.

So off he set and came to this inn of the Clyde fords, and then he heard that on the evening before such a cavalcade had passed as he sought But he learned something more the next morn; namely, that my cousin's power was wholly broken and that now I was freed from all suspicion of danger. Once more he fell into a confusion, but the one thing clear was that he must find me at all costs. He had heard of me last at the town of Biggar not fifteen miles off; when I heard the great news he guessed that I would ride straight for Smitwood; I would hear the tidings that the folk there had to tell, and, if he knew aught of me, I would ride straight, as he had done, on the track of the fugitives. So he turned back to the inn, and abode there awaiting me, and, lo! at nightfall I had come.

Then for long we spoke of my own wanderings, and I told him many tales of my doings and sufferings up hill and down dale, as did Ulysses to the Ithacan swineherd. But ere long we fell to discussing that far more momentous task which lay before us. It behoved us to be up and doing, for I had a horrid fear at my heart that my cousin might seek to reach the western sea coast and escape to France or Ireland, and thus sorely hinder my meeting with my love. I had no fear but that I should overtake him sooner or later, for fate had driven that lesson deep into my heart, and to myself I said that it was but a matter of days, or weeks, or maybe years, but not of failure. I was for posting on even at that late hour, but Nicol would have none of it.

"Look at your face i' the gless, sir," said he, "and tell me if ye look like muckle mair ridin' the day. Ye're fair forwandered wi' weariness and want o' sleep. And what for wad ye keep thae queer-like claes? I'll get ye a new suit frae the landlord, decent man, and mak ye mair presentable for gaun intil the Wast."

I looked as he bade me in the low mirror, and saw my dark face and wind-tossed hair, and my clothes of flaming crimson. Something in the odd contrast struck my fancy.

"Nay," I said grimly, "I will bide as I am. I am going on a grim errand, and I will not lay aside these rags till I have done that which I went for to do."

"Weel, weel, please yersel'," said my servant jauntily, and he turned away, whistling and smiling to himself.

CHAPTER II

AN OLD JOURNEY WITH A NEW ERRAND

I slept like a log till the broad daylight on the next morn woke me, and with all speed I got up and dressed. I found myself much refreshed in body. My weariness was gone, and the dull languor which had oppressed me had given place to a singular freshness of spirit.

When I went below I found my servant ready and waiting, with the horses saddled and my meal prepared. The soldiers had gone early, paying no score; for when their liquor had left them they had wakened up to the solemn conviction that this country-side was not like to be a pleasant habitation for them for many months to come. So they had gone off to Heaven knows where, cutting my bridle-rein as a last token of their affection.

It was near ten o'clock ere we started, the two of us, on our road to the West. I had travelled it many times, for it was the way to Glasgow, and I found myself calling up, whether I would or no, a thousand half-sad and half-pleasing memories. At this place I had stopped to water my horse, at this cottage I had halted for an hour, at this hostel I had lain the night. Had I not looked at my comrade every now and then, I might have fancied that I was still the schoolboy, with his wide interest in letters and life, and little knowledge of either, with half a dozen letters in his pocket, looking forward with fear and hope to town and college. Heigh-ho! Many things had come and gone since then, and here was I still the same boy, but ah! how tossed and buffeted and perplexed. Yet I would not have bartered my present state for those careless and joyous years, for after all this is a rugged world, with God knows how many sore straits and devilish temptations, but with so many fair and valiant rewards, that a man is a coward indeed who would not battle through the one for the sweet sake of the other.

As we went Nicol talked of many things with a cheery good-humour. His was an adventure-loving mind, and there were few things which he would not brave save the routine of settled life. Now, as the November sun came out, for the morn was frosty and clear, his face shone with the sharp air and the excitement of the ride, and he entertained me to his views on the world and the things in it. The ground was hard as steel underfoot, the horses' hooves crackled through the little ice-coated pools in the road, and a solitary thrush sang its song from a wayside wood and seemed like a silver trump calling to action and daring.

"What think ye o' the hills, Laird?" said my servant. "Ye've been lang among them, and ye'll ken them noo in anither way than if ye had just trampit ower them after wild-juks or ridden through them to Yarrow or Moffatdale. I've wandered among them since I was a laddie five 'ear auld, and used to gang oot wi' my faither to the herdin'. And since then I've traivelled up Tweed and doun Tweed, and a' ower the Clydeside and the Annanside, no to speak o' furrin pairts, and I can weel say that I ken naucht sae awfu' and sae kindly, sae couthy and bonny and hamely, and, at the same time, sae cauld and cruel, as juist thae green hills and muirs."

"You speak truly," said I. "I've seen them in all weathers and I know well what you mean."

"Ay," he went on, "thae lawlands are very bonny, wi' the laigh meadows, and bosky trees and waters as still as a mill-pound. And if ye come doun frae the high bare lands ye think them fair like heev'n. But I canna bide lang there. I aye turn fair sick for the smell o' moss and heather, and the roarin' and routin' o' the burn, and the air sae clear and snell that it gars your face prick and your legs and airms strauchten oot, till ye think ye could run frae here to the Heads o' Ayr."

"I know all of that," said I, "and more."

"Ay, there's far mair," said he. "There's the sleepin' at nicht on the grund wi' naething abune you but the stars, and waukin' i' the mornin' wi' the birds singin' i' your lug and the wind blawin' cool and free around you. I ken a' that and I ken the ither, when the mist crowds low on the tap o' the hills and the rain dreeps and seeps, or when the snaw comes and drifts sae thick that ye canna stand afore it, and there's life neither for man nor beast. Yet wi' it a' I like it, and if I micht choose the place I wad like best to dee in, it would be in the lee side o' a muckle hill, wi' nae death-bed or sic like havers, but juist to gang straucht to my Makker frae the yirth I had aye traivelled on. But wha kens?" and he spurred up his horse.

"Nicol," said I, after a long silence, "you know the errand we go on. I have told you it, I think. It is to find my cousin and Mistress Marjory. If God grant that we do so, then these are my orders. You will take the lady home to Tweeddale, to Dawyck, which is her own, and leave me behind you. I may come back or I may not. If I do, all will be well. If I do not, you know your duty. You have already fulfilled it for some little time; if it happens as I say, you will continue it to death. The lass will have no other protector than yourself."

"E'en as ye say," cried he, resuming his hilarity, though whether it was real or no I cannot tell. "But dinna crack aboot siccan things, Laird, or ye'll be makkin' our journey nae better than buryin'. It's a wanchancy thing to speak aboot death. No that a man should be feared at it, but that he should keep a calm sough till it come. Ye mind the story o' auld Tam Blacket, the writer at Peebles. Tam was deein', and as he was a guid auld man the minister, whae was great at death-beds and consolation, cam to speak to him aboot his latter end. 'Ye're near death, Tammas,' says he. Up gets auld Tam. 'I'll thank ye no to mention that subject,' he says, and never a word wad he allow the puir man to speak."

So in this way we talked till we came to where the road leaves the Clyde valley and rises steep to the high land about the town of Hamilton. Here we alighted for dinner at an inn which bears for its sign the Ship of War, though what this means in a town many miles from the sea I do not know. Here we had a most excellent meal, over which we did not tarry long, for we sought to reach Glasgow ere nightfall, and at that season of the year the day closes early.

As we rode down the narrow, crooked street, I had leisure to look about me. The town was in a ferment, for, as near the field of Bothwell Brig where the Whigs had suffered their chiefest slaughter, it had been well garrisoned with soldiers, and the news of the Prince of Orange's landing put the place into an uproar. Men with flushed, eager faces hurried past with wonder writ large on their cheeks; others stood about in knots talking shrilly; and every now and then a horseman would push his way through the crowd bearing fresh tidings to the townsfolk or carrying it thence to the West country.

Suddenly, in the throng of men, I saw a face which brought me to a standstill. It was that of a man, dark, sullen, and foreign-looking, whose former dragoon's dress a countryman's coat poorly concealed. He was pushing his way eagerly through the crowd, when he looked into the midstreet and caught my eye. In an instant he had dived into one of the narrow closes and was lost to sight.

At the first glance I knew my man for that soldier of Gilbert's, Jan Hamman, the Hollander, whom already thrice I had met, once in the Alphen Road, once at the joining of the Cor Water with Tweed, and once at the caves of the Cor, when so many of his Majesty's servants went to their account. What he was about in this West country I could not think, for had he been wise he would have made for the eastern sea coast or at least not ventured into this stronghold of those he had persecuted. And with the thought another came. Had not he spoken bitterly of his commander? was he not the victim of one of my fair cousin's many infamies? had he not, in my own hearing, sworn vengeance? Gilbert had more foes than one on his track, for here was this man, darkly malevolent, dogging him in his flight. The thought flashed upon me that he of all men would know my cousin's plans and would aid me in my search. I did not for a moment desire him for an ally in my work; nay, I should first frustrate his designs, before I settled matters with Gilbert, for it was in the highest degree unseemly that any such villain should meddle in matters which belonged solely to our house. Still, I should use him for my own ends, come what might.

I leaped from my horse, crying on Nicol to take charge of it, and dashed up the narrow entry. I had a glimpse of a figure vanishing round the far corner, and when I had picked my way, stumbling over countless obstacles, I found at the end an open court, roughly paved with cobblestones, and beyond that a high wall. With all my might I made a great leap and caught the top, and lo! I looked over into a narrow lane wherein children were playing. It was clear that my man had gone by this road, and would now be mixed among the folk in the side street. It was useless to follow farther, so in some chagrin I retraced my steps, banning Nicol and the Dutchman and my own ill-luck.

I remounted, making no answer to my servant's sarcastic condolences—for, of course, he had no knowledge of this fellow's purport in coming to the Westlands, and could only look on my conduct as a whimsical freak. As we passed down the street I kept a shrewd lookout to right and left if haply I might see my man, but no such good luck visited me. Once out of the town it behoved us to make better speed, for little of the afternoon remained, and dusk at this time of year fell sharp and sudden. So with a great jingling and bravado we clattered through the little hamlets of Blantyre and Cambuslang, and came just at the darkening to the populous burgh of Rutherglen, which, saving that it has no college or abbey, is a more bustling and prosperous place than Glasgow itself. But here we did not stay, being eager to win to our journey's end; so after a glass of wine at an inn we took the path through the now dusky meadows by Clydeside, and passing through the village of Gorbals, which lies on the south bank of the river, we crossed the bridge and entered the gates just as they were on the point of closing.

251

During the latter hours of the day I had gone over again in mind all the details of the doings of past weeks. All seemed now clear, and with great heartiness I cursed myself for errors, which I could scarce have refrained from. The steps in Gilbert's plan lay before me one by one. The letter had given him only the slightest of clues, which he must have taken weeks to discover. When at last it had been made clear to him, something else had engaged his mind. He must have had word from private sources, shut to the countryfolk, of the way whither events were trending in the state. His mind was made up; he would make one desperate bid for success; and thus he shaped his course. He sent men to Smitwood with the plausible story which I had already heard from my servant, how all breach was healed between us, and how this was her escort to take her to me. Then I doubted not he had bidden the men show her as proof some letter forged in my name on the model of the one I had lost on Caerdon, and also give her some slight hint of the great change in the country to convince her that he could do no ill even had he desired it, and that I was now on the summit of fortune. The poor lass, wearied with anxiety and long delay, and with no wise Nicol at hand to give better counsel, had suffered herself to be persuaded, and left the house with a glad heart. I pictured her disillusion, her bitter regrets, her unwilling flight. And then I swore with redoubled vehemence that it should not be for long.

We alighted for the night at the house of that Mistress Macmillan where I lodged when I first came to college. She welcomed us heartily, and prepared us a noble supper, for we were hungry as hawks, and I, for one, tired with many rough adventures. The house stood in the Gallow Gate, near the salt market and the college gardens; and as I lay down on the fresh sheets and heard the many noises of the street with the ripple of the river filling the pauses, I thanked God that at last I had come out of beggary and outlawry to decent habitation.

CHAPTER III

THE HOUSE WITH THE CHIPPED GABLES

The next morn the weather had changed. When I looked forth through the latticed panes to the street, it was a bleak scene that met my eyes—near a foot of snow, flakes tossing and whirling everywhere, and the roofs and gables showing leaden dull in the gloom. Had I been in another frame of mind I should have lost my spirits, for nothing so disheartened me as heavy, dismal weather. But now I was in such a temper that I welcomed the outlook; the grey, lifeless street was akin to my heart, and I went down from my chamber with the iron of resolution in my soul.

My first care was to inquire at Mistress Macmillan if she knew aught of my cousin's doings, for the town house of the Eaglesham Burnets was not two streets distant. But she could give me no news, for, said she, since the old laird died and these troublous times succeeded, it was little that the young master came near the place. So without any delay I and my servant went out into the wintry day, and found our way to the old, dark dwelling in the High Street.

The house had been built near a hundred years before, in the time of Ephraim Burnet, my cousin's grandfather. I mind it well to this day, and oft as I think of the city, that dreary, ancient pile rises to fill my vision. The three Burnet leaves, the escutcheon of our family, hung over the doorway. Every window was little and well barred with iron, nor was any sign of life to be seen behind the dreary panes. But the most notable things to the eye were the odd crow-step gables, which, I knew not from what cause, were all chipped and defaced, and had a strange pied appearance against the darker roof. It faced the street, and down one side ran a little lane. Behind were many lesser buildings around the courtyard, and the back opened into a wynd which ran westward to the city walls.

I went up the steps and with my sword-hilt thundered on the

door. The blows roused the echoes of the old place. Within I heard the resonance of corridor and room, all hollow and empty. Below me was the snowy street, with now and then a single passer, and I felt an eerie awe of this strange house, as of one who should seek to force a vault of the dead.

Again I knocked, and this time it brought me an answer. I heard feet—slow, shuffling feet, coming from some room, and ascending the staircase to the hall. The place was so void that the slightest sound rang loud and clear, and I could mark the progress of the steps from their beginning. Somewhere they came to a halt, as if the person were considering whether or not to come to the door, but by-and-by they advanced, and with vast creaking a key was fitted into the lock and the great oak door was opened a little.

It was a little old woman who stood in the opening, with a face seamed and wrinkled, and not a tooth in her head. She wore a mutch, which gave her a most witch-like appearance, and her narrow, grey eyes, as they fastened on me and sought out my errand, did not reassure me.

"What d'ye want here the day, sir?" she said in a high, squeaking voice. "It's cauld, cauld weather, and my banes are auld and I canna stand here bidin' your pleesur."

"Is your master within?" I said shortly. "Take me to him, for I have business with him."

"Maister, quotha!" she screamed. "Wha d'ye speak o', young sir? If it's the auld laird ye mean, he's lang syne wi' his Makker, and the young yin has no been here thae fower years. He was a tenty bit lad, was Maister Gilbert, but he gaed aff to the wars i' the abroad and ne'er thinks o' returnin'. Wae's me for the puir, hapless chiel." And she crooned on to herself in the garrulity of old age.

"Tell me the truth," said I, "and have done with your lies. It is well known that your master came here in the last two days with two men and a lady, and abode here for the night. Tell me instantly if he is still here or whither has he gone."

She looked at me with a twinkle of shrewdness and then shook her head once more. "Na, na, I'm no leein'. I'm ower neer my accoont wi' the Lord to burden my soul wi' lees. When you tae are faun i' the hinner end o' life, ye'll no think it worth your while to mak up leesome stories. I tell ye the young maister hasna been here for years, though it's blithe I wad be to see him. If ye winna believe my word, ye can e'en gang your ways."

Now I was in something of a quandary. The woman looked to be speaking the truth, and it was possible that my cousin had left the city on one side and pushed straight on to his house of Eaglesham or even to the remoter western coast. Yet the way was a long one, and I saw not how he could have refrained from halting at Glasgow in the even. He had no cause to fear my following him there more than another place. For that I would come post-haste to the Westlands at the first word he must have well known, and so he could have no reason in covering his tracks from me. He was over-well known a figure in his own countryside to make secrecy possible; his aim must be to outrace me in speed, not to outwit me with cunning.

"Let me gang, young sir," the old hag was groaning. "I've the rheumaticks i' my banes and I'm sair hadden doon wi' the chills, and I'll get my death if I stand here longer."

"I will trust you then," said I, "but since I am a kinsman of your master's and have ridden far on a bootless errand, I will even come in and refresh myself ere I return."

"Na, na," she said, a new look, one of anxiety and cunning, coming into her face, "ye maun na dae that. It was the last word my maister bade me ere he gaed awa'. 'Elspeth,' says he, 'see ye let nane intil the hoose till I come back.' "

"Tut, tut, I am his own cousin. I will enter if I please," and calling my servant, I made to force an admittance.

Then suddenly, ere I knew, the great door was slammed in my face, and I could hear the sound of a key turning and a bar being dropped.

Here was a pretty to-do. Without doubt there was that in the house which the crone desired to keep from my notice. I sprang to the door and thundered on it like a madman, wrestling with the lock, and calling for the woman to open it. But all in vain, and after a few seconds' bootless endeavour, I turned ruefully to my servant.

"Can aught be done?" I asked.

"I saw a dyke as we cam here," said Nicol, "and ower the back o't was a yaird. There was likewise a gate i' the dyke. I'm thinkin' that'll be the back door o' the hoose. If ye were awfu' determined, Laird, ye micht in in there."

I thought for a moment. "You are right," I cried. "I know the place. But we will first go back and fetch the horses, for it is like there will be wild work before us ere night."

But lo and behold! when we went to the inn stable my horse was off. "I thocht he needit a shoe," said the ostler, "so I just sent him doun to Jock Walkinshaw's i' the East Port. If ye'll bide a wee, I'll send a laddie doun to bring him up."

Five, twenty, sixty minutes and more we waited while that accursed child brought my horse. Then he came back a little after midday; three shoes had been needed, he said, and he had rin a' the way, and he wasna to blame. So I gave him a crown and a sound box on the ears, and then the two of us set off.

The place was high and difficult of access, being in a narrow lane where few passers ever went, and nigh to the city wall. I bade Nicol hold the horses, and standing on the back of one I could just come to within a few feet of the top. I did my utmost by springing upward to grasp the parapet, but all in vain, so in a miserable state of disappointed hopes I desisted and consulted with my servant. Together we tried the door, but it was of massive wood, clamped with iron, and triply bolted. There was nothing for it but to send off to Mistress Macmillan and seek some contrivance. Had the day not been so wild and the lane so quiet we could scarce have gone unnoticed. As it was, one man passed, a hawker in a little cart, seeking a near way, and with little time to stare at the two solitary horsemen waiting by the wall.

Nicol went off alone, while I kept guard—an aimless guard—by the gate. In a little he returned with an old boat-hook, with the cleek at the end somewhat unusually long. Then he proposed his method. I should stand on horseback as before, and hang the hook on the flat surface of the wall. When, by dint of scraping,

I had fixed it firmly, I should climb it hand over hand, as a sailor mounts a rope, and with a few pulls I might hope to be at the summit.

I did as he bade, and, with great labour, fixed the hook in the hard stone. Then I pulled myself up, very slowly and carefully, with the shaft quivering in my hands. I was just gripping the stone when the wretched iron slipped and rattled down to the ground, cutting me sharply in the wrist. Luckily I did not go with it, for in the moment of falling I had grasped the top, and hung there with aching hands and the blood from the cut trickling down my arm. Then, with a mighty effort, I swung myself up and stood safe on the top.

Below me was a sloping roof of wood which ended in a sheer wall of maybe twelve feet. Below that in turn was the great yard, flagged with stone, but now hidden under a cloak of snow. Around it were stables, empty of horses, windy, cold, and dismal. I cannot tell how the whole place depressed me. I felt as though I were descending into some pit of the dead.

Staunching the blood from my wrist—by good luck my left— as best I might with my kerchief, I slipped down the white roof and dropped into the court. It was a wide, empty place, and, in the late afternoon, looked grey and fearsome. The dead black house behind, with its many windows all shuttered and lifeless, shadowed the place like a pall. At my back was the back door of the house, like the other locked and iron-clamped. I seemed to myself to have done little good by my escapade in coming thither.

Wandering aimlessly, I entered the stables, scarce thinking what I was doing. Something about the place made me stop and look. I rubbed my eyes and wondered. There, sure enough, were signs of horses having been recently here. Fresh hay and a few oats were in the mangers, and straw and dung in the stalls clearly proclaimed that not long agone the place had been tenanted.

I rushed out into the yard, and ran hither and thither searching the ground. There were hoofmarks—fool that I was not to have marked them before—leading clearly from the stable door to the gate on the High Street. I rushed to the iron doors and tugged at them. To my amazement I found that they yielded, and I was staring into the darkening street.

So the birds had been there and flown in our brief absence. I cursed my ill-fortune with a bitter heart.

Suddenly I saw something dark lying amid the snow. I picked it up and laid it tenderly in my bosom. For it was a little knot of blue velvet ribbon, such as my lady wore.

CHAPTER IV

UP HILL AND DOWN DALE

I rushed up the street, leaving the gates swinging wide behind me, and down the lane to where Nicol waited. In brief, panting words I told him my tale. He heard it without a movement, save to turn his horse's head up the street. I swung myself into the saddle, and, with no more delay, we made for our lodgings.

"There is but one thing that we may do," said I. "The night is an ill one, but if it is ill for us 'tis ill for them." And at the words I groaned, for I thought of my poor Marjory in the storm and cold.

At Mistress Macmillan's I paid the lawing, and having eaten a hearty meal, we crammed some food into our saddle-bags and bade the hostess goodbye. Then we turned straight for the west port of the city.

It was as I had expected. The gates were just at the closing when the twain of us rode up to them and were suffered to pass. The man looked curiously at my strange dress, but made no remark, as is the fashion of these taciturn westland folk, and together we rode through and into the bleak night. The snow had ceased to fall early in the day, but now it came on again in little intermittent driftings, while a keen wind whistled from the hills of the north. The land was more or less strange to me, and even my servant, who had a passing acquaintance with many country-sides, professed himself ignorant. It was the way to the wild highlands—the county of Campbells and Lennoxes—and far distant from kindly Christian folk. I could not think why my cousin had chosen this path, save for the reason of its difficulty and obscurity. I was still in doubt of his purpose, whether he was bound for his own house of Eaglesham or for the more distant Clyde coast. He had clearly gone by this gate from the city, for this much had we learned from the man at the port. Now, if he sought Eaglesham, he must needs cross the river, which would give us some time to gain on his track. But if he still held to the north, then there was naught for it but to follow him hotfoot and come up with him by God's grace and our horses' speed.

I have been abroad on many dark nights, but never have I seen one so black as this. The path to the west ran straight from our feet to the rugged hills which dip down to the river edge some ten miles off. But of it we could make nothing, nor was there anything to tell us of its presence save that our horses stumbled when we strayed from it to the moory land on either side. All about us were the wilds, for the town of Glasgow stood on the last bounds of settled country, near to the fierce mountains and black morasses of the Highlandmen. The wind crooned and blew in gusts over the white waste, driving little flakes of snow about us, and cutting us to the bone with its bitter cold. Somewhere in the unknown distances we heard strange sounds—the awesome rumble of water or the cry of forlorn birds. All was as bleak as death, and, in the thick darkness, what might otherwise have seemed simple and homelike was filled with vague terrors. I had shaped no path—all that I sought was to hasten somewhere nearer those we followed, and on this mad quest we stumbled blindly forward.

When we had gone some half-dozen miles a light shone out from the wayside, and we descried a house. It was a little, low dwelling, with many sheds at the rear; clearly a smithy or a humble farm. My servant leaped down and knocked. The door was opened; a warm stream of light lay across the snowy road. I had a glimpse within, and there was a cheerful kitchen with a fire of logs crackling. A man sat by the hearth, shaping something or other with a knife, and around him two children were playing. The woman who came to us was buxom and comely, one who delighted in her children and her home. The whole place gave me a sharp feeling of envy and regret. Even these folk, poor peasants, had the joys of comfort and peace, while I, so long an outlaw and a wanderer, must still journey hopeless seeking the lost.

"Did any riders pass by the road today?" I asked.

"Ay, four passed on horses about midday or maybe a wee thing after it, twae stoot fellows, and a braw-clad gentleman and a bonny young leddy. They didna stop, but gaed by at a great rate."

"What was the lady like?" I asked breathlessly.

"Oh, a bit young thing, snod and genty-like. But I mind she looked gey dowie and I think she had been greetin'. But wherefore d'ye speir, sir? And what are ye daein' oot hereaways on siccan a nicht? Ye best come in and bide till mornin'. We've an orra bed i' the house for the maister, and plenty o' guid saft straw i' the barn for the man."

"Did they go straight on?" I cried, "and whither does this way lead?"

"They went straight on," said she, "and the road is the road to the toun o' Dumbarton." And she would have told me more, but with a hasty word of thanks, I cut her short, and once more we were off into the night.

From this place our way and the incidents thereof are scarce clear in my memory. For one thing the many toils of the preceding time began at last to tell upon me, and I grew sore and wearied. Also a heavy drowsiness oppressed me, and even in that cold I could have slept on my horse's back. We were still on the path, and the rhythmical jog of the motion served to lull me, till, as befell every now and then, there came a rut or a tussock, and I was brought to my senses with a sharp shock. Nicol rode silently at my side, a great figure in the gloom, bent low, as was always his custom, over his horse's neck. In one way the state was more pleasing than the last, for the turmoil of cares in my heart was quieted for the moment by the bodily fatigue. I roused myself at times to think of my purpose and get me energy for my task, but the dull languor would not be exorcised, and I always fell back again into my sloth. Nevertheless we kept a fair pace, for we had given the rein to our animals, and they were fresh and well-fed.

Suddenly, ere I knew, the way began to change from a level road into a steep hill-path. Even in the blackness I could see a great hillside rising steeply to right and left. I pulled up my horse, for here there would be need of careful guidance, and was going on as before when Nicol halted me with his voice.

"Laird, Laird," he cried, "I dinna ken muckle aboot the Dumbarton road, but there's yae thing I ken weel and that is that it keeps i' the laigh land near the waterside a' the way, and doesna straiggle ower brae faces."

This roused me to myself. "Did we pass any crossroad?" I asked, "for God knows the night is dark enough for any man to wander. Are you sure of what you say?"

"As sure as I am that my fingers are cauld and my een fair dazed wi' sleep," said he.

"Then there is naught for it but to go back and trust to overtaking the path. But stay, are these not the hills of Kilpatrick, which stretch down from the Lennox to the Clyde and front the river at this very Dumbarton? I have surely heard of such. Our highway must lie to our left, since we clearly have turned to the right, seeing that if we had turned to the left we should have reached the water. If then we strike straight from here along the bottom of this slope, will we not reach the town? The chances are that we should never find our path, whereas this way will bring us there without fail, if we can stomach some rough riding."

"Weel, sir, I'm wi' ye wherever ye like to gang. And I'll no deny but that it's the maist reasonable road to tak, if ye're no feared o' breakin' your craig ower a stane or walkin' intil a peat-bog. But we maun e'en lippen to Providence and tak our chance like better men."

So wheeling sharply to our left, we left the path and rode as best we could along the rough bottom of the hills. It was a tract of rushy ground where many streams ran. Huge boulders, tumbled down from the steeps, strewed it like the leaves of a hazel wood in autumn. On one hand the land lay back to the haughlands and ordered fields, on the other it sloped steeply to the hills. Stumps of birk trees and stray gnarled trunks came at times, but in general the ground was open and not unsuited for horses in the light of day. Now it was something more than difficult, for we came perilous near oftentimes to fulfilling my servant's prophecy. Once, I remember, I floundered fair into a trench of moss-water with a vile muddy bottom, where I verily believe both horse and man would have perished, had not Nicol, who saw my misfortune and leaped his beast across, pulled me fiercely from my saddle to the bank, and the twain of us together extricated the horse. In this fashion, floundering and slipping, we must have ridden some half-dozen miles. All drowsiness had vanished with the rough mode of travel.

Now, however, we were suddenly brought to an end in our progress. Before us lay a little ravine, clogged with snow, in whose bottom a burn roared. It was a water of little size, and, in summer weather, one might have leaped it. Now the snow had swollen it to the semblance of a torrent, and it chafed and eddied in the little gorge, a streak of dark, angry water against the dim white banks. There was nothing for it but to enter and struggle across, and yet, as I looked at the ugly swirl, I hesitated. I was nigh numbed with cold, my horse was aching from its stumbling, there was little foothold on the opposing bank. I turned to Nicol, who sat with his teeth shaking with the bitter weather.

"There is naught for it," said I, "but to risk it. There is no use in following it, for we shall find no better place in a ravine like this."

Even as I spoke my servant had taken the plunge, and I saw horse and man slip off the snowy bank into the foam. I followed so closely that I lost all sight of them. To this day I remember the feelings of the moment, the choking as an icy wave surged over my mouth, the frantic pulling at the bridle-rein, the wild plunging of my horse, the roar of water and the splash of swimming. Then, with a mighty effort, my brave animal was struggling up the farther side, where my servant was already shaking the water from his clothes.

This incident, while it put me in better heart, vastly added to my bodily discomfort. An icy wind shivering through dripping garments may well chill the blood of the stoutest. And for certain the next part of the way is burned on my memory with a thousand recollections of utter weariness and misery. Even my hardy servant could scarce keep from groaning, and I, who was ever of a tenderer make, could have leaned my head on my horse's neck and sobbed with pure feebleness.

The country was now rough with tanglewood, for we were near the last spur of the hills, ere they break down on the river. Somewhere through the gloom lights were shining and moving, as I guessed from a ship on the water. Beyond were still others, few in number, but fixed as if from dwelling-houses. Here at last, I thought, is the town of Dumbarton which I am seeking, and fired with the hope we urged on the more our jaded beasts.

But lo! when we came to it, 'twas but a wayside inn in a little clachan, where one solitary lamp swung and cast a bar of light over the snowy street. I hammered at the door till I brought down the landlord, shivering in his shirt. It might be that my cousin had halted here, so I asked the man if he had any travellers within.

"Nane, save twae drunk Ayr skippers and a Glesca packman, unless your honour is comin' to keep them company."

"Has any one passed then?" I cried.

"How could I tell when I've been sleepin' i' my bed thae sax 'oor?" he coughed, and, seeing we were no sojourners, slammed the door in our face.

We were numb and wretched, but there was naught for it but to ride on farther to the town. It could not be far, and there were signs of morn already in the air. The cold grew more intense, and the thick pall of darkness lifted somewhat towards the east. The blurred woods and clogged fields at our side gradually came into view, and as, heart-sick and nigh fordone with want of sleep, we rounded the great barrier-ridge of hill, an array of twinkling lights sprang up in front and told us that we were not far from our journey's end. Nevertheless, it was still dark when we rode into a narrow cobbled street and stopped at the first hostelry.

Now, both the one and the other were too far gone with weariness to do more than drop helplessly from the horses and stagger into the inn parlour. They gave us brandy, and then led us to a sleeping-room, where we lay down like logs and dropped into a profound slumber.

When we awoke the morning was well advanced. I was roused by Nicol, who was ever the more wakeful, and without more delay we went down and recruited our exhausted strength with a meal. Then I summoned the landlord, and asked, more from habit than from any clear expectation, whether any travellers had lodged overnight.

The man answered shortly that there had been a gentleman and a maid, with two serving-men, who had but lately left.

In a great haste I seized on my hat and called loudly for the horses. "Where did they go?" I said; "by what way? Quick, tell me."

"They took the road doun to the ferry," said he, in great amazement. "It's no an 'oor since they went."

Thereupon I flung him his lawing, and we rushed from the house.

CHAPTER V

EAGLESHAM

It was dawning morn, grey and misty, with a thaw setting in on the surface of the snow. Down the narrow, crooked streets, with a wind shivering in our teeth, we went at a breakneck gallop. I lashed my horse for its life, and the poor brute, wearied as it was by the toils of the night, answered gallantly to my call. Sometimes, in a steep place, we slipped for yards; often I was within an ace of death; and at one street turning with a mighty clatter Nicol came down, though the next minute he was up again. A few sleepy citizens rubbed their eyes and stared from their windows, and in the lighted doorway of a tavern a sailor looked at us wonderingly.

In less time than it takes to tell we were at the water-edge. Here there is a rough quay, with something of a harbour behind it, where lie the sugar-boats from the Indies, when the flood-tide is too low to suffer them to go upstream to the city. Here, also, the ferry four times daily crosses the river.

Before us the water lay in leaden gloom, with that strange, dead colour which comes from the falling of much snow. Heavy waves were beginning to roll over the jetty, and a mist was drooping lower and ever lower. Two men stood by an old anchor coiling some rope. We pulled up our horses, and I cried out in impatience where the ferry might be.

"Gone ten meenutes syne," said one, with no change on his stolid face. "There she is gin ye hae een i' your heid to see."

And he pointed out to the waste of waters. I looked and saw a sail riding and sinking in the trough of the waves.

"When does she return?" I cried out, with many curses on our laggard journey.

"Whiles in an 'oor, whiles in twae. She'll be twae the day ere she's back, for the ferryman, Jock Gellatly, is as fou as the Baltic wi' some drink that a young gentleman gave him."

So we turned back to the harbour tavern, with all the regrets of unsuccess.

The man had said two hours, but it was nearer three ere that wretched shell returned, and, when it came, 'twas with a drunken man who could scarce stagger ashore. I was in no mood for trifling.

"Here, you drunken swine," I cried, "will you take us across and be quick about it?"

"I maun hae anither gless o' Duncan's whusky," said the fellow, with a leer.

"By God, and you will not," I cried. "Get aboard and make no more delay, or, by the Lord, I'll throw you into the stream."

The man hiccuped and whined. "I canna, I canna, my bonny lad. I had ower muckle guid yill afore I sterted, and I maun hae some whusky to keep it doon. I'm an auld man, and the cauld air frae the water is bad for the inside. Let me be, let me be," and he lay down on the quay with the utter helplessness of a sot.

"Here is a devil of a mess," I cried to Nicol. "What is to be done?"

"I'll hae to tak the boat mysel', Laird," said my servant quietly. "If I droon ye, dinna complain."

Indeed, I was in no mood for complaining at anything which would carry me farther on my quest. With some difficulty we got the horses aboard and penned them in the stalls. Then Nicol hoisted the sail, and we shoved off, while I kept those at bay with a boat-hook who sought to stop us. Once out on the stormy waters I was beset with a thousand fears. I have ever feared the sea, and now, as we leaped and rolled among the billows, and as the wind scoured us like a threshing-floor, and, above all, as the crazy boat now almost lay sideways on the water, I felt a dreadful sinking of my courage, and looked for nothing better than immediate death. It was clear that Nicol, who knew something of seamanship as he knew of most things, had a hard task to keep us straight, and by his set face and white lips I guessed that he, too, was not without his fears. Nevertheless, the passage was narrow, and in less time than I had expected we saw a dim line of sand through the fog. Running in there, we beached the coble, and brought the horses splashing to shore.

The place was dreary and waste, low-lying, with a few huts facing the river. Beyond the land seemed still flat, though, as far as the mist suffered me to see, there seemed to be something of a rise to the right. My feet and hands were numbed with cold, and the wound in my wrist, which I got scaling the wall, smarted furiously. I was so stiff I could scarce mount horse, and Nicol was in no better plight.

We rode to the nearest cottage and asked whither the four had gone who landed with the last ferry. The woman answered gruffly that she had seen none land, and cared not. At the next house I fared little better; but at the third I found a young fisher-lad, who, for the sake of a silver piece, told me that they had headed over the moor about three hours ago. "And what lies beyond the moor?" I asked. "Beyond the muir," said he, "is a muckle hill they ca' Mistilaw, a' thick wi' bogs, and ayont it there are mair hills and mosses, and syne if ye ride on ye'll come to Eaglesham, whaur the muirs end and the guid lands begin. I yince was ower there wi' my faither, aboot a cowt, and a braw bit place it is, and no like hereaways."

So Nicol and I, with dogged hearts and numbed bodies, rode

into the black heath where there was no road. The snow had lost all hardness and was thick and clogging to our horses' feet. We made as good speed as we could, but that, after all, was little. About midday we had done the first part of our journey and were clambering and slipping over the shoulder of Mistilaw. This hill is low and trivial contrasted with our great Tweedside hills, but it well deserves its name, for it is one vast quagmire, where at all seasons mists and vapours hang. Beyond it, and all through the afternoon, we struggled among low hills and lochs. We halted at a solitary shepherd's hut among the wilds, and ate a vile meal of braxy and oaten cake. Then again we set forth, and in the darkening came to the wide moor which is the last guard of the wastes and borders the pleasant vale of the Cart.

Now here I fell into a great fit of indecision. It was clear that Gilbert and Marjory were but a little way off in the House of Eaglesham, and I had almost reached the end of my travels. But here my plans came to a sudden end. Was I to ride forward and boldly require my cousin to let her go? I knew my cousin's temper; he could make but one reply, and at last some end would be placed to our feud. But with this came another thought. Gilbert was not a man of one device but of many. If I sought to wrest my lady from his hands by force, it was most likely that he would be the winner. For he was ever ripe for high, bold, and dastardly policies, and at such a time was little likely to be punctilious.

So in my extremity I fell to consulting with Nicol, and between us we devised a plan. I liked it so well that I lost all dismal forebodings and proceeded to put it in action. Night fell just as we came to the meadows above the village, and the twinkling lights of the place served as our guides. There was an inn there which I remembered of old time, for the innkeeper had come originally from Tweeddale. At first I would have shunned it, but then I remembered that the man was dead these half-dozen years, and all the place so changed that I was secure from recognition, even had I not been so disguised and clad. So without any fear we rode up to the door and sought admittance.

The place was roomy and wide; a clean-swept floor, with a fire blazing on the hearth, and a goodly smell of cooked meat everywhere. They brought us a meal, which we ate like hungry men who had been a long day's journey in a snowbound world. Then I lay back and stared at the firelight, and tried hard to fix my mind on the things which were coming to pass. I found it hard to determine whether I was asleep or awake, for the events of the past hours were still mere phantasmagoria in my memory. Through all the bewildering maze of weariness and despair and scrupulosity of motive, there was still that one clear thought branded on my mind. And now, as I sat there, the thought was alone, without any clear perspective of the actors or the drama to be played. I scarce thought of Marjory, and Gilbert was little in my mind, for the long series of cares which had been mine for so many days had gone far to blunt my vision, and drive me to look further than the next moment or the next hour. I was dull, blank, deadened, with this one unalterable intention firm in my heart, but, God knows, little besides.

About nine or ten, I know not rightly, my servant roused me and bade me get ready. He had ordered the landlord to have the horses round to the door, giving I know not what excuse. I mounted without a thought, save that the air was raw and ugly. We rode down the silent street out on to the heath, where the snow was deeper, and our steps all but noiseless. The night was clear and deadly chill, piercing to the marrow. A low snow-fog clothed the ground, and not a sound could we hear in that great, wide world, save our own breathing and our horses' tread. A sort of awe took me at the silence, and it was with solemn thoughts that I advanced.

In a mile we left the heath, and, dipping down into the valley of the stream, entered a wood of pines. Snow powdered us from the bare boughs, and a dead branch crackled underfoot. Then all of a sudden, black and cold and still, from the streamside meadows and all girt with dark forest, rose the house. Through the tree-trunks it looked ghostly as a place of the dead. Then I remembered that this was the hill front, where no habitable rooms were; so, marvelling no more at the dearth of light, we turned sharp to the left and came on the side looking to the river.

Two lights twinkled in the place, one in the basement, and one in the low, first storey. I cast my memory back over old days. One was from the sitting parlour where the old Gilbert Burnet had chosen to spend his days, and the other—ah, I had it, 'twas from the sleeping-room of the old Mistress Burnet, where she had dragged out her last years and drawn her last breath. But for these there was no other sign of life in the house.

We crossed the snowy slope to the black shadow of the wall, where we halted and consulted. By this time some life and spirit had come back to my movements, and I held myself more resolutely. Now I gave my servant his orders. "If so happen we get Mistress Marjory safe," said I, "you will ride off with her without delay, down the valley to the Clyde and then straight towards Tweeddale. You will get fresh horses at Hamilton, and till then these will serve your purpose. Once in her own country-side there remains nothing for you save to see that you do her bidding in everything. If God so will it, I will not be long in returning to you."

Then, with no more words, we set our faces to our task.

The light in the window above us still shone out on the white ground. Many yards to our left another patch of brightness marked where the other lamp burned. There was need of caution and stillness, else the master of the place would hear. I kicked my shoes from my feet, though it was bitter cold, and set myself to the scaling of the wall. The distance was little, scarce twenty feet, and the masonry was rough-hewn and full of projecting stones, yet I found the matter as hard as I could manage. For my hands were numbed with the excessive chill, and the cut in my wrist still ached like the devil. I was like to swoon twenty times ere I reached the corner of the window. With a sob of exhaustion I drew myself up and stared at the curtained window.

Very gently I tapped on the pane, once, twice three times. I heard a quick movement of surprise within, then silence once more, as if the occupant of the room thought it only the snow drifting. Again I rapped, this time with a sharp knock, which men use who wait long outside a gate in a windy night. Now there could be no doubt of the matter. A hand drew the curtain aside, and a timid little face peered out. Then of a sudden the whole folds were swept back and my lady stood before me.

She wore her riding dress still, but a shawl was flung around her shoulders. There she stood before my sight, peering forth into the darkness, with surprise, fright, love, joy chasing one another across her face, her dear eyes sad and tearful, and her mouth drawn as with much sorrow, and her bright hair tossed loosely over her shoulders. It was many lone and dismal months since I had seen her, months filled with terrors and alarms and heart-sickening despair. And now, as she was almost within my reach at last after so many days, my heart gave a great bound, and with one leap the burden of the past shook itself from my shoulders.

"Open the window, dear," I said, and with trembling hands she undid the fastenings and swung the lattice open. The next moment I had her in my arms, and felt her heart beating close to mine, and the soft, warm touch of her neck. "Marjory lass," I cried, "how I have missed you! But now I have you and shall never leave you more." And I drew her closer to me while she could only sob the more.

Then, with an effort, I recalled myself to the immediate enterprise. The sound of the horses shuffling the snow without forced on me the need of action.

"My servant is without with horses," I said. "You must go with him, dear. It is our only safety. By tomorrow you will be in Tweeddale, and in a very little while I will come to you."

"But do you not go now?" she cried in anxiety, still clinging to me.

"No, Marjory dear," said I, soothing her as best I could, "I cannot come yet. There are some things which need my special care. If you think yourself, you will see that."

"Is it aught to do with Gilbert Burnet? Oh, I dare not leave you with him. Come with me, John, oh, come. I dare not, I dare not." And the poor child fell to wringing her hands.

"Marjory," I said, "if you love me do as I bid you. I will come to no scath. I promise you I will be with you at Dawyck ere the week is out."

So she put a brave face on the matter, though her lips still quivered. I went to the window and looked down to where Nicol stood waiting with the horses. Then I thought of a plan, and, finding none better, I cried to him to mount to the window-sill, for I knew his prowess as a climber, and the uncommon toughness of his arm. The horses were too jaded and spiritless to need any watching.

I caught up my lady in my arms and stepped out upon the ledge. Then very carefully and painfully I lowered myself, still clinging to the sill, till I found a foothold in a projecting stone. Below us were Nicol's arms and into them I gave my burden. I heard him clambering down by degrees, and in a very little, for the height was small, he had reached the ground. Then I followed him, slipping the last few feet, and burying myself in a bank of snow.

I had brought a heap of warm furs from the room, and these I flung round my love's shoulders. My heart ached to think of her, weary from the day's hard riding, setting forth again into the cold of a November night.

"Oh John," she said, "no sooner met than parted. It is ever our fate."

"It will be the last time, dear," I said, and I kissed her face in her hood.

Then, with many injunctions to my servant, I bade them goodbye, and watched the figure which I loved best in all the world disappear into the darkness. With a sad and yet cheerful heart I turned back and clambered again into the chamber.

There were Marjory's things scattered about, as of one who had come from a long journey. Something on a table caught my eye, and, taking it up, I saw it was a slip of withered heather. Then I minded how I had given it her one summer long ago on the Hill of Scrape.

I kicked off my boots, and in utter weariness of body and mind, I flung myself on the bed and was soon asleep.

271

CHAPTER VI

I MAKE MY PEACE WITH GILBERT BURNET

I slept till dawn the dreamless sleep of those who have drowned care in bodily exertion. It was scarce light when I awoke, and, with the opening of the eyes, there came with a rush the consciousness of my errand. I leaped out of bed, and sitting on the edge considered my further actions.

First I sought to remove from my person some of the more glaring stains of travel. There was water in the room, bitter cold and all but frozen, and with it I laved my face and hands.

Then I opened the chamber door and stepped out into one of the long corridors. The house was still, though somewhere in the far distance I could hear the bustle of servants. I cast my mind back many years, and strove to remember where was the room where the morning meal was served. I descended the staircase to the broad, low hall, but still there were no signs of other occupants. One door I tried, but it was locked; another, with no better fate, till I began to doubt my judgment. Then I perceived one standing ajar, and, pushing it wide, I looked in. Breakfast was laid on the table, and a fire smoked on the hearth. I entered and closed the door behind me.

There was a looking-glass at the far end, and, as I entered, I caught a glimpse of my figure. Grim as was my errand, I could have laughed aloud at the sight. My hair unkempt, my face tanned to the deepest brown, my strange scarlet clothes, marred as they were by wind and weather, gave me a look so truculent and weird that I was half afraid of myself.

I warmed my hands at the blaze and waited. The minutes dragged slowly, while no sound came save the bickering of the fire and the solemn ticking of a clock. I had not a shade of fear or perturbation. Never in all my life had my mind been so wholly at ease. I waited for the coming of my enemy, as one would wait on a ferry or for the opening of a gate, quiet, calm, and fixed of

272

purpose.

At last, and it must have been a good hour, I heard steps on the stair. Clearly my cousin had slept long after his exertions. Nearer they came, and I heard his voice giving some orders to the servants. Then the door was opened, and he came in.

At first sight I scarcely knew him, so changed was he from the time of our last meeting. He was grown much thinner and gaunter in countenance, nor was his dress so well cared for and trim as I remembered him. The high, masterful look which his face always wore had deepened into something bitter and savage, as if he had grown half-sick of the world and cared naught for the things which had aforetime delighted him. His habit of scorn for all which opposed him, and all which was beneath him, had grown on him with his years and power, and given him that look as of one born to command, ay, and of one to whom suffering and pain were less than nothing. As I looked on him I hated him deeply and fiercely, and yet I admired him more than I could bear to think, and gloried that he was of our family. For I have rarely seen a nobler figure of a man. I am not little, but in his presence I felt dwarfed. Nor was it only in stature that he had the pre-eminence, for his step was as light and his eye as keen as a master of fence.

He had expected a very different figure to greet him at the other side of the table. In place of a lissom maid he saw a grim, rough-clad man waiting on him with death in his eyes. I saw surprise, anger, even a momentary spasm of fear flit across his face. He looked at me keenly, then with a great effort he controlled himself, and his sullen face grew hard as stone.

"Good morning to you, Master John Burnet," said he. "I am overjoyed to see you again. I had hoped to have had a meeting with you in the past months among your own hills of Tweedside, but the chance was denied me. But better late than never. I bid you welcome."

I bowed. "I thank you," I said.

"I have another guest," said he, "whom you know. It is a fortunate chance that you should both be present. This old house of Eaglesham has not held so many folk for a long day. May I ask when you arrived?" The man spoke all the while with great effort, and his eyes searched my face as though he would wrest from me my inmost thoughts.

"An end to this fooling, Gilbert," I said quietly. "Marjory Veitch is no more in this house; with the escort of my servant she is on her road to Tweeddale. By this time she will be more than halfway there."

He sprang at me like a wild thing, his face suddenly inflaming with passion.

"You, you—" he cried, but no words could come. He could only stutter and gape, with murder staring from his visage.

As for me, the passion in him roused in me a far greater.

"Yes," I cried, my voice rising so that I scarce knew it for mine. "You villain, liar, deceiver, murderer, by the living God, the time has now come for your deserts. You tortured my love and harassed her with hateful captivity; you slew her brother, your friend, slew him in his cups like the coward you are; you drove me from my house and lands; you made me crouch and hide in the hills like a fox, and hunted me with your hellhounds; you lied and killed and tortured, but now I am free, and now you will find that I am your master. I have looked for this day, oh, for so long, and now you shall not escape me. Gilbert Burnet, this earth is wide, but it is not wide enough for you and me to live together. One or other of us shall never go from this place."

He made no answer but only looked me straight in the face, with a look from which the rage died by degrees. Then he spoke slowly and measuredly. "I think you are right, Cousin John," said he; "the world is too small for both of us. We must come to a settlement." And in his tone there was a spice of pity and regret. Then I knew that I had lied, and that this man was stronger than I.

For a little we stood looking across the table at each other. There was an extraordinary attraction in him, and before the power of his keen eyes I felt my wits trembling. Then, with his hand, he motioned me to sit down. "The morning air is raw, Cousin John. It will be better to finish our meal," and he called to his servant to bring in breakfast.

I have never eaten food in my life under stranger circumstances. Yet I did not fear aught, but satisfied my hunger with much readiness. As for him, he toyed and ate little. Once I caught him looking over at me with a shade of anxiety, of dread in his gaze. No word passed between us, for both alike felt the time too momentous for any light talk. As the minutes fled I seemed to discern some change in his manner. His brows grew heavier and he appeared to brood over the past, while his glance sought the pictures on the walls, and my face in turn, with something of fierceness. When all was over he rose and courteously made way for me to pass, holding the door wide as I went out. Then he led me to a little room at the other side of the hall, whence a window opened to the garden.

"You wish to be satisfied," he said, "and I grant you that the wish is just. There are some matters 'twixt me and thee that need clearing. But, first, by your leave, I have something to say. You believe me guilty of many crimes, and I fling the charge in your teeth. But one thing I did unwittingly and have often repented of. Michael Veitch fell by his own folly and by no fault of mine."

"Let that be," said I; "I have heard another tale."

"I have said my say; your belief matters naught to me. One thing I ask you. Where has the girl Marjory gone? If fate decides against you, it is but right I should have her."

"Nay," I cried passionately, "that you never shall. You have caused her enough grief already. She hates the sight of you even as I, and I will do nothing to make her fall into your hands."

"It matters little," he said, with a shrug of his great shoulders. "It was only a trifling civility which I sought from you. Let us get to work."

From a rack he picked a blade, one such as he always used in any serious affray, single-edged and basket-hilted. Then he signed to me to follow, and opened the window and stepped out.

The morning was murky and damp. Fog clothed the trees and fields, and a smell of rottenness hung in the air. I shivered, for my clothes were thin and old.

Gilbert walked quickly, never casting a look behind him. First we crossed the sodden pleasance, and then entered the pine wood, which I had skirted on the night before.

In a little we heard the roaring of water and came to the banks of the stream, which, swollen by the melting snows, was raving wildly between the barriers of the banks. At the edge was a piece of short turf, some hundred yards square and drier than the rest of the ground which we had traversed. Here Gilbert stopped and bade me get ready. I had little to do save cast my coat, and stand stripped and shivering, waiting while my enemy took his ground.

The next I knew was that I was in the thick of a deadly encounter, with blows rattling on my blade as thick as hail. My cousin's eyes glared into mine, mad with anger and regret, with the unrequited love and aimless scheming of months concentrated in one fiery passion. I put forth my best skill, but it was all I could do to keep death from me. As it was I was scratched and grazed in a dozen places, and there was a great hole in my shirt which the other's blade had ripped. The sweat began to trickle over my eyes with the exertion, and my sight was half dazed by the rapid play.

Now it so happened that I had my back to the stream. This was the cause of my opponent's sudden violence, for he sought to drive me backwards, that, when I found myself near the water, I might grow bewildered. But I had been brought up to this very trick, for in the old days in Tweeddale, Tam Todd would take his stand near the Tweed and strive to force me back into the great pool. In my present danger these old memories came back to me, and in a second I was calm again. This, after all, was only what I had done a thousand times for sport. Could I not do it once for grim earnest?

In a very little I saw that my cousin's policy of putting all his strength out at the commencement was like to be his ruin. He was not a man built for long endurance, being too full in blood and heavy of body. Soon his breath came thick and painfully; he yielded a step, then another, and still a third; his thrusts lacked force, and his guards were feeble. He had changed even from that tough antagonist whom I had aforetime encountered, and who taxed my mettle to the utmost. Had it not been that my anger still held my heart, and admitted no room for other thoughts, I would even have felt some compunction in thrusting at him. But now I had no pity in me. A terrible desire to do to him as he had done to my friends gripped me like a man's hand. The excitement of the struggle, and, perhaps, the peril to my own life, roused my dormant hate into a storm of fury. I know not what I did, but shrieking curses and anathemas, I pressed on him relentlessly. Before my sword-point I saw his face growing greyer and greyer with each passing minute. He was a brave man, this I have always said for him; and if any other in a like position, with an enemy at his throat and the awful cognizance of guilt, still keeps his stand and does not flee, him also I call brave.

Suddenly his defence ceased. His arm seemed to numb and his blade was lowered. I checked my cut, and waited with raised point. An awful delight was in my heart, which now I hate and shudder to think on. I waited, torturing him. He tried to speak, but his mouth was parched and I heard the rattle of his tongue. Still I delayed, for all my heat seemed turned into deadly malice.

Then his eyes left my face and looked over my shoulders. I saw a new shade of terror enter them. I chuckled, for now, thought I, my revenge has come. Of a sudden he crouched with a quick movement, bringing his hands to his face. I was in the act of striking, when from behind came a crack, and something whistled past my ear. Then I saw my cousin fall, groaning, with a bullet through his neck.

In a trice my rage was turned from him to the unknown enemy behind. With that one shot all rancour had gone from my heart. I turned, and there, running through the trees up the river bank, I saw a man. At the first look I recognized him, though he was bent wellnigh double, and the air was thick with fog. It was the fellow Jan Hamman.

I ran after him at top speed, though he was many yards ahead of me. I have never felt such lightness in my limbs. I tore through thicket and bramble, and leaped the brooks as easily as if I were not spent with fighting and weak from the toils of months. This man had dared to come between us; this man had dared to slay one of my house. No sound escaped my lips, but silently, swiftly, I sped after the fleeing figure.

277

He ran straight up stream, and at every step I gained. Somewhere at the beginning he dropped his pistol; soon he cast away his cap and cloak; and when already he heard my hot breathing behind him he cried out in despair and flung his belt aside. We were climbing a higher ridge beneath which ran the stream. I was so near that I clutched at him once and twice, but each time he eluded me. Soon we gained the top, and I half stumbled while he gained a yard. Then I gathered myself together for a great effort. In three paces I was on him, and had him by the hair; but my clutch was uncertain with my faintness, and, with a wrench, he was free. Before I knew his purpose he swerved quickly to the side, and leaped clean over the cliff into the churning torrent below.

I stood giddy on the edge, looking down. There was nothing but a foam of yellow and white and brown from bank to bank. No man could live in such a stream. I turned and hastened back to my cousin.

I found him lying as I had left him, with his head bent over to the side and the blood oozing from his neck wound. When I came near he raised his eyes and saw me. A gleam of something came into them; it may have been mere recognition, but I thought it pleasure.

I kneeled beside him with no feelings other than kindness. The sight of him lying so helpless and still drove all anger from me. He was my cousin, one of my own family.

He spoke very hoarsely and small.

"I am done for, John. My ill-doing has come back on my own head. That man—"

"Yes," I said, for I did not wish to trouble a man so near his end with idle confessions, "I know, I have heard, but that is all past and done with."

"God forgive me," he said, "I did him a wrong, but I have repaid it. Did you kill him, John?"

"No," I said; "he leaped from a steep into the stream. He will be no more heard of."

"Ah," and his breath came painfully, "it is well. Yet I could have wished that one of the family had done the work. But it is

278

no time to think of such things. I am going fast, John."

Then his speech failed for a little and he lay back with a whitening face.

"I have done many ill deeds to you, for which I crave your forgiveness."

"You have mine with all my heart," I said hastily. "But there is the forgiveness of a greater, which we all need alike. You would do well to seek it."

He spoke nothing for a little. "I have lived a headstrong, evil life," said he, "which God forgive. Yet it is not meet to go canting to your end, when in your health you have crossed His will."

Once again there was silence for a little space. Then he reached out his hand for mine.

"I have been a fool all my days. Let us think no more of the lass, John. We are men of the same house, who should have lived in friendship. It was a small thing to come between us."

A wind had risen and brought with it a small, chill rain. A gust swept past us and carried my cast-off cloak into the bushes. "Ease my head," he gasped, and when I hasted to do it, I was even forestalled. For another at that moment laid His hand on him, and with a little shudder his spirit passed to the great and only Judge of man's heart.

I walked off for help with all speed, and my thoughts were sober and melancholy. Shame had taken me for my passion and my hot fit of revenge; ay, and pity and kindness for my dead opponent. The old days when we played together by Tweed, a thousand faint memories came back to me, and in their light the last shades of bitterness disappeared. Also the truth came home to me as I went, how little the happiness of man hangs on gifts and graces, and how there is naught in the world so great as the plain virtues of honour and heart.

CHAPTER VII

OF A VOICE IN THE EVENTIDE

Of the events of the time following there is little need to give an exact account. There was some law business to be gone through in connection with my cousin's death and the disposing of the estate, which went to an East country laird, a Whig of the Whigs, and one like to make good and provident use of it. Then, when I would have returned to Tweeddale, I received a post from my good kinsman, Dr. Gilbert Burnet, which led me first to Edinburgh and then so far afield as London itself. For it was necessary, in the great confusion of affairs, that I should set myself right with the law and gain some reparation for my sometime forfeited lands.

So to the great city I went, posting by the main road from Edinburgh, and seeing a hundred things which were new and entertaining. I abode there most all the winter, during the months of December, January, February, and March, for there was much to do and see. My lodging was in my kinsman's house near the village of Kensington, and there I met a great concourse of remarkable folk whose names I had heard of and have heard of since. Notably, there were Master John Dryden, the excellent poet, my Lord Sandwich, and a very brisk, pleasing gentleman, one Mr. Pepys, of the Admiralty. I had opportunity of gratifying my taste for books and learned society, for my kinsman's library was an excellent one, and his cellars so good that they attracted all conditions of folk to his house. Also I had many chances of meeting with gentlemen of like degree with myself, and many entertaining diversions we had together. Nor did I neglect those in Tweeddale, for I sent news by near every post that went to the North.

But when the spring came, and there was no further need for tarrying in the South, with a light heart I set off homewards once more. I journeyed by Peterborough and York in the company of one Sir C. Cotterell, a gentleman of Northumberland, and abode two days at his house in the moors, where there was excellent fishing. Then I came northwards by the great Northumberland road by the towns of Newcastle and Morpeth, and crossed the Cheviot hills, which minded me much of my own glens. At Coldstream I forded the Tweed, which is there grown a very broad, noble river, and then rode with all speed over the Lammermoors to Edinburgh. I stayed there no longer than my duty demanded; and when all was settled, one bright spring day, just after midday, set out for Barns.

The day, I remember, was one of surprising brightness, clear, sunshiny, and soft as midsummer. There are few ways I know better than that from the capital to my home—the bare, windy moorlands for one half, and the green glens and pleasant waters of the other. It was by this road that I had come to Leith to ship for Holland; by this road that I had ridden on that wild night to Dawyck. Each spot of the wayside was imprinted on my memory, and now that my wanderings were over, and I was returning to peace and quiet, all things were invested with a new delight. Yet my pleasure was not of the brisk, boisterous order, for my many misfortunes had made me a graver man, and chastened my natural spirits to a mellow and abiding cheerfulness.

At Leadburn was the inn where I had first met my servant Nicol, my trusty comrade through so many varying fates. I drank a glass of wine at the place for no other cause than a sentimental remembrance. The old landlord was still there, and the idle ostlers hung around the stable doors, as when I had passed before. Down in the bog-meadow the marsh-marigolds were beginning to open, and the lambs from the hillside bleated about their mothers. The blue, shell-like sky overhead arched without a cloud to the green, distant hills.

When I came to the place on the Tweedside road, called the Mount Bog, I dismounted and lay down on the grass. For there the view opens to the hills of my own countryside. A great barrier of blue, seamed with glens, all scarred in spots with rock and shingle, lifting serene brows from the little ridges to the wide expanse of the heavens. I named them one by one from east to

281

west—Minchmoor, though it was hidden from sight, where fled the great Montrose after the fatal rout of Philiphaugh; the broad foreheads of the Glenrath heights above my own vale of Manor, Dollar Law, Scrape, the Drummelzier fells, the rugged Wormel, and, fronting me, the great Caerdon, with snow still lining its crannies. Beyond, still farther and fainter lines of mountain, till like a great tableland the monstrous mass of the Broad Law barred the distance. It was all so calm and fragrant, with not a sound on the ear but the plash of little streams and the boom of nesting snipe. And above all there was the thought that now all peril had gone, and I was free to live as I listed and enjoy life as a man is born to do, and skulk no more at dykesides, and be torn no longer by hopeless passion.

When I rode through the village of Broughton and came to the turn of the hill at Dreva, the sun was already westering. The goodly valley, all golden with evening light, lay beneath me. Tweed was one belt of pure brightness, flashing and shimmering by its silver shores and green, mossy banks. Every wood waved and sparkled in a fairy glow, and the hills above caught the radiance on their broad bosoms. I have never seen such a sight, and for me at that hour it seemed the presage of my home-coming. I have rarely felt a more serene enjoyment, for it put me at peace with all the earth, and gilded even the nightmare of the past with a remembered romance. To crown it there was that melodious concert of birds, which one may hear only on such a night in this sweet time o' year. Throstles and linnets and the shriller mountain larks sang in the setting daylight, till I felt like some prince in an eastern tale who has found the talisman and opened the portals of the Golden Land.

Down the long, winding hill-path I rode, watching the shadows flit before me, and thinking strange thoughts. Fronting me over the broad belt of woodland, I saw the grey towers of Dawyck, and the green avenues of grass running straight to the hill.

By-and-by the road took me under the trees, among the cool shades and the smell of pine and budding leaves. There was a great crooning of wood-doves, and the sighing of the tenderest breezes. Shafts of light still crept among the trunks, but the soft darkness of spring was almost at hand. My heart was filled with a great exaltation. The shadow of the past seemed to slip from me like an old garment.

Suddenly I stopped, for somewhere I heard a faint melody, the voice of a girl singing. 'Twas that voice I would know among ten thousand, the only one in all the world for me. I pulled up my horse and listened as the notes grew clearer, and this was what she sang:

> "First shall the heavens want starry light,
>   The sea be robbèd of their waves;
> The day want sun, the sun want bright,
>   The night want shade, and dead men graves;
> The April, flowers and leaf and tree,
>   Before I false my faith to thee,
>   To thee, to thee."

There came a pause, and then again, in the fragrant gloaming, the air went on:

> "First shall the tops of highest hills
>   By humble plains be overpry'd;
> And poets scorn the Muses' quills,
>   And fish forsake the water-glide;
> And Iris lose her colour'd weed
>   Before I fail thee at thy need."

I stood in shadow and watched her as she came in sight, sauntering up the little green glade, with a basket of spring flowers swinging on her arm. Her hat of white satin hung loose over her hair, and as she walked lightly, now in the twilight, now in a sudden shaft of the western sun, she looked fairer than aught I had ever seen. Once more she sung with her clear voice:

> "First direful Hate shall turn to Peace,
>   And Love relent in deep disdain;
> And Death his fatal stroke shall cease,
>   And Envy pity every pain;
> And Pleasure mourn, and Sorrow smile,
>   Before I talk of any guile."

But now the darkness had come in good earnest, and I could scarce see the singer. "First Time shall stay," the voice went on:

> "First Time shall stay his stayless race,
>   And Winter bless his brows with corn;
> And snow bemoisten July's face,
>   And Winter, Spring and Summer mourn."

Here the verse stopped short, for I stepped out and stood before her.

"Oh, you have come back," she cried. "At last, and I have looked so long for you."

"Indeed, dear lass, I have come back, and by God's grace to go no more away."

Then leading my horse, I walked by her side down the broad path to the house. We spoke nothing, our hearts being too busy with the delights of each other's presence. The crowning stone was added to my palace of joy, and in that moment it seemed as if earth could contain no more of happiness, and that all the sorrows of the past were well worth encountering for the ecstasy of the present. To be once more in my own land, with my own solemn hills looking down upon me, and that fair river wandering by wood and heather, and my lady at my side, was not that sufficient for any man? The purple, airy dark, odorous with spring scents, clung around us, and in the pauses of silence the place was so still that our ears heard naught save the drawing of our breath.

At the lawn of Dawyck I stopped and took her hands in mine.

"Marjory," I said, "once, many years ago, you sang me a verse and made me a promise. I cannot tell how bravely you have fulfilled it. You have endured all my hardships, and borne me company where I bade you, and now all is done with and we are returned to peace and our own place. Now it is my turn for troth-plighting, and I give you it with all my heart. God bless you, my own dear maid." And I repeated softly:

> "First shall the heavens want starry light,
>   The seas be robbèd of their waves;

The day want sun, the sun want bright,
The night want shade, and dead men graves;
The April, flowers and leaf and tree,
Before I false my faith to thee."

And I kissed her and bade farewell, with the echo still ringing in my ears, "to thee, to thee."

I rode through the great shadows of the wood, scarce needing to pick my path in a place my horse knew so well, for once again I was on Maisie. The stillness clung to me like a garment, and out of it, from high up on the hillside, came a bird's note, clear, tremulous, like a bell. Then the trees ceased, and I was on the shorn, green banks, 'neath which the river gleamed and rustled. Then, all of a sudden, I had rounded the turn of the hill, and there, before me in the dimness, stood the old grey tower, which was mine and had been my fathers' since the first man tilled a field in the dale. I crossed the little bridge with a throbbing heart, and lo! there was the smell of lilac and gean-tree blossom as of old coming in great gusts from the lawn. Then all was confusion and much hurrying about and a thousand kindly greetings. But in especial I remember Tam Todd, the placid, the imperturbable, who clung to my hand, and sobbed like the veriest child, "Oh, Laird, ye've been lang o' comin'."

CHAPTER VIII

HOW NICOL PLENDERLEITH
SOUGHT HIS FORTUNE ELSEWHERE

Now, at last, I am come to the end of my tale, and have little more to set down. It was on a very fresh, sweet May morning, that Marjory and I were married in the Kirk of Lyne, which stands high on a knoll above the Lyne Water with green hills huddled around the door. There was a great concourse of people, for half the countryside dwelled on our land. Likewise, when all was done, there was the greatest feast spread in Barns that living man had ever seen. The common folk dined without on tables laid on the green, while within the walls the gentry from far and near drank long life and health to us till sober reason fled hotfoot and the hilarity grew high. But in a little all was over, the last guest had clambered heavily on his horse and ridden away, and we were left alone.

The evening, I remember, was one riot of golden light and rich shadow. The sweet-scented air stole into the room with promise of the fragrant out-of-doors, and together we went out to the lawn and thence down by the trees to the brink of Tweed, and along by the great pool and the water meadows. The glitter of that brave, romantic stream came on my sight, as a sound of old music comes on the ears, bringing a thousand half-sad, half-joyful memories. All that life held of fair was in it—the rattle and clash of arms, the valour of men, the loveliness of women, the glories of art and song, the wonders of the great mother earth, and the recreations of the years. And as we walked together, I and my dear lady, in that soft twilight in the green world, a peace, a delight, a settled hope grew upon us, and we went in silence, speaking no word the one to the other. By-and-by we passed through the garden where the early lilies stood in white battalions, and entered the dining-hall.

A band of light lay on the east wall where hung the portraits of my folk. One was a woman, tall and comely, habited in a grey satin gown of antique fashion.

"Who was she?" Marjory asked softly.

"She was my mother, a Stewart of Traquair, a noble lady and a good. God rest her soul."

"And who is he who stands so firmly and keeps hand on sword?"

"That was my father's brother who stood last at Philiphaugh, when the Great Marquis was overthrown. And he with the curled moustaches was his father, my grandfather, of whom you will yet hear in the countryside. And beyond still is his father, the one with the pale, grave face, and solemn eyes. He died next his king at the rout of Flodden. God rest them all; they were honest gentlemen."

Then there was silence for a space, while the light faded, and the old, stately dames looked down at us from their frames with an air, as it seemed to me, all but kindly, as if they laughed to see us playing in the old comedy which they had played themselves.

On the morning of the third day from the time I have written of, I was surprised by seeing my servant Nicol coming into my study with a grave face, as if he had some weighty matter to tell. Since I had come home, I purposed to keep him always with me, to accompany me in sport and see to many things on the land, which none could do better than he. Now he sought an audience with a half-timid, bashful look, and, when I bade him be seated, he flicked his boots uneasily with his hat and looked askance.

"I hae come to bid ye fareweel, sir," at length he said slowly.

I sprang up in genuine alarm.

"What nonsense is this?" I cried. "You know fine, Nicol, that you cannot leave me. We have been too long together."

"I maun gang," he repeated sadly; "I'm loath to dae 't, but there's nae help for 't."

"But what?" I cried. "Have I not been a good friend to you, and your comrade in a thousand perils? Is there anything I can do more for you? Tell me, and I will do it."

"Na, na, Maister John, ye've aye been the best o' maisters. I've a'thing I could wish; dinna think I'm no gratefu'."

"Then, for Heaven's sake, tell me the reason, man. I never thought you would treat me like this, Nicol."

"Oh, sir, can ye no see?" the honest fellow cried with tears in his eyes. "Ye've been sae lang wi' me, that I thocht ye kenned my natur'. Fechtin' and warstlin' and roamin' aboot the warld are the very breath o' life to me. I see ye here settled sae braw and canty, and the auld hoose o' Barns lookin' like itsel' again. And I thinks to mysel', 'Nicol Plenderleith, lad, this is no for you. This is no the kind of life that ye can lead. Ye've nae mair business here than a craw among throstles.' And the thocht maks me dowie, for I canna get by 't. I whiles think o' mysel' bidin' quiet here and gettin' aulder and aulder, till the time passes when I'm brisk and venturesome, and I'm left to naething but regrets. I maun be up

287

and awa', Laird, I carena whither. We're a' made different, and I was aye queer and daft and no like ither folk. Ye winna blame me."

I tried to dissuade him, but it was to no purpose. He heard me patiently, but shook his head. I did not tax him with ingratitude, for I knew how little the charge was founded. For myself I was more sorry than words, for this man was joined to me by ties of long holding. I longed to see him beside me at Barns, an unceasing reminder of my stormy days. I longed to have his sage counsel in a thousand matters, to have him at my hand when I took gun to the hills or rod to the river. I had grown to love his wind-beaten face and his shrewd, homely talk, till I counted them as necessary parts of my life. And now all such hopes were dashed, and he was seeking to leave me.

"But where would you go?" I asked.

"I kenna yet," he said. "But there's aye things for a man like me somewhere on the earth. I'm thinkin' o' gaun back to the abroad, whaur there's like to be a steer for some time to come. It's the life I want and no guid fortune or bad fortune, so I carena what happens. I trust I may see ye again, Maister John, afore I dee."

There was nothing left for it but to agree, and agree I did, though with a heavy heart and many regrets. I gave him a horse to take him to Leith, and offered him a sum of money. This he would have none of, but took instead a pair of little old pistols which had been my father's.

I never saw him again, though often I have desired it, but years after I heard of him, and that in the oddest way. I corresponded to some little extent with folk in the Low Countries, and in especial with one Master Ebenezer van Gliecken, a learned man and one of great humour in converse. It was at the time when there was much fighting between the French and the Dutch, and one morn I received a letter from this Master van Gliecken, written from some place whose name I have forgot, a rascally little Holland town in the south. He wrote of many things—of some points in Latin scholarship, of the vexatious and most unpolitic state of affairs in the land, and finally concluded with this which I transcribe. . . . . "Lastly, my dear Master John, I will tell you a tale which, as it concerns the glory of your countrymen, you may think worth hearing. As you know well, this poor town of ours has lately been the centre of a most bloody strife, for the French forces have assaulted it on all sides, and though by God's grace they have failed to take it, yet it has suffered many sore afflictions. In particular there was a fierce attack made upon the side which fronts the river, both by boat and on foot. On the last day of the siege, a sally was made from the gate of the corner tower, which nevertheless was unsuccessful, our men being all but enclosed and some of the enemy succeeding in entering the gate. One man in particular, a Scot, as I have heard, Nicolo Plenderleet by name, with two others who were both slain, made his way to the battlements. The gate was shut, and, to all appearance, his death was certain. But they knew not the temper of their enemy, for springing on the summit of the wall, he dared all to attack him. When the defenders pressed on he laid about him so sturdily that three fell under his sword.

"Then when he could no longer make resistance, and bullets were pattering around him like hail, and his cheek was bleeding with a deep wound, his spirit seemed to rise the higher. For, shouting out taunts to his opponents, he broke into a song, keeping time all the while with the thrusts of his sword. Then bowing gallantly and saluting with his blade his ring of foes, he sheathed his weapon, and joining his hands above his head, dived sheer and straight into the river, and, swimming easily, reached the French lines. At the sight those of his own side cheered, and even our men, whom he had so tricked, could scarce keep from joining.

"Touching the editions which you desired I have given orders to the bookseller on the quay at Rotterdam to send them to you. I shall be glad indeed to give you my poor advice on the difficult matters you speak of, if you will do me the return favour of reading through my excursus to Longinus, and giving me your veracious opinion. Of this I send you a copy.

"As regards the Scot I have already spoken of, I may mention for your satisfaction that in person he was tall and thin, with black hair, and the most bronzed skin I have ever seen on a man. . . . "

When I read this letter to Marjory, her eyes were filled with tears, and for myself I would speak to no one on that day.

CHAPTER IX

THE END OF ALL THINGS

I am writing the last words of this tale in my house of Barns after many years have come and gone since the things I wrote of. I am now no more young, and my wife is no more a slim maid, but a comely woman. The years have been years of peace and some measure of prosperity. Here in Tweeddale life runs easily and calm. Our little country matters are all the care we know, and from the greater world beyond there comes only chance rumours of change and vexation. Yet the time has not been idle, for I have busied myself much with study and the care of the land. Many have sought to draw me out to politics and statecraft, but I have ever resisted them, for after all are these things of such importance that for them a man should barter his leisure and peace of mind? So I have even stayed fast in this pleasant dale, and let the bustle and clamour go on without my aid.

It is true that more than once I have made journeys even across the water, and many times to London, on matters of private concern. It was during one of these visits to Flanders that I first learned the importance of planting wood on land, and resolved to make trial on my own estate. Accordingly I set about planting on Barns, and now have clothed some of the barer spaces of the hills with most flourishing groves of young trees, drawn in great part from the woods of Dawyck. I can never hope to reap the benefit of them myself, but haply my grandchildren will yet bless me, when they find covert and shade where before was only a barren hillside.

Also in Tweed I have made two caulds, both for the sake of the fish and to draw off streams to water the meadows. In the wide reaches of water in Stobo Haughs I have cut down much of the encumbering brushwood, and thus laid the places open for fishing with the rod. Also with much labour I have made some little progress in clearing the channel of the river in places where it is foully overlaid with green weed. The result, I am pleased to think, has been good, and the fish thrive and multiply. At any rate, I can now make baskets that beforetime were counted impossible. My crowning triumph befell me two years ago in a wet, boisterous April, when, fishing with a minnow in the pool above Barns, I landed a trout of full six pound weight.

The land, which had fallen into neglect in my father's time and my own youth, I did my utmost to restore, and now I have the delight of seeing around me many smiling fields and pleasant dwellings. In the house of Barns itself I have effected many changes, for it had aforetime been liker a Border keep than an orderly dwelling. But now, what with works of art and things of interest gathered from my travels abroad, and above all, through the deft fingers of my wife, the place has grown gay and well-adorned, so that were any of its ancient masters to revisit it they would scarce know it for theirs.

But the work which throughout these years has lain most near to my heart has been the studies which I have already spoken of. The fruit of them, to be sure, is less than the labour, but still I have not been idle. I have already in this tale told of my exposition of the philosophy of the Frenchman Descartes, with my own additions, and my writings on the philosophy of the Greeks, and especially of the Neo-Platonists—both of which I trust to give to the world at an early time. As this story of my life will never be published, it is no breach of modesty here to counsel all, and especially those of my own family, who may see it, to give their attention to my philosophical treatises. For though I do not pretend to have any deep learning or extraordinary subtlety in the matter, it has yet been my good fate, as I apprehend it, to note many things which have escaped the eyes of others. Also I think that my mind, since it has ever been clear from sedentary humours and the blunders which come from mere knowledge of books, may have had in sundry matters a juster view and a clearer insight.

Of my own folk I have little to tell. Tam Todd has long since gone the way of all the earth, and lies in Lyne kirkyard with a flat stone above him. New faces are in Barns and Dawyck, and there scarce remains one of the old serving-men who aided me in my time of misfortune. Also things have changed in all the country-side, and they from whom I used to hear tales as a boy are now no more on the earth. In Peebles there are many new things, and mosses are drained and moors measured out, till the whole land wears a trimmer look. But with us all is still the same, for I have no fancy for change in that which I loved long ago, and would fain still keep the remembrance. Saving that I have planted the hillsides, I have let the moors and marshes be, and today the wild-duck and snipe are as thick on my land as of old.

As for myself, I trust I have outgrown the braggadocio and folly of youth. God send I may not have also outgrown its cheerfulness and spirit! For certain I am a graver man and less wont to set my delight in trifles. Of old I was the slave of little things—weather, scene, company; but advancing age has brought with it more of sufficiency unto myself. The ringing of sword and bridle has less charm, since it is the reward of years that a man gets more to the core of a matter and has less care for externals. Yet I can still feel the impulses of high passion, the glory of the chase, the stirring of the heart at a martial tale. Now, as I write, things are sorely changed in the land. For though peace hangs over us at home, I fear it is a traitor's peace at the best, and more horrific than war. Timeservers and greedy sycophants sit in high places, and it is hard to tell if generous feeling be not ousted by a foul desire of gain. It is not for me to say. I have no love for King or Parliament, though much for my country. I am no hotheaded king's man—nay, I never was; but when they who rely upon us are sold for a price, when oaths are broken and honour driven away, I am something less of one than before. It may be that the old kings were better, who ruled with a strong hand, though they oft ruled ill. But indeed I can say little; here in this valley of Tweed a man hears of such things only as one hears the roar of a stormy sea from a green inland vale.

As I write these last words, I am sitting in my study at Barns, looking forth of the narrow window over the sea of landscape. The afternoon is drawing to evening, the evening of a hot August day, which is scarce less glorious than noon. From the meadow come the tinkling of cattle bells and the gentle rise and fall of the stream. Elsewhere there is no sound, for the summer weather hangs low and heavy on the land. Just beyond rise the barrier ridges, green and shimmering, and behind all the sombre outlines of the great hills. Below in the garden my wife is plucking flowers to deck the table, and playing with the little maid, who is three years old today. Within the room lie heavy shadows and the mellow scent of old books and the faint fragrance of blossoms.

And as I look forth on this glorious world, I know not whether to be glad or sad. All the years of my life stretch back till I see as in a glass the pageant of the past. Faint regrets come to vex me, but they hardly stay, and, as I look and think, I seem to learn the lesson of the years, the great precept of time. And deep in all, more clear as the hours pass and the wrappings fall off, shines forth the golden star of honour, which, if a man follow, though it be through quagmire and desert, fierce faces and poignant sorrow, 'twill bring him at length to a place of peace.

But these are words of little weight and I am too long about my business. Behold how great a tale I have written unto you. Take it, and, according to your pleasure, bless or ban the narrator. Haply it will help to while away a winter's night, when the doors are barred and the great logs crackle, and the snow comes over Caerdon.